T0171450

A FOOT IN TWO WORLDS

A Pastor's Journey From Grief to Hope

Vincent D. Homan

WestBow
PRESS
A DIVISION OF THOMAS NELSON

Copyright © 2013 Vincent D. Homan

All rights reserved. No part of this book may be used or reproduced by any means, graphic, electronic, or mechanical, including photocopying, recording, taping or by any information storage retrieval system without the written permission of the publisher except in the case of brief quotations embodied in critical articles and reviews. WestBow Press books may be ordered through booksellers or by contacting:

WestBow Press
A Division of Thomas Nelson
1663 Liberty Drive
Bloomington, IN 47403
www.westbowpress.com
1-(866) 928-1240

Because of the dynamic nature of the Internet, any web addresses or links contained in this book may have changed since publication and may no longer be valid. The views expressed in this work are solely those of the author and do not necessarily reflect the views of the publisher, and the publisher hereby disclaims any responsibility for them. Any people depicted in stock imagery provided by Thinkstock are models, and such images are being used for illustrative purposes only.
Certain stock imagery © Thinkstock.

All scripture quotations, unless otherwise indicated, are taken from the Holy Bible, New International Version®, NIV®. Copyright ©1973, 1978, 1984, 2011 by Biblica, Inc.™ Used by permission of Zondervan. All rights reserved worldwide. www.zondervan.com The "NIV" and "New International Version" are trademarks registered in the United States Patent and Trademark Office by Biblica, Inc.™

Scripture quotations marked NLT are taken from the Holy Bible, New Living Translation, copyright 1996, 2004. Used by permission of Tyndale House Publishers, Inc., Wheaton, Illinois 60189. All rights reserved.

Scripture quotations marked The Message are taken from The Message. Copyright (c) by Eugene H. Peterson 1993, 1994, 1995, 1996, 2000, 2001, 2002. Used by permission of NavPress Publishing Group.

Scripture quotations marked NRSV are taken from the Holy Bible, New Revised Standard Version Bible, copyright 1989, Division of Christian Education of the National Council of the Churches of Christ in the United States of America. Used by permission. All rights reserved.

Scripture quotations marked TLB are taken from The Living Bible copyright © 1971. Used by permission of Tyndale House Publishers, Inc., Carol Stream, Illinois 60188. All rights reserved.

Scripture quotations marked (GNT) are from the Good News Translation in Today's English Version- Second Edition Copyright © 1992 by American Bible Society. Used by Permission.

Because of the active nature of the Internet, any web addresses or links contained in this book may have changed since publication and may no longer be valid.

ISBN: 978-1-4497-7479-0 (e)
ISBN: 978-1-4497-7480-6 (sc)
ISBN: 978-1-4497-7481-3 (hc)
Library of Congress Control Number: 2012921890

Printed in the United States of America
WestBow Press rev. date: 09/26/2013

DEDICATION

This book is dedicated
to everyone who has walked through
the valley of tears and sorrows
and yet found the courage to hope again.

Blessed are those who mourn, for they
will be comforted (Matthew 5:4).

TABLE OF CONTENTS

ACKNOWLEDGMENTS

I will always believe God had a significant hand in the selection of Vicki to be my partner, friend, and love in my life. We have celebrated much joy and happiness in our years together, and now we have known a great darkness and sadness. Yet, we are resolved to face our future together with good spirit and great hope. This is a journey I could not walk alone. I am grateful for the tireless love and support of my wife. She is a gift.

As I cherished my son Gabe, I cherish my daughters Valerie and Tiffany. They are loving, kind, and gracious souls who have wept much. For the joy and life they have brought me, I am ever grateful. I also am thankful for the gift of their husbands, my fine sons-in-law, Alan and Ryan. They are terrific young men, and a welcome gift to me in the wake of Gabe's death. I love them as sons.

My grandchildren are the light of my life and a very tangible presence of God's love that helped me believe in goodness again. Lily, Kain, Graham, and Sutton (so far) bring me joy and great love, as did Gabe, Valerie, and Tiffany many years ago. I thank God every day for these children.

I also acknowledge the community of bereaved hearts, especially those who have lost children of any age. I knew many bereaved parents before, and I've met many more since we lost Gabe. I treasure these people. Among them was the support group we attended for several years that was simply a lifesaver to me. To lose a child is a savage heartache; it's a break in the natural order of life—a chaos, conflict, and crisis that affects everything from health, to family, to faith. To all who have grieved the loss of a loved one, especially those who have buried a child of any age, we stand with you, encourage you, and offer you our ongoing love and prayers. You are not alone. We found a large and loving community of people who had walked where we now walk, who came to our aid and comfort, and who encouraged us to live again.

I equally offer these writings to those who had faith in a good God tested by tragedy. Spirituality can be clouded by loss. Our faith seems muddled, becoming packaged up with much mystery, question, and emotion. Still, we can no more abandon our faith than we can abandon the grief that holds us so tight. Our grief and our faith stand side by side as partners in our journey. Likewise, I recognize the caregiver and comforter. We were most grateful for those who came to our aid and gave us their love, support and prayers. I thank God for kind souls who provide comfort to sorrow-filled hearts. Grief offers opportunities to do acts of great mercy and love. Let this book be an encouragement to remember the bereaved long term.

I also acknowledge those who supported and encouraged me to keep working on this book: My editor, Connie Anderson (Words & Deeds, Inc.), who went the extra mile to keep this project on task. I similarly thank Mary Lynn Gehrett and Hans Cornelder, who proofread the book. Their expertise and generosity with time were great gifts. Several friends have done the loving work of reading through my manuscript, also giving feedback and support: Rhonda Eakins, Nancy Bell, Jan Wallerich, Angie Alderson, and Neil Montz. They, plus a great community of loving friends and family, have provided much love and encouragement, both with our book project and our lives after loss. I thank God for them all.

Finally, I have had the good fortune to pastor the same little, rural, and loving United Methodist Churches in Delta and What Cheer for many years. They are filled with kind and gracious people. In the months and years after we lost Gabe, I was an unpredictable pastor. Often, I simply couldn't do the job. Sometimes I was moody, angry, or absent. They saw me during a very dark time and loved me throughout. It was true Christian charity. I am grateful for their patience and love, while they waited for their pastor's heart to start working again.

Vincent D. Homan

INTRODUCTION

We are not the first; we won't be the last. Death does not respect age. It does not matter—normalcy has been lost. When our son died, we suddenly found ourselves awash in an emotional sea of duress. Before death knocked down our door, I simply wasn't aware that life could so quickly become undone. But it has.

In the years since Gabe's death, we have tried valiantly to recover, make some sense of it all, live again, reestablish a degree of purpose, and reclaim faith. But parental grief has proven to be a formidable opponent. Any sense of recovery seemed vain. Life became filled with regret, guilt, and an insufferable sadness. No meaning or reason could be retrieved from such tragedy, but perchance, is there a purpose? Perhaps life's very path could be redirected in the jetsam of tragic loss. And faith? That became my Everest, my high place I would once more have to ascend—like Moses on Sinai, and there to again contend with my God. I knew our faith would be vital to surviving what had befallen us.

My Christian faith provides the strength and direction for my life. It is the first place I turn during times of trial. Yet my faith was clouded for a season by grief. I felt on the edge of a dark abyss. But God provided signposts that kept me close to grace. One came from a spiritual advisor who told me every believer must ultimately answer two questions: "Is God good?" and "Does God work for good in our lives?" I have never questioned God's existence or goodness. I think, as it was for Jeremiah, I knew it while still in the womb. I have always deeply believed. But life was suddenly, fiercely, in conflict with my belief.

As so many before, I couldn't reconcile the death of an innocent young man with a "good God." I couldn't understand how this could all be part of some great plan. I didn't know to what degree this could be punishment, consequence, sovereignty, or simply chance. Internal conflicts like these led to my writing this book.

Over time as I read and kept journals on a myriad of grief books, some helpful, some not, I began to sense a pattern. Authors, scholars, and counselors who had not suffered a tragic loss were more likely to have a path to recovery. It wasn't an exclusive list but enough to see the pattern. Though expressed in a framework of compassion and intellectualism, most offered a series of formulaic steps that would bring one back from the dark precipice of despair to the sunny vistas of betterment and empowerment. I felt I was reading instruction manuals on how to fly from people who had never been off the ground. But the books I read that came from broken, embittered, and bereaved hearts were more real. They didn't offer easy answers. They simply invited you to sit and weep with them, and they with you. They were more real, intimate, and welcoming, offering chances to visit and come near their grief, while not fully entering into it.

You cannot entirely enter another person's grief. It is intensely private. To each person, his or her grief is the worst.

Something about grief magnifies and crystallizes every encounter, every thought, and every word that the eye, heart, and ear ingest. Today, I still think about little vignettes of that first year. Specific words, phrases, encounters, glances, exchanges, and responses— these remain frozen in my memory. After hearing an excess of well-intentioned but often inappropriate remarks, my youngest daughter Tiffany and I quipped that we would one day write a book on what not to say and do around grieving people. This is not that book (though a few remarks are disparagingly included).

This is not a to-do list of recovery steps or a prescription for healing. I know of no antibiotic for a grieving heart or easy answers to life-and-death problems, and this is certainly not an attempt to give any. I would not insult our holy faith by trying to find a quick spiritual fix to burying a child. This is not even a detailed account of our story. It is too personal. Rather, this is an invitation for you to walk with me, to ponder with me, to weep with me, to tremble and yet hope, to stand in utter darkness and somehow still see light. I am not an author, a scholar, or a counselor. My theology and articulation are not textbook examples; neither are my faith and life. None of those things are the point of this book.

Rather I want this to be an honest, open, and *very* human discussion. I am a bereaved father. But I am also a person of faith. And I have spent these past years trying to reconcile the two. As a pastor for over twenty years, I've grown accustomed to writing comforting, and assuring words about faith and God. I couldn't give you my recipe for pancakes without a verse from the Psalms and at least two gospel references. My faith will be a very present voice in these writings and will stand alongside my grief. In fact, that is the precise point of the book: I am caught between grief and hope. That is where I now live my life. I have a foot in two worlds. It is to that end that these writings are offered.

> Bereaved moms or dads must know they are not alone. The large community of the bereaved is sometimes silent and sometimes invisible, but uniquely bonded.

Race, social status, age, or gender cannot divide it. Perhaps you might even find some level of comfort or solace in these words. I particularly offer these writings to those who struggle to reconcile their faith in a good God with tragic loss. Come journey to Sinai with me. And to the community who knows and cares for the bereaved families in your lives, I offer this as an encouragement that you would not forget them but hold them close in your hearts and lives. Please remember, you may have moved on from their loss, but they have not. It is a lifetime loss.

Finally, I confess, I write this book as my own catharsis. It has given me a place to sit down for a while, sort out my heart, and grieve. Before my life was divided by death, I used to see grief as an enemy—something to be avoided or gotten over quickly. But that is simply not a faithful response. With time, I have come to see grief as a friend—perhaps even a gift from God. It is not a means to an end. It is simply a means—a *way* to process what has happened to us. I invite you to walk that way with me.

CHAPTER 1

INTO THE STORM

THE STORM

It was a dark and rolling thing that crept,
In such a way that gave a sense of awe.
And stands as no surprise that no one saw
The power and grace with which it took each step.
For such was not what caught one's wondering eye,
Or caused each heart to beat more than it should,
But clothed in billowed black and shrouded hood,
Its jagged sparks forewarned that dread is nigh.
Then leashed its pregnant swell loose on the earth,
While thunder pealed away its rhythmic beat.
No army could have brought the squall defeat,
Nor slowed its tempest blast of self-made worth.

And when its lungs are emptied of their ill;
The air is sweet, and fresh—and all is still.

Vincent D. Homan

THE YEARS THAT HAVE passed since the death of our son Gabe have become something of a blur. The only thing that has separated one from another is when I grievously report in my annual Christmas letter, "This is now the second Christmas without our beloved Gabe." Then it is the third, the fourth, the fifth …. I have likened it to a storm with long sieges of blowing, thundering, and deep darkness. Sometimes, the gray and black clouds roll by quickly, like in the spring. We've also had times of sunshine, even bright sunshine, where we can hear birds singing, moments that have lasted for extended periods of time. Stretches like these allow me to think life is again normal, even joyful—and sometimes it is. Then suddenly we hear thunder roll again, and dark clouds gather, and we know normal has left our life. Storms have the power to take away normal. But they also can allow people to create a new normal, one that generates space for both storms and sunshine in a life and humility to seek the value in each.

On Saturday, June 18, 2005, his best friend, Russell, came to our door with the news: Gabe had collapsed while out fishing, and he had no pulse. I have relived that moment in its most dramatic and dreadful detail a million times, often in the dark of night. In exactly two weeks, we were to celebrate the wedding of our daughter Valerie. What was intended to be a joyful family time suddenly became a savage heartbreak. I could not process or believe the injustice of it all. I've always thought storms were at their worst in the darkness. June 18 was my entrance into a lifetime storm and my invitation to understand what made no sense. Even now, I can barely speak of it. This storm became a dull ache that haunts my life day and night. It divided me.

My existence suddenly became a hybrid of two parts, even two lives: the before and the after. The before remains a sacred and joyful memory; the after becomes a painful and heartrending reality.

Gabe was the eldest of our three children, and more a man than a boy at the time of his death. But he will always be *my boy*. Born September 8, 1975, Gabe was four years older than Valerie and eight years older than Tiffany, his other sister. They were the textbook trio, and my house was happy and full. I couldn't say one of their names without saying all three. Gabe, Val, and Tiff flowed like one name to me. I felt like the most blessed man on earth. My family seemed perfect. The psalmist wrote, "Children are a gift from the Lord; they are a reward from him. Children born to a young man are like arrows in a warrior's hands. How joyful is the man whose quiver is full of them!" (Psalm 127:3–5b, NLT). I was joyful and thankful. When Gabe was born, like many young dads, I was overcome by the miracle. I had to pull my car onto the shoulder and stop while driving home from the hospital. My eyes were full of tears. I wept that day with thanks for the gift of a son. And I wept with sorrow—great sorrow on the day Gabe died. And I wept for years.

First Steps After Loss

People treat you differently after losing a child. No one knows how to respond or what to say, so they often do neither. It made me feel *shunned*. Likewise, I marveled at how others used my storm to measure me: Will he be able to get back to work? Will they divorce? Will he be the same old Vince? Will he still go fishing? Will he still be my friend? Meanwhile, I was wondering simply how to breathe again, how to live, how to hope, how to believe, how to function, and how to continue. That is precisely the reason I invested myself in writing this book.

Many good souls endure terrible storms, and they, too, must find ways to breathe again, to live again, to hope again, to believe again, to function again, and to continue. I humbly submit my story, and my heart to those who have been invaded by life's winds and waves.

You who love, support, and try to understand the bereaved are much needed. Each person, ultimately, must weave and dodge storm clouds—with many left feeling the full brunt of the tempest, some more tragically than others. And when the winds and rains have accomplished their untimely crime, they leave. In their wake, the rubble remains to be sorted out by grief and time. Like Christian perfection, grief never arrives; rather it becomes a learning process. We each must ultimately learn to live with loss, for life and loss are part and parcel of this earth. We are all vulnerable. No one spends life in a storm shelter—nor would most choose to (as if we had that God-like choice).

I have always resisted preachers, counselors, and theologians who try to tidy up profoundly grievous and complicated life issues. Actually, I have grown weary of them and find many insulting. There are life moments that defy explanation and tidy endings. Moreover, it is an affront to the moment to suggest the possibility. That is certainly not my intention here. I am not inviting you to take my methodical remedy for sorrow or loss of any kind, much less that of parental bereavement. Rather, I am inviting you to walk with me, to ask questions, to wrestle with heartache, and to live in the tension between faith and doubt.

Living with loss in the wake of a storm requires immediate confrontations with emotions previously uncontested. Guilt, anger, bitterness, helplessness, emptiness, injustice, and fear—these and more come calling in dreaded, inexhaustible waves. The loss of a child is a sorrow unimaginable. The sudden death of a child is a bewailing lament. Nothing seems more cruel or final. Suddenly, a great void forces its way into every thought, action, breath, and emotion. The void intrusively ravages the soul and body.

Losing a child is a violation of the natural order of life. What was hoped and dreamed for is left in ashes and tears. Drs. Brook Noel and Pamela D. Blair realistically speak to the carnage and devastation that surround the broken hearts of a family that has buried its child:

It has been said that there is no loss as devastating as the loss of a child. Sudden death is a mix-up of everything we know to be true in life. Losing a child to sudden death is a break in the natural law and order of life. The child we have spent our time loving and caring for and planning to watch well into adulthood has been taken. It is heartache like no other. Those who live through and survive such an ordeal without becoming bitter have the strongest, most loving souls of all people walking on the planet.[1]

A future has suddenly become a past: graduations, weddings, holidays, family pictures, grandchildren, a passing of our lineage, all are now gone. Guilt, an insufferable sadness, and anger become the norms. Life is forever altered. Nothing can replace what you have lost. No amount of filling up the void with other people, guidance, activity, or even religion offers any respite. Friends change. Despair and helplessness reign. In my opinion, anyone who continues after such an ordeal is among the parade of saints. If one can continue living in the wake of the ultimate storm, then one has found a great nobility and strength.[2] It takes the nobility of kings and princes and the strength of Goliath to put a smile on your face and walk out the door every morning after your heart is taken from you. Learning to live with loss is not easy.

A Community Storm

People are well intentioned and helpful when storms hit. Years ago our community was struck by a powerful wind. Sitting in my office, I received a phone call that 100-mph, straight-line winds were approaching my hometown of Sigourney, Iowa. I closed my office and jumped in the car.

By the time I arrived in town, the storm had already passed, but the damage was evident. Our quaint downtown square was in disarray. Many beautiful trees in the courtyard were stripped and scattered from one end of the block to the other. I thought the square would never look the same again. The roads were covered with downed trees, branches, and overhead lines. I couldn't even get home.

Parking on the nearby highway, I ran up the alley to my yard. But my yard, looking much the same as the courtyard, was the least of my concerns. None of my kids were home. They had gone to the pool and, thankfully, were safe. What amazed me, though, was what happened later that day. Volunteers from all over town brought their pickups, chain saws, rakes, and bushel baskets. Within a couple of days, the cleanup was mostly done, and the square and town soon started looking normal. And, as is nature's way, time brought the trees and landscape back to life.

Today you would never know that awful storm passed through our town. I wondered if the same could be true for the storms of grief and loss. Do neighbors, nature, and time make any real difference? In the horrible early moments and days after Gabe died, many friends, family, church members, and neighbors came. They did not bring chain saws, pickup trucks, or rakes. But they did bring food, hugs, and tears. I recall very little of what happened in those early days, except for the good people who sat and cried with us; among them were Marsha and Terry, Claudia, and Jan. They wept like we wept. I then understood the Bible verse, "Rejoice with those who rejoice and mourn with those who mourn" (Romans 12:15). I treasured these people much. They offered no religious platitudes, no attempts to compare wounds, no empty council—just tears. They were salve to my wounded heart. I could distinctly feel their tears mingling with my own as we wept, cheek to cheek.

However, that would not always be the case. Despite the well-intentioned hearts who reached out to us, I found myself slowly, and secretly, resenting some of my comforters, particularly those who said they understood our loss or there was some divine reason for it. Many of these consolers were caring people who had substantial losses themselves, but I was numb to them. They said they knew what we were going through. "No, you don't!" my inner voice would scream. Those who attempted to comfort me with their stories of loss, however significant, were met with a brewing storm of my own. People would say things like, "I lost my grandmother. I understand." "My spouse lost a grown child during a previous marriage. I understand." "My uncle, who I looked up to like a dad died. I understand." "My wife of sixty-two years died. I understand." One person at the visitation even said, "We lost our dog that we had for many years. We understand." "No, you don't! No, you don't!" I know their losses were all painful but I couldn't hear them. My stifling grief had closed off my ears—and my heart.

> I began to contemptibly believe that unless you lost your only son or daughter to sudden death, you could never understand.

A lady from our church approached my weeping mother at Gabe's visitation, and said, "Imogene, why are you crying so? It's not like it was one of your children." My mom said, "My grandchildren *are* my children!" And now being a grandfather, I fully know this to be true. I'm surprised my sainted and spirited mother didn't slap that misguided woman. Oh, the words people say. If you are hearing the sacred confessions of another's loss, *please* don't see it as an opportunity to tell them yours; just listen—please.

At that time, my normal compassionate and congenial demeanor surrendered to disdain and disgust. How dare others compare their losses to mine. Old people are supposed to die, I reasoned. Not all losses are as keenly felt. Not all are as tragic. The Bible says we are given seventy years (see Psalm 90:10). Those living beyond that age had their time. Their deaths come in the proper order of things. But people, who die before seventy, even as children—how do we reconcile this? What sense can it possibly make? Their deaths surely cause the earth itself to weep more. Yet, time has graciously allowed me to rethink that sentiment, while subconsciously asking forgiveness from those to whom I held unnecessary harsh feelings.

I've come to discover it is not fair to expect anyone to understand that which is not understandable, neither they for me, nor I for them. Though I still resent people comparing their very different losses to mine, I've mercifully reclaimed the respectful knowledge that everyone's loss is the worst to them. Every life is sacred and intrinsically valuable, and each end is grievously painful in its own right. The point of this book is not to garner sympathies for our loss or to measure it against another's. Rather, I want to give you a brief glance into the long, narrow, dark valley through which we have traveled and through which we travel still—and in the journey find a way to live again.

Struggling with Spirituality

I have always been a person of faith. I grew up in the church, and now I lead one as its pastor. I have always lived with the concrete sense that there was a right and a wrong, a good and a bad, and an up and a down to this world. When a mentor once advised me never to preach absolute truth in a sermon, I had to breathe into a paper bag for three minutes. I believe life has a sense of purpose and cycle to it, found somewhere between God's supreme design and our self-made reality. And I believe the universe has an intended order involved, like that of a honeycomb, or a microchip. These things I believe are of God.

Likewise, the scriptures intrigue me, not in a way that makes me question, but in a way that gives me pause. Despite the occasional waver to my walk, I try to live my life by them. Their stories are my stories, and their lessons are my lessons—all of this, of course, before the storm of June 18, 2005. After the storm passed, spiritual matters became hard for me. My faith seemed awash. My spirituality suddenly became packaged up with so much emotion, question, and vagueness that I felt it better left alone.

As pastor of a church I was in a significant dilemma. I didn't feel capable of the critical thought necessary to formulate a sermon, a Bible study, or even a conversation. My District Superintendent informed me that one well-intentioned member in my parish thought I should just *swallow the lump in my throat* and jump back in the pulpit. For a moment, I hated that person. But I know that he just didn't know, he couldn't know. I minister with my heart. I preach with my heart. I counsel with my heart. I lead with my heart. I teach with my heart. I love with my heart. And as my daughter Tiffany reminded me, my heart wasn't working. It had been broken. It had been crushed.

Two weeks after Gabe's death, I pressed out a letter to be read in church. It was not the kind of thing church-growth gurus would have you do to inspire the masses and attract new converts. I think the fallout of the letter left our good people wondering about the welfare and future of their pastor. It caused one person to leave the church. He heard me talking for years about the goodness of God in all seasons and how nothing in life or death could separate us from God's love. Now he thought I didn't practice what I had preached. And for a while—I didn't. The letter read:

July 3, 2005

Dear Church Family,

I wanted to express our deep gratitude for your profound love and concern for our family, at the untimely and unexplained loss of our beloved son Gabe. Many of you came to our home immediately after church on that dark Sunday, two weeks ago. You simply came with your tears and your love and sat by our side. Thank you. I will never find the words to express the shadows and sorrow that continue to surround us. The pain has been suffocating. However, I have been unable to pray a single time. So your prayers are needed now more than ever. I have come to the realization that I know little about life at all and little about faith. I have to be honest with you, my life has partly ended. I feel cheated and robbed, not so much for myself, but for my son. Providence has seemed especially cruel and unjust. I have lost my joy, my hope, and (in part) my faith. At this time I have nothing to offer you, and I will not be back to church until I do.

So this weekend, by God's grace, we will rejoice in the marriage of our dear daughter, Valerie, and our fine son-in-law, Alan. They are good people whose lives together will be a healing balm for us all. I also take solace from the fact that our church has good leaders. I am confident to leave matters in their hands. In fact, I have been thinking about something else lately. Perhaps my absence is now necessary for another reason. Maybe the church had become too much about what I thought and did—too much about me. That day is over. God has not called just me. It is time we all did the work of the church. The church is a body, not a person.

This morning I offer you what I know. I still believe in love, in kindness, in forgiveness, and in compassion. So be good to each other. Be gentle and gracious with each other. Lay down any hardness of heart you might have. Hold each other close. This life is full of shifting shadows. Be careful to spend your days wisely. I've been thinking of this text lately, "Beloved, let us love one another, for love is from God; and everyone who loves is born of God and knows God. The one who does not love does not know God, for God is love" (1 John 4:7–8). That is the message I've always tried to say. In this hour of darkness it remains the only message I can speak and embrace.

Grace and Peace,

Vince

After about eight weeks of bereavement leave, I did decide to step back into the pulpit, not knowing if it was my return or my final Sunday. I was going to let the day decide my future. When our lives are in crisis or conflict, so often is our faith.

This was the case for John Wesley (1703–1791), the unintentional founder of the Methodist church. As a young, Anglican priest, serving far from Mother England in distant Georgia, Wesley's mission was failing and, like me, began to doubt the depth of his faith. His flock had not behaved as had his holy clubs back at Oxford. Also, a young woman he had courted married another. Wesley determined his one-time love was superficial and denied her communion. Sued for defamation, Wesley became embittered and returned to England. There, he came under the tutelage of Moravian mentor, Peter Boehler. Boehler advised him to preach faith until you have it—then because you have it, you will preach faith. Preach faith until you have it! Doing is transformed into being. So I preached—not because I had something to offer, but because I was seeking something myself.

Being a predictable Methodist, I often rely on the lectionary calendar to guide my scripture selections. And there it was, in that Sunday's reading, in Matthew's gospel—the disciples, those innocuous followers of Jesus, locked in a life-and-death struggle with a storm (see Matthew 14:22–33). This story holds a number of mysteries and risks for me. Wearied by the sad news of the death of John the Baptist, and the feeding of the five thousand, Jesus sent the multitudes away. Then he specifically made the disciples get into a boat and head out to sea without him. The *King James Version* says he "constrained them." The word has to do with compulsion, as if there were no other option or choice. Why? Did he know that dreadful storm was about to come? Did he want to test them? Was it to see how the discipleship training was going? Was the dreadful moment crafted by heaven to see if the twelve were worthy of carrying the torch? It was the fourth watch, the graveyard shift, between 3 and 6 a.m., the time when night can be especially frightful—even without storms. And Jesus came to them, walking on the water. But his presence didn't still their terrors; it magnified them. "It is a ghost!" They cried out for fear (Matthew 14:26b). And I ask: Why could they recognize Jesus in the calm of the land, but not in the storm of the sea? Do storms disguise God? Is God less or more visible when dread and uncertainty come calling?

One commentator suggests that to understand the story, we must realize that at the time of Jesus' appearance on the sea, the boat would have been far from land, and driven and tossed by the waves. If that was so, it may mean that Jesus' miracle of walking on the water was not intended to just show off who he was, but to come to the aid of his threatened disciples.[3] Again I ask: Jesus, why did you send your disciples out into the storm, if you only had to rescue them later? Couldn't the whole matter have been addressed satisfactorily with a Bible study on the shores of Galilee, while munching on the leftovers of the loaves and fishes?

Between Faith and Doubt

But something else is here. If to love is to take risks, then surely faith becomes the greatest risk of all. While this story is also told by Mark and Luke, only Matthew included the account of Peter. "Lord, if it is you, command me to come to you on the water." "Come," said Jesus (Matthew 14:28-29). And Peter sank. This story graphically depicts what it means to be a Christian caught between faith and doubt. Tennyson said there was more faith in honest doubt than in half the church's creeds. Peter represents to me everyone who has dared to believe in a good God revealed in a kind and gentle Son who cares about this world. It is called faith for a reason. Without seeing, yet we are to entrust ourselves and our families to an invisible God and dare to believe a day of justice is coming when that God will wipe away every tear from our eyes. Death will be no more on that day. In the words of John the Revelator, there shall be no mourning, no crying or pain, no sorrow or sighing, for the things that have haunted humanity are past and are gone (see Revelation 21:4). But until that day, we are sent into storms, crises come, life hangs in the balance—we sink. But Peter, oh Peter, when all seemed lost, you cried out, you remembered, you reached out. It wasn't that you found Jesus' big hand. No. He found your little hand, "And immediately Jesus stretched out his hand and took hold of him" (Matthew 14:31). To be a person of faith is to be a risk-taker. Faith is the belief that when you are sinking below the waves, a hand will be there to take you, to raise you back up.

Former Senate Chaplain Peter Marshall once wrote, "I give gratitude for that constant sense of need that keeps me close to thy side. Help me to keep my hand in thine and my ears open to the wisdom of thy voice."

Like Peter, I found myself caught between faith and doubt, sinking, reaching for that hand, listening for that voice. Surely he will find me.

On June 12, 2008, a tornado randomly dipped down upon a Boy Scout outing at the Little Sioux Scout Ranch near Little Sioux, Iowa. An EF3 twister with wind speeds of 145 mph cut a path about fourteen miles long. When the storm moved on, a pickup truck had been tossed on its side. Tree limbs rested on top of the Scout tents. Trees were flattened, and debris filled the landscape. The meeting room where the scouts had sought shelter was a pile of rubble, bricks, and cinderblocks. And the lives of four elite Scouts, two aged 14 and two aged 13, had been taken, along with the buildings and branches. In moments, with little warning, four boys were dead. Just like that, four families were thrust violently into the depths. I sat in stunned silence when news of that pointless tragedy broke on my television set. Somehow, I felt it my tragedy, too. I knew what those calls to family were like. I knew what would happen in those homes in the coming days. I knew about picking out clothes for your child's funeral. I knew the sorrowful cries, the blind and blunt force that dislodges every crumb of normalcy. Suddenly, I was there again. And I hated storms.

If only the kids hadn't gone to the camp. If only the warning signals had worked better or the boys had heeded them better. If only the event had been postponed or cancelled. If only the protective dads had been there. If only those boys had been somewhere else, anywhere else. As I have said, the Bible's stories are my stories. One that has long mystified me is of a father who had a boy paralyzed by demonic seizures (Mark 9:14-27). With no resource, no refuge, sinking beneath the waves, he came to Jesus. With honest doubt, the father said to Jesus: "If you can do anything, take pity on us and help us!" Just like Peter's beckoning words from the tempest tossed boat, "If you are the Lord, command me to come on the water" (Matthew 14:28). One little word, if: it is one tiny nugget of humanity amidst the divinity; it is a welcome mat among the scriptures that bids me come; it is anathema to the health-and-wealth preachers, but pure nectar to this seeker. Jesus said to him, "If you can! All things are possible to him who believes." It is a staggering thought. The father surely wondered why his son's healing was dependent on his ability to believe. What kind of God is this? What sort of conditional bargaining does heaven require of us?

Do I have to be sent out into a storm in order to know I can be rescued from it? How does one call upon faith, when all traces of it are gone? Yet, perhaps that is the nature of the whole matter. The father honestly breathed out the words: "I do believe; help me overcome my unbelief" (Mark 9:24). Yes! I do believe. I still believe. Yet—I sink amidst the winds and the waves of my storm. Lord, help my unbelief.

The father received back the fruit of his honest doubt; the demon was cast out. Peter rose back to the top of the sea. What, then, for those of us who have not received our sons and daughters back? The storm has subsided, yet the devastation remains. We are caught between faith and doubt, and both are legitimate. Like Little Sioux Scout Ranch, the carnage seems irreconcilable. Sometimes lives are not spared, and children do not come back. There is a litany of mistreated martyrs listed in the letter to the Hebrews; a terrifying piece really; patriarchs and matriarchs of the faith, good people—and they suffer untimely and (ostensibly) unjust ends. But it all comes seemingly with God's approval. The eleventh chapter concludes with an enigmatic line, "These were all commended for their faith, yet none of them received what had been promised. God had planned something better for us so that only together with us would they be made perfect" (Hebrews 11:39–40). Untimely and unjust death seems a steep price to pay for perfection.

The death of our child reshapes our priorities, our goals, our purpose, our desires, our ideology, and what is left of our faith. Like clay on the potter's wheel, the reshaping is out of our hands, both in timing and design. From the clay's perspective, it seems most arbitrary and uninvited. Yet, after a season, somehow those things began to reemerge in spite of us, and new shapes begin to form. There is a before and after here, with the lingering image of who we have been now overshadowed by the likeness of who we are becoming.

The Importance of Self-Care

I have often heard bereaved parents say at various groups such things as "After our son/daughter died, our friends and interests changed. We moved, we stopped or started going to church. We threw ourselves into a project, or we withdrew into an introvert's world." It's understandable. Everything about life changes when our children die, and that is as it should be. This kind of storm cannot be cleaned up. Chain saws or rakes will not make this mess go away. There must be some sense of re-creation instead, a new normal. The storm becomes woven into who you are becoming. It is in you, the real you. The fabric of our being has changed, and the pattern reflects the change. Whether or not our families and friends understand and accept that change is extrinsic to our lives. They can and must take second place to our grief. Here is one place we are allowed to be selfish. We don't need to explain why we're different. We don't need to justify our emerging new identity. We don't need to apologize for its changes. We have been through enough. It is simply sufficient to say, "I have been caught up in a storm, and it's not over." Our churches, our neighbors, our families, and our friends will either receive us as storm damaged or they won't. But while they're deciding, we'll be just surviving.

> The bereaved need to know they have no one else they must please. And a freedom comes with this realization. We simply exist, for one breath, then another. As the breaths increase, they do what breath has always done—bring life to the clay of our humanity.

Our first year, I became a phone acquaintance with a woman who lost her daughter in an auto accident. What penetrated my heart concerning her was in the how and when of her daughter's death. Concerned about bad roads, Mom called her traveling daughter on the cell phone and begged her to reconsider a trip halfway across the state to see her boyfriend. While she was on the phone, the car spun out of control on a patch of black ice and into the path of an oncoming truck. And the phone went dead. I have lost contact with that woman now, but I'll never forget what her ghost-like whispering voice told me during one of our last conversations. She said, "I live a forced life now. I make myself live, breathe, work, eat, and sleep." We must not underestimate our opposition. These are the kinds of storms that demand the sanctity of self-care. It must come before all other responses.

Putting yourself first is a seemingly unchristian act. But in the initial seasons of parental grief, it is all we can do; it is all we must do. For entire days I was simply unable to function at any level. Phone calls came, and I would hold the phone but could not offer any response. People came to my house, expecting to see how a Christian pastor, victorious in his faith, handled loss. They found a disheveled, dispirited, soulless man who was just surviving. I know some left thinking my faith a sham. And I admit, I wondered the same thing.

I had never taken sleeping pills in my life, but my sleeping patterns changed that day of my storm, and they have remained changed. So I discovered in order to sleep at all (and one must sleep to cope with grief), sleep aids were essential. Even personal hygiene and eating were major hurdles in those initial months. I was constantly tired because everything was an overwhelming task. I was drained not only by the effort of the task, but also by the effort needed to work up to the task. It is crucial to make a way toward self-care. Without it, the storms of life can crush you. Storms must be accepted for what they are. You cannot change their path, purpose, or strength. I have learned to accept the storms which came my way, and after they passed, to cleanup or rebuild.

But parental grief is a different kind of storm indeed. It is hard to accept and impossible to rebuild afterward. A friend of mine who lost a beloved daughter some years ago told of a conversation she had with a middle-aged widow. The widow advised this dear bereaved mom to get going again. She told how she had gone to a dance to meet and dance with other men. "You can't just stay home and mope, you know," she offered. "You have to 'get out there.'" My dear friend told me later she couldn't even respond to such thoughtlessness. "What did she want me to do? I can't just go out to a bar and pick up another daughter." People who have not lost a child don't understand the heart of such separation. Our children are not replaceable. We can't get another. Even if we have more or adopt more, it doesn't bring back the children we have buried. This is death at its worse—absolute cessation.

Another difference between meteorological and parental storms is in the preparation. With our technology, we are usually informed of an oncoming storm and can "take cover." When severe weather is threatening, local news is quick to break in to our favorite shows, showing us the path and ferocity of the coming storm. Plans change; events are cancelled—all because we have discovered that threatening weather is on its ugly way. In affected parts of the world, houses are now built with hurricane straps, a means of bonding the roof to the walls, so they can withstand hurricane-force winds.

Storm shutters are available for those who live in hurricane alley. There is no shortage of means and ways to get ready for a storm's brunt force. Still, despite their best preparative efforts, many suffer much loss and storm damage.

No one can prepare for the death of a son or daughter. It is a damnable and destructive ogre that leaves self-will so dead there is no longing to make things better again. So we must care for ourselves in grief. We do so in the common, ordinary ways. But that only initializes the process; it comes as a start. Tiny steps make up the beginning, and numerous steps are necessary to complete the process. A journey such as this begins, and then eventually leads us towards that secret and sacred place inside of us. Our hopes and dreams reside in this place, as well as our deepest longings, sacred confessions and darkest fears. And, out of this place our determination will resurrect, with a desire to live again after the storm.

A Large Community

I know our family is not the first one to have suffered such a loss. We quickly became aware of how large the community of bereaved parents was. One group who visited us shortly after Gabe's death said, "No one wants to be in this damnable fraternity, but now that you're here, you need to know some things." And what I have learned is there are sorrows that can hold us as tight now as our cherished ones did then. I know there is not a time limit on any grief or a defined set of rules and responses in a tidy how-to manual on the bookstore shelf. Each person needs to experience significant trial and error to progress through grief. Nonetheless, I know each person's sorrows are the worst to them. And I know that every life has a storm. If we live long enough, we each will be sent out into the storm. Is it only to see if we'll be rescued? I still don't know. But I do know we cannot do this by ourselves. We learn to live in that teeter-totter center between solitude and community in order to coexist with our losses. Experience teaches that many become caught in the web between doubt and faith. This self-realization allowed me to bear my storm. And raindrop by raindrop, I am enduring and aspiring for some semblance of sunshine and with it a renewed faith and life.

CHAPTER 2

GRIEF AND REDEMPTION

O Never Star

O never star
Was lost; here
We all aspire to heaven and there is heaven
Above us.
If I stoop
Into a dark tremendous sea of cloud,
It is but for a time; I press God's lamp
Close to my breast; its splendor soon or late
Will pierce the gloom.
I shall emerge someday.

Robert Browning[4]

IT STILL TROUBLES ME; the assumption that all things happen for a reason. As stated, much of what passed for comfort was loathsome to me. I didn't seem capable of receiving consolation. Gradually I became more gracious toward those who misspoke *words of assurance*; still I was amazed they could be so misinformed. After all, haven't we all been scarred by death's torment? Haven't we learned the impotence of platitudes? Haven't words rung hollow when we were near death's ugly sights and smells? Particularly, I resented the idea that there was a purpose in people's deaths. Everyone who has buried a family member has heard the litany of *other-worldly* motives: things happens for a reason; God knows what God is doing; something good comes out of everything; it was just their time; God needed them in heaven; God only takes the best; there is a purpose in everything—*ad nauseam*.

Perhaps it is our own fragile humanity, the desperate need to make sense of the nonsensical that gives wings to our feeble attempts at verbal consolation. Even I, a man of words, have many times found myself to be wanting in the face of sorrow and tragedy. If I could hit replay, I know I would hear a multitude of meaningless platitudes pouring out of my mouth in the direction of wounded and sorrowing people, more as a means of concession than inspiration. We just want to help, and words become our only means to project our feelings of empathy and compassion onto another. If for no other reason than the knowledge that no one gets out of this life unscathed, we should be patient with the bearers of insensitive words. After all, their intent wasn't unkind, only their effect. Nonetheless, that realization hasn't tempered my ill will even now when I hear similar conciliatory words, but I have learned to keep my resentment to myself and let others struggle through how best to give and receive comfort.

But the whole matter has required me to contemplate God's authority, especially regarding its role in untimely death. I have spent considerable time and deep introspection, debating the idea.

The years have allowed me to step back and rethink the possibilities. What I have allowed myself to consider has more to do with the future than with the past. Whether or not there is some divine reason for anguish of this level, I still do not know. I have come to make room for the possibility of good coming from bad. It's not that God causes (or allows) bad to accomplish good (though that still may be), rather that God can redeem something bad in such fashion that it is reshaped into something good. I must allow for the possibility that God could take my private world of grief and refashion it in a way that is redemptive and emancipating; or more simply stated, in God's world, perhaps some things *do* happen for a reason. Can God even redeem grief? Can virtue be rescued from the pit of sorrow? These are questions life would force me to consider, with no easy answers.

Lessons in Grief

I am a deliberate learner in matters of loss, yet I am slowly learning. I am learning these lessons:

- Parental grief is a formidable opponent that stalks its victims night and day.

- Grief recovery (perhaps an oxymoron) is a very long-term process.

- People in grief are not themselves and perhaps will never again be themselves.

- People in grief are prone to sieges of sadness, anger, insensitivity, fatigue, depression, sullenness, bitterness, and a profound sense of helplessness.

- People in grief fight having resentment for those who are not.

- Friends and acquaintances simply cannot understand the depths of this kind of pain.

And I am learning that the whole world hasn't stopped—only our part of it has. All these are necessary lessons before one can consider the possibility of God's intervention for good. But one thing I have already learned and I learned it early: if you intend to befriend or be in the company of a bereaved person, be prepared to be in the presence of someone who is learning lessons.

I have also learned lessons regarding what I will not do the next time I am with a grieving person.

- I will not tell them I understand.

- I will not tell them to be strong.

- I will not expect them to "get over it" quickly, if at all.

- I will not avoid honest conversation regarding their loss.

- I will not laugh or make light conversation at the wake, visitation, or funeral.

- I will not be offended if they speak or act irrationally.

- I will not be negligent in showing my care and compassion.

- I will not neglect my responsibility as their friend, their neighbor, their pastor, or simply as a Christian.

The tragic death of our child (of any age), or any immediate member of our family, unhinges our world. Everything suddenly goes crazy. Many sound and balanced people simply can no longer cope nor make sense of their world. Caregivers do them no favors by projecting normalcy on them, or making it seem as if everything is all right. In addition to the divine reasons for death that seemed to flow so effortlessly from those consolers, I also grew to particularly scorn the response, "They're in a better place now." People who offered that comforting retort often got only steely silence from me— if they were lucky. From our earthly vantage point, the best place for our loved one is with us. I understand and have been there when some people, like the elderly, those who have suffered much pain, or those abandoned, lonesome, and alone have died. Perhaps they do go to a better place—but not my son. His place was here.

> If I could change one thing about the responses many made to our loss, it would simply be, you don't need to say anything other than "I'm sorry." Some things cannot be tidied up by a well-turned or a well-intentioned phrase.

Grief is a very private thing. It is ours, not theirs. My wife Vicki and I both grieved passionately, but differently. She was more accepting. Not me. I would lament, "Why us?" She would return, "Why not us?" I thought I was losing my mind. Some days I couldn't breathe. I didn't eat. I rarely slept for days and days. I was so sad I simply sat in my tears. One night a church member called me. Vicki mercifully answered the phone and handed it to me. I tried, valiantly but impotently, to compose myself. Pain and brokenness filled my voice as I said hello. It could not be disguised. "What's wrong, Vince?" the caller broke in. Incredulous, I barked back, "My son died!" How could this person not know this? Do people simply think this goes away like a cold? If this kind of loss doesn't evoke extended compassion from the people in your life, what possibly could?

Likewise, I soon discovered friends, family, and colleagues got over our loss much sooner than we did (and we have wonderful friends, family, and colleagues). A few months after Gabe's death, Vicki contacted a one-time colleague of mine to whom I'd been very close to disclose our sad news. He offered to meet me halfway for a visit, to which I reluctantly agreed. I met him at a county park, near a lake, and poured out my grief. With a pastor's proficiency he comforted me with a prayer, a book, and a promise to revisit me on a monthly basis. I never heard from him again. That would be the pattern of many well-intentioned comforters. On the first dreadful anniversary of Gabe's death, we suffered alone. Only a few family members reached out to us. By the next anniversary, only a couple did. By the third year there were none. They had mostly moved on or forgotten. I understood their absence. But we couldn't move on. We couldn't forget.

Trying to Understand and Be Understood

Desperate for some perspective, I began to search for someone who really understood. And I knew this meant I had to find counsel from others like me—people who had lost their children. My search uncovered a number of organizations that were initiated by and for parents who had lost children. *Bereaved Parents of the USA* and *The Compassionate Friends* were two groups that spoke directly to me and became very helpful. Though I never met a single person who was part of these groups, they became instrumental in my grief. It was evident that the people behind them and other similar groups had walked where I walked. I am indebted to the good people behind these organizations. They understood me.

I have an old plaque on my desk entitled, *Indian Prayer.* I've kept it all these years, not because of its authorship but because of its sentiment. The prayer is simply: "O Great Father, never let me judge another man until I have walked in his moccasins for two weeks." The prayer says we should not criticize others until we have walked in their shoes. It implies we should not project our assumptions upon those whose life experience is vastly different than ours. I quickly learned to spot authors, speakers, preachers, counselors, and support people who spoke only from clinical experience. They said little to me. A radio preacher and author who had been a long-time favorite of mine gave a sermon on grief that I heard one day. I suddenly realized he didn't have a clue about grief. He spoke out of a historical, academic, and theological tradition. But he had never picked out a casket for his child. Some things cannot be learned without having been experienced.

We've all had those undesirable times when we are telling a friend or acquaintance about something in our lives, a trip we've been on, or what our kids are doing. Then, in the middle of our discourse, they interrupt, and *one-up* us. They, of course, understand our story and can do us one better. For friendship sake we tolerate this because, after all, such is human nature. We are all guilty of some little social indiscretion. But such crassness crosses a line when it invades our private world of grief. Here is sacred ground, and others' opinionated counsel is often as irritating as a neighbor's barking dog or the fingernail on the blackboard.

I used to resent the notion among certain social, civil, and political groups that only like-minded, like-gender, and like-ethnicity could truly be representative of their agendas. But I've come to believe they may be onto something. My experience was that unless you've walked through the valley of tears that I've walked in, you just don't know.

In an effort to educate both myself, and those who seek to comfort people in grief, I compiled a little list that was representative of the advice I received from *The Compassionate Friends, Bereaved Parents of the USA*[5] et al. The list was of tips for those whose circle of friends and family included bereaved parents. However, it seems these apply to any family loss. Even in the center of that swirling debris of loss and grief, I knew I really wasn't despising my consolers. I thanked God for them. It was more that I was so desperately vulnerable that any misplaced word bit with venom. You don't get a rulebook when your children are born (with apologies to Dr. Spock), and neither is there one should they die. I tried to fix that, even though parental grief protocol was difficult to nail down. Nevertheless, with some risk involved, I offered these suggestions to my churches, my friends, and my family:

- Do not avoid a family because you feel helpless in the light of a tragic loss. They will benefit long term from whatever support and understanding you give. Offer to do practical things like mowing the yard, washing the car, running errands, providing childcare. Do not just say, "Call me if you need anything." That statement requires them to make the effort at a time when they have no extra energy. You take the lead in helping them.

- Mention the name of the one who has died. The bereaved long to hear the name of their loved one mentioned again. Don't fear it will only lead to further pain. The opposite is often true. Share your stories and memories of your time with them.

- Please avoid pretentious sayings or religious platitudes like, "I know how you feel," or "everything happens for a reason." These will seem presumptuous and will likely undo any good or comfort your visit has brought.

- Learn how to simply say, "I'm so sorry." There are no magic words in moments like these, and you don't need to feel compelled to find some. This kind of pain is not appeased by what you say. A hug, a touch, and a simple "I'm so sorry," will do. Don't be afraid to cry with them.

- Become a good listener. This means not responding every time a thought comes to your mind. The bereaved will need people who will just listen and to whom they can unload their thoughts. Your ability to receive their words will be more cathartic than your desire to speak. Just being there is sometimes the best comfort. Don't be afraid to ask if they want you to stay.

- Do not judge them. Bereaved people will say and do many irrational things. Mood swings are normal. They may even say cruel things about you or your family. Anger and bitterness can be the norm. Intense sadness may prevail. Regardless, your gift is your presence, not your judgment.

Bereaved parents do not "get over" the death of their children nor "snap out of it," as the outside world often seems to think they can and should do. The death of our children is not an illness or a disease from which we recover. It is a life-altering change with which we must learn to live. It is impossible to continue with "business as usual."

The community of the bereaved often must find a new normal. Tragic grief can also set a person in contrast with our superficial world that measures itself by appearance, performance, and achievement. Culture cleverly seduces us into thinking our academic, athletic, domestic, economic, and occupational prowess determines our worth. It does not. Each person who visits our planet is a gift from God and has an intrinsic value all of his or her own. If life does not teach us that, death will, for it is the great leveler. This is the life the bereaved often live. And if you will care for them, you must understand that truth. We are "caught," living in the theological and domestic middle. Yet, that is precisely the point. It is living in that tension between doubt and faith that calls for the question: *Can there be anything redemptive in the untimely death of our loved ones?* Were those who comforted me right? Do things have a plan and purpose to them—even death? Is God able to restore what death removes? It was after the death of his son that Rabbi Kushner famously framed the question this way in his book *Why Do Bad Things Happen to Good People?* Such soul searching is like having one foot stuck in the pit while the other searches for higher ground.

In my twenty plus years as a pastor, I have stood before a grieving family, by an open grave, near enough to smell the earth, some four hundred times. There I have humbly uttered the timeless words, "In the midst of life we are in death; from whom can we seek our help? Our help is in the name of the Lord, who made heaven and earth."[6] To say such a thing on behalf of another seems presumptuous enough. To believe it for oneself seems inordinate. But I do believe there is help in the Lord—even in the face of death. I must believe. How do we face grief of this magnitude without the belief that someone is behind the scenes working on our behalf? It's not because I've discovered such faith, rather it is within me, imparted to me, by the foremothers and forefathers of the church, by my pastors and teachers, by my mother and father, and by those who surround me now. Maybe it is also intuitive, placed by God within me like breath.

Redemption as a Community

If God is a *glass half full* kind of God, then even the suffering and sorrowful are invited to share God's provision and consolation. I cannot allow for God's grace being less comforting to some than others. If there is to be a redeeming future for those besieged by sorrow, it must surely come (in part) through those with whom we share our lives. Consolers and caregivers do make a difference. They have that power, and that choice. Perhaps it is an incarnation thing, as if God has no hands or heart but ours upon the earth. If so, then complete aloneness is one foe we can eliminate from our list of grievous opponents. Though sorrow and solitude will always be strangely linked, redemptive grief is less alone. People in grief need others who genuinely care. With that realization, our resistance to others' good-intentioned care is lessened, and we begin to embrace the fact that others do care about us—and our journey. As has been said, *a joy shared is twice a joy, but a burden shared is half a burden*. Perhaps it is what it means to be carried. It is the power of community, and it is surely redemptive.

I have friends who cannot open their windows during the summer. They live on a gravel road, and with every gust of wind or passing car, the dust finds its way into the house. Dust gets into everything, the carpet, the blinds, the furniture, the light fixtures, and the kitchen—everywhere. Grief is like that. It gets into everything in your life, and like dust, it subtly reveals itself.

My grief showed up during my annual physical. My doctor asked me what was wrong, and I told him. While I appreciated his inquiry, I didn't expect his response. He told me he had lost a daughter in a car wreck on Christmas Eve at the tender age of fourteen. He said he entered into a deep depression for ten years that cost him his marriage, his personal life, and nearly his career. He cautioned me of the same possibilities saying "Make your grief work a priority in your life because it affects everything."

Redemption as a Promise

Such is grief—human and unredeemed. The idea of grief being unredeemable seemed hopeless, and it became a primary conflict within me. It seemed nothing but darkness, sadness, and death could come from what had happened. And even if the promise of a reunion in the sweet bye-and-bye were realized, it wouldn't be enough compensation for what had been taken from us. But redemption's song has to do with making good on a promise or a pledge, like paying off a mortgage. It also connotes making up for something lost. I will always believe Gabe was God's gift to us. Yet, it appeared the promise was only given in part. If our children are gifts from God, their untimely death makes the gift seem incomplete. We wanted more. The death of your child leaves a great *undone-ness* to your life. Yet, I reasoned, if my faith is anything more than words, then I must allow for a completion of redemption's work. With God's help, by faith our lost children remain gifts, received in part—one day received in full!

Dr. Ralph Sockman, the onetime "Dean of the American Pulpit," wrote of being thankful for God's gifts in his book, *The Meaning of Suffering*:

> Instead of dwelling on the loss we have suffered in the death of our loved ones, we can think gratefully of the gift we have received from God in sharing their lives. Some years ago a young man died at twenty-one just after he had finished a long and expensive education. The bereaved parents will never forget the words spoken to them at the time by the late Dr. Walter A. Jessup, former president of the University of Iowa. Dr. Jessup told of a father who had lost two sons just as they were about to launch forth on their lifework. That father said that his boys had given him far more satisfaction than could be measured by any money and efforts spent on them and hence he still felt indebted to God for their lives.[7]

Could this also be the redemptive power of grief? Could our focus shift from the enduring suffering of loss to indebtedness for the gift, however long we had it? And from there, to the hope of what is yet to come? It would take redemption.

In a theological context the word also has to do with the idea of a ransom or deliverance. In the church it is central to our understanding of salvation. The apostle Paul wrote in Romans, "... for all have sinned and fall short of the glory of God, and are justified freely by his grace through the redemption that came by Christ Jesus" (Romans 3:23–24). (Justified: made right with God—freely—through redemption.) Amazing. Does the same God allow the same formula for the bereaved? (Comforted: ransomed from sorrow—lovingly—through redemption.) It would be amazing indeed.

Redemption as a Fellowship

There is also a fellowship in grief that is redemptive—a *brotherhood of the bereaved*, if you will. Thorton Wilder wrote a short play entitled, *The Angel That Troubled the Water*. It is based on the legend of the pool of Bethesda, where you could be healed if you enter the pool when an angel appears and stirs the water. The play has three characters: 1) a doctor with a secret burden, praying that the angel will come; 2) a confirmed invalid, who has waited long for healing, and scolds the doctor for seeking the pool of healing: "You are able to walk about. Go back to work and leave these miracles to us who need them," and 3) the angel. Before he enters the pool of healing, he speaks to the doctor:

> Draw back physician, this moment is not for you. Without your wound, where would your power be? It is your very remorse that makes your low voice tremble into the hearts of men. The very angels themselves cannot persuade the wretched and blundering children on earth as can one human being broken on the wheels of living. In Love's service only the wounded soldier can serve. [8]

Again I ask, is this the redemptive power of grief? Is some great work accomplished in us that give us ears we haven't had before, compassion we hadn't understood, care we haven't given? Does grief transform us in any redemptive way? What kind of change is wrought in us, birthed by sorrow, shaped by redemption? I think of the predictable changes I've morphed through in my years since Gabe died: profound sadness, raging anger, self-centered bitterness, spiritual crisis, destructive behavior, and then a great aloneness. I found I could not run from grief, anesthetize myself from it, or forget about it. And I valiantly tried them all. Yet with time, unexpected emotional companions began to intrude upon my pain: compassion, sensitivity, humanity, mercy, and sympathy. As one began to loosen its grip, another took its place. It was like being ransomed. Like a chrysalis, do we even realize we are changing? Does memory and experience keep us tethered to what we have been, rather than what we are becoming? Does redemption have that rescuing power to ultimately shape this aching experience into something transformative—even something good?

I could not see it at first. Even now it is shaded and disguised, but I think grief might have a redemptive side. It can cause us to be more sensitive to another's pain, it gives empathy, and it bids us welcome into the suffering of others. I have never been a person who reads the obituaries. In fact, I've always thought it a tawdry practice. It seemed invasive and rude. I felt it was like peeking into someone else's private stories. But after Gabe's death, I found myself drawn to them, but only to certain ones. I might glance over most of them, but I seemed to be drawn to the obituaries of young people, recognizing them even before I read them. It was almost as if it was an intuitive thing. If their pictures were there I would study their face, as if I had known them. I would ask myself why this abrupt change. Usually my weekend morning paper-reading routines were predictable. I stayed with the fluff: sports, funnies, ads, opinions, and puzzles. Life was serious enough; I wanted my paper to be a diversion, not a means of adding to the weight of the world. But I knew the reason for the morning shift in reading protocol. I identified with each untimely loss, as if it were part mine. In the same manner as the invisible and universal church, the community of bereaved parents remains a single body—though we've never met each other.

Redemption Through a Support Group

Some months after Gabe's death, a Bereaved Parent's Support Group, a monthly group that met in the boardroom at the Mahaska County Hospital in Oskaloosa, contacted us. I don't know how they got our names, but every month we received a letter of invitation, accompanied by a little piece of timely and welcoming prose or poetry. When I received the first letter, I knew I would someday go, but I was not ready yet. I was in no shape to tell my story to a bunch of grieving parents or to hear theirs. I secretly feared that their sorrows would exceed my own or at least take me back to the beginning. I was not prepared for such a setback. So month after month the invitation came. And month after month I carefully and respectfully read them and then threw them away. Then one month, just over a year into our journey of sorrows, I found myself traveling to Oskaloosa. It was the second Tuesday, the regular meeting night, and I would be in plenty of time for the 7:00 meeting. I don't know why, but I know I went alone this first time. Vicki either couldn't or wasn't ready to attend. Some of these highly charged emotional experiences have become clouded by shades of gray, perhaps mercifully so. But I do recall this much, I went but did not participate in the meeting, nor did I stay long. I later reasoned it was just too soon. By the next meeting, however, or maybe the next, Vicki and I would attend, and stay. Vicki didn't always go, but for about the next five years I attended regularly.

A gracious and caring lady named Elaine led the group. Elaine's husband Bert started coming not long after we did. They had lost a dear daughter in a car wreck, some twenty years earlier, and the loss had endured all those years. Nevertheless, something purposeful came out of their grief, something redemptive. Elaine gave of herself to provide a safe place for others who have known this hell to come find sanctuary. She kept a firm, steady hand on the wheel during many emotionally charged nights. I could tell immediately that her loss and sorrow were as real and keenly felt as mine, but she was channeling her grief into something useful. Everyone who attended these meetings was just like us—they had buried a son or daughter. Sometimes grandparents also came. This was one of the few places I still could feel normal. This was my world, and everyone here understood me, and I them. I can still recognize all the faces, if no longer all the names, although I will never forget a certain few. At each meeting Elaine asked each of us to tell our stories. I knew that meant once a month I would have to retell the dreadful details of the day Gabe died and give an update on our journey. I dreaded that part of the meeting. But somehow, like lancing a boil, I felt better the next day for having done so.

However, with the telling of our story, came listening to the stories of others, a painstaking process, no doubt. Oddly, neither

Vicki nor I remember all the names, but we do recall the stories and the faces. There were suicides, cancer, and car wrecks, each story told with trembling syllables and breaths, one moment at a time. As we came to know each other, there became a family feeling to this gathering; it was a true community. As months rolled along, new parents came on board. Some, like me, had allowed some time to elapse before they were ready to talk about what had befallen them. Some came immediately. It didn't matter; they became part of our brotherhood of the bereaved.

One dear lady came with her mother the first night, and she wailed, passionately, for hours. Vicki hadn't come this night, and I was wishing I had stayed home as well. Through her tears a story began to unfold; a dreadful story. Her loss was only a week old. I marveled that she could be here at all. No way could I have done this that soon. Perhaps this was the only straw she had to grasp. She had lost her daughter in a car wreck, her beloved daughter—who was nine months pregnant with her grandchild—and now they were both dead. Elaine just gently loved her. We all did. We all loved each other with compassionate hearts. If there is a safety net for such melancholy, apart from our faith, then surely like-minded support groups are it. I am most grateful for this community of broken hearts. I have finally stopped attending this group. I'm not sure why, but I knew when to go, and I knew when to quit. Regardless, they became a precious family to me, and I found redemption in their midst.

The psalmist understood mourning and deliverance. Many Psalms are a litany of sorrow, mistrust, wrongdoing, repentance, and redemption, as if this were some natural progression in life. I often center myself in a particular Psalm during times of trial and tribulation. About six months after Gabe's death I found Psalm 31, particularly the 9th and 10th verses, "Be merciful to me, O Lord, for I am in distress; my eyes grow weak with sorrow, my soul and body with grief. My life is consumed by anguish and my years by groaning; my strength fails because of my affliction, and my bones grow weak." I thought to myself: this man knows. This is how I feel. All of my life is consumed by my grief. No part of my living is unaffected. My eyes were weak, my body and soul wracked with sorrow, and I felt powerless. In distress I, too, looked for mercy, if there was any to be found. But what good could mercy do me now? I needed mercy before June 18, 2005. Yet, when all else is gone, only one place is left to go. I have always known this.

Redemption Through Faith

Jesus once crossed the Sea of Galilee to Capernaum to escape the pressing crowds. He had fed them loaves and fishes and they wanted more. Jesus said they followed him because he provided food. However, he was now offering them another type of bread and another type of drink. His own body and blood—living bread, he called it, "… unless you eat the flesh of the Son of Man and drink his blood, you have no life in you" (John 6:53). This wasn't the kind of sermon that wins friends or influences people. In fact, the offended crowd deserted Jesus. But this brings me to the precious point of the story, Jesus then turning to the remaining disciples asked, "You do not want to leave too, do you?" Again it was Peter, blessed Peter, who answered him, "Lord, to whom shall we go? You have the words of eternal life" (John 6:60–69). This is what the psalmist knew—and I did too. Even in the center of failing strength and groaning years we must look up, as we have nowhere else to go. Redemption is found in no other place. Broken hearts know this to be intuitively true.

Nevertheless, reclaiming faith in the center of grief is struggle enough; it is all a good soul can do. Doing ministry in the center of grief is overwhelming. On more than one occasion, I had decided to quit being a pastor. Though, like Peter, I was reconciling myself to the growing awareness that I had nowhere else to go, I could not conceive the same possibility regarding the pastorate. Staying with the Lord and staying with the church were separate aspirations. Even though I had gone back, I was an empty suit. I really wasn't doing my job. During this time we were advised to visit with our Conference Pastoral Counselor, a nice woman employed by our church leaders to provide counsel to clergy and staff. I had no expectations as Vicki and I drove to Des Moines for our initial visit. She was a welcoming person and knew some of our story. Her office was typical for a counselor's office, and we sat on a small couch as she lit a candle in front of us. I felt like I was back in the sixties. A counselor's ability to truly listen is a great gift, maybe as helpful as her guidance. Perhaps that is the nature of the occupation. We only met with this person twice. I had known one self-doubting pastor who was a regular here. He had some deep need to sit on that couch in front of that candle and have the counselor listen to him, which he did again and again. But this task-oriented preacher wanted to get the job done right away. Candles only burn so long, and so does my patience.

Ministry by Rote

Still, a couple of important things came from our two visits with her. First, I deeply appreciated her honesty. She said up front that she had never known our deep grief and would not pretend that she understood. She sat as an outsider and observer. Her counsel would come from that position. I really valued that honest word. She didn't project any knowing on us. She was taught well. May her kind increase. I have been reminded many times when people have come into my office with an obvious burden, listening (really listening) to another's heart is a great gift to give. The second thing she did would have a life-direction effect on me. She told me in a very matter-of-fact manner that I could not leave the ministry. In the way a mother tells her child to brush his teeth, she told me to remain in the church. "Your son died, your calling didn't," she offered. "But how can you expect me to keep them separate? How do I do these things with my heart out of commission?" I replied. And she offered a simple word; something that would never have occurred to me. She told me to do ministry by rote. "By rote," I asked, "How do you do heart things by rote?" She had a laundry list ready: stay behind your desk, delegate, don't work with kids, don't do funerals, stay out of living rooms, go home early, administrate, do the *nuts-and-bolts* things. Is this possible, I thought? Can you do a heart job mechanically?

I haven't always been a minister. I have an alter ego. I am an electrician, a trade I inherited from my wonderful father. I started wiring houses and grain bins before I could drive a car, in fact, before I had a permit. This was a nuts-and-bolts job. Once you knew the mechanics of it, you were off and running. No heart was required here, although my father had a deep and caring heart. You can wire houses even while in grief. Still, in my many years of business, and like my father before me, deep friendships and relationships were often forged with my customers. In that manner, running a small business and running a small church is not that dissimilar. Nevertheless, in matters of the heart, in life-and-death matters—they are legions apart. Yes, you can wire houses while in grief. But can you do ministry? Regardless, I always tried to do what my mother told me (err … mostly), and I would try to do what this mother-like counselor told me. I would try to do ministry by rote.

And for over a year, I did. Colleagues did the funerals, a decision I particularly regretted when a special lady in our church died. A secretary by nature and occupation, she had the gift of encouragement, and she fulfilled that calling with a secretary's efficiency. She sent out cards to any and every one, for everything. Her card ministry was a great reassurance to many, me included. I felt guilty for not doing her funeral, but I stayed true to the counselor's advice. Once it seemed safe enough to make a visit to an elderly couple, members of the church. With caring and noble intentions, they surrounded me on the couch, so close their legs were touching mine. The man placed his hand on my knee and said, "So, Vincent, how are you doing?" I know he meant the best for me, but I felt trapped and jumped up and bolted out the door. After this, I stayed out of living rooms. I stayed away from the kids and youth. I stayed behind my desk. I delegated. I went home as soon as I could. And I did this until I knew it was okay to resume my pastoral duties.

Sometimes redemption needs a breather. It can't be forced. It has an agenda, and a little well-intentioned regimented mechanics can give it time to take root, like a seed germinating. Regardless, I felt there was a sense of determinism about my brief time with our pastoral counselor. My life could have veered off into another path during those days, but she wouldn't let me. So I did ministry by rote, until my heart started working again.

Redemption as a Path

I will never know if it is God or chance that allows us places in life to redirect our path. Frost said it was the *Road Less Traveled* that has made all the difference. Give me Yogi Berra's wise counsel: "When you come to a fork in the road—take it." Regardless, most of us come to forks in the road, places where life can have decidedly different implications. Sometimes we are allowed to back up and chose a different path, but sometimes our choice of path seems irrevocable. What if one path led to redemption, despite a formidable outset? Would we risk a roll of the dice if it meant the end of the journey was better than its beginning? If I thought this blessed opportunity for redemption came at the expense of sorrow, I would never choose it. But if I thought it a means of grace in response to my sorrow, then it would be a gift indeed, and I would ultimately redirect and reclaim my hope and my purpose.

> I see this as an act of redemption: to believe that when you let go and fall into a new path, arms will be there to hold you and to guide you.

With some integrity, I can say it has taken me a while to realize this—but I am coming to believe God may have a redemptive design to my sorrow; a path to take. I have always fought with some internal rebellion. But there has been a circle-like pattern to my journey of grief, and having come back to the fork, I am more ready to relinquish and allow the flow to direct my steps than before. What I don't know is the number of revolutions on the circle or the redemptive moments along the way. Will God seem nearer or farther—or both? I don't know. The psalmist concludes, "In my alarm I said, 'I am cut off from your sight!' Yet you heard my cry for mercy when I called to you for help. Be strong and take heart, all you who hope in the Lord" (Psalm 31:22, 24). It is as if to say there is a confidence there for those wounded souls who make God their security. I suppose God's role in my fork in the road is irrelevant. What matters is God's guidance in the choices now being made; a sovereign hand to shepherd us from our painful past to a purposeful future. Perhaps this is where I need redemption most. Like Peter, I feebly utter, "Lord, to whom shall we go? You have the words of eternal life" (John 6:68).

The idea of a redeeming power in grief has helped me in one last way, and that is in how I felt about God. Gabe died suddenly, without warning. The autopsy was negative. There was no heart attack, no stroke, no pulmonary embolism, no bleeding—nothing. For some time I tersely told people who asked what he died of that "God assassinated him." And for some time, that is what I felt. God took my son—and I wanted to hurt God back. I contemplated and somewhat dabbled in destructive and demeaning behaviors intended to hurt God. I felt out of control. I am now amazed I ever thought like this. When alone, I would vent my fury at God. I vowed I would never sing songs like *Our God Is an Awesome God* ever again. There could be nothing awesome about a God who took my son, I reasoned. A spiritual advisor even told me that whatever I felt about God concerning Gabe's death, I had to allow for the possibility that God at least allowed it. I'm not sure if anger or bitterness is sufficient to explain how I felt. Partly it was anger, then bitterness, but it was also a great sense of God having failed us, of being abandoned. I resented God for it. But staying mad at God is like staying mad at your mother; you just can't do it for long—and you don't want to anyway.

Author and editor, Carol Luebering, tells the story of Carl, a man who encountered a fierce anger and bitterness after his son's death. Carl grew to resent God. After a long, painful illness, his son had died, and Carl's resentment toward God intensified. Walking into an empty church one day, Carl had his moment. It was something akin to *High Noon*. He screamed his pain and anger to God. He likened him to a bully who mistreated and tortured the innocent. Carl railed with a bitter contempt that made him think he'd be struck dead. Finally, exhausted and empty, he collapsed in an empty pew. There, in silence, redemption introduced itself. "'I didn't hear a thundering from the sky,' he said. 'But in my heart I sensed that God was agreeing that my son's death was a terrible tragedy. I suddenly felt that God was raging and weeping with me.'"[9]

In my attempts to contend with the demon now a part of my life, to find like-minded support, and to equip those around me for the sake of my care, I found the unexpected—redemption. It is an unfinished work, but it is underway. My old District Superintendent once said of a hymn, "Here we are singing beyond where we are living." Amen.

Grief and redemption are like that. We are always speaking beyond where our experience currently is. That was certainly my experience. Yet, I speak (then and now) corporately, not as one but as one of many. That is the power of community and the power of redemptive faith. If there is a more sacred ministry of the church than to the dying and the bereaved, I know not what it could be. Love and compassion for the dying and the bereaved must have a special place in the Christian congregation. I believe Christ comes near in such suffering. Only the suffering cannot feel or see such a visit; only their anguish is visible. So the community comes, with their calls, their cards, their sympathies, their casseroles, their intercessions, and their caring. This is the advocacy of the community of the bereaved. This is the power of faith. This is ministry. It is to be a bridge from what is not—to what might yet be. This is redemption.

Our family continues with its journey through grief, knowing it is best to keep surrounded by compassionate friends, family, faith, and counsel. Finding the path toward redemption while feeling your way through shadows and sorrows requires a sense of purpose to our redirection. But it is there to be found, among the shadows: community, indebtedness, deliverance, fellowship, abandonment, faith, and emancipation. It is there.

Do things happen for a reason? I still don't know. But can redemption be found in all things? That is the possibility, the higher ground that my foot reaches for, while the other remains in the mire. Even in the mystery of grief, redemption says there will be a dawn following each day of darkness. Oscar Wilde wrote, "Where there is sorrow, there is holy ground."[10] Holy ground indeed—a place where lessons are taught and lessons are learned. And there, by God's help, is also redemption.

CHAPTER 3

PAIN AND PURPOSE

Gracious God

Often, the patterns of our lives seem to spin
Out of control.
Our well-designed patterns have come unwoven.
The very fabric of our soul has warped,
And is without texture.

In our pain—weave a thread of hope,
Mend our brokenness,
Trim away our despair.

And, in Your mercy,
Lead us by faith to a new pattern,
Where we are held and kept by
Your hand.
Where the measure of our lives
Is not in what we have lost,
But in what we have found.
Amen.

Vincent D. Homan

PAIN IS A MYSTERIOUS companion in so many lives. It comes cloaked in an array of known and unknown trappings: sickness, loss, alienation, aloneness, grief, divorce, disability, addictions, and depression. Sometimes it affixes itself to our being like a yoke to oxen—and sometimes we submit to its debilitating powers like slave to master. Regardless, much of human living is done in the shadow of pain. Those who have been shaped in its crucible know their lives haven't been defined by the experience. Pain doesn't have that kind of power.

I have witnessed others endure tremendous pain, yet they live their lives without a whimper—even at times victoriously. It is a humbling and wonder-filled experience. Are life's purpose and pain mutually exclusive ideals, or do they weave themselves together in some sovereign harmonious design? It seems blasphemous to consider that pain and purpose could somehow be linked. Natural selection would surely weed out the infirm, and only the strong would survive. Yet, for me, that possibility has intruded into my comfortable life.

Like so many others, pain has been my companion for much of my life. Diagnosed with pronounced scoliosis while in mid-adolescence, I learned both the social and physical pain of wearing a brace that extended from pelvis to chin—and traveled with me everywhere. I simply could not believe that as a young lad, with all those exciting years just ahead, I was about to be locked up in that portable prison. What in the world had I done to deserve such a fate? Those high school years, usually difficult anyway, would now be insufferable. I couldn't even look down at my desk to read a book. I felt any hope for a social life or a high school romance was futile. I even had to learn to sleep in that thing. It might have been made more bearable had I thought it was actually healing my body, but that wasn't the brace's mission. Its job was simply to keep me from getting worse. That it did, though it took years, until the doctors told me as a young man I could finally divorce myself from my mate of polypropylene and metal.

Those years locked inside that exoskeleton of torment shaped me in a number of ways. They seemed to heighten my awareness of anxiety, introduce me to loss, and cultivate a deep hatred for inequity. Even so, those feelings were tempered by a belief that everything would somehow work out in the end. An old scripture I often heard quoted during times of trial and tribulation reinforced my optimistic dogma. "And we know that in all things God works for the good of those who love him ..." the apostle wrote (Romans 8:28a). I began to realize that I still had a life ahead, and my time in the brace would end. With that growing awareness, I was discovering pain and suffering do not necessarily have to preempt my hopes and dreams. It also became clear to me that my brace, as much as I despised it, was somehow good for me.

Another victim of scoliosis, a few years older than I, also grew up in my small hometown. He didn't want to exchange his present for his future, so (as I was told) he seldom wore his brace. As adolescence gave way to young adulthood, his physique became substantially worse. This man became a very good friend, and I cared for him deeply. He died in mid-age, mostly because of the terrible pain he endured. His deformity had successfully robbed him of the dignity that life's simple pleasures should afford. One week before his death, I was a Saturday evening visitor in his home. I grilled us steaks, but he was in too much pain to be able to eat. I remember kneeling by his wheelchair and rubbing his feet, which were full of pain. He died one week later, early on Sunday morning. I officiated at his funeral. I felt a kinship with this man. His family were good folks. Neither they nor he deserved such a fate, but then who does deserve pain.

I've seen enough movies to know that Hollywood justice demands bad guys get theirs in the end—and I also want that. But I don't yet understand God's justice, or why good guys seem to suffer as much (or more) than bad guys. I don't know whether wearing the brace more faithfully would have helped him, but I know it helped me, despite the terrible pain it caused.

A Community of Pain

Life quickly teaches us that we are not the only ones in pain. We learned the road to Children's Hospital in Iowa City quite well because of the need for constant check-ups and adjustments to my brace. Other lessons and lives revealed in those trips stood in contrast to my own. Each trip unveiled a whole community of children with cleft palates, missing limbs, pronounced deformities, loss of mobility—a community of pain. Yet, they remained children, full of promise and purpose. It was hard to remain transfixed on my own pain in their midst. I recognized that truth even as a child.

Now, with over five decades in my rearview mirror, I still recognize the child-like power of attitude and community to disarm ache or anguish. I am not without physical pain a single day. My back is an ever-growing reminder of life's ability to afflict. Each year it seems to get worse, though a kind therapist encourages me to continue stretching and exercising, promising to postpone chronic pain and immobility for later in life. Despite that hopeful assurance, my reality is I can't even pick up my stepladder anymore, and standing for more than twenty minutes seems impossible. An occupational health therapist told me if I wanted to walk in my sixties, I shouldn't lift more than twenty-five pounds—a stunning reminder of my growing frailness. I had planned on treating myself to a new fishing boat upon retirement as a reward for a life of labor—but I bought it already, last spring. I decided I better start using my boat now, while I am still able as each year has taken away increments of mobility and strength. I am also saddened not to be able to hold my grandchildren more than a few minutes at a time.

Vicki has to do most of the physical things that need doing around a house these days, as I do less and less. Should I get a couple good days and invest myself in some welcome physical work, which is real therapy, I pay for it later. My evening cocktail can often consist of painkillers or muscle relaxers. Sleep is a privilege, not a given. I have some serious reservations about what my sixties will look like. Daughter Valerie has commented that she is amazed I can be so upbeat when she knows I hurt. But pain is a great teacher, and its primary lesson is not to let what's happening inside dictate what's happening outside. If we look closely a community of pain surrounds us still, and it is rarely far away. I will not forget the "children of promise" I met on my many visits to Iowa City. If heart and soul allow, it is still hard to remain transfixed on my own pain with the ever-present memory of those children and their pain. As an adult, what I observed and learned in Children's Hospital endures as a plumb-line for my tribulations, and I refuse to allow pain to rob me of life.

This is the reason I decided to remain so transparent with our deep, Job-like pain after losing our son Gabe.

> I now know that pain, of every kind and magnitude, does not necessarily have to rob us of our purpose and plan for life. Rather, my pain became a lens that enabled me to see my purpose and life in a new light.

Western civilization has done an admirable job at desensitizing us to human pain. If it's all the same, we'd prefer a life without it—a life with few ripples in our water. After all, nobody wants party poopers at their party. Festivity and fallibility are poor bedfellows. We love to tarry at the altar of meaningless diversion but rush through the valley of tears where real living can sometimes occur.

Pain and Theology

Too often the church follows suit. I could be prejudiced, but one could get the impression that culture *and* religion view pain and suffering as enemies with which we must contend, defeat, and put behind us. This seems particularly egregious concerning those in grief. It was my experience, and I'm sure it was not unique, to have confidants and friends advise me to quickly put away my sadness. They reasoned we would all be better off if I would just go back to being my old self, as if grief was something we could wipe off like water after a shower. In the church of the 21st century, which can seem more interested in how we manage our money and get along with our boss than in solitude, suffering, and self-denial, faith and pain no longer speak to each other.

> It's easier on our theology if we simplify it to good vs. bad. Faith is good, and pain is bad. So good people have faith, and bad people have pain. Likewise, it seems an easier version of God if we assume faith automatically separates one from all pain, with pain being that final litmus test of whether one has faith.

But my mantra hasn't changed; most folk's pain and suffering are either here, or they are on the way. If you live long enough, you will know some measure of pain and suffering. It is, perhaps, what it means to be fully human, when the brokenness and frailty of the human condition overtakes our often-smooth passage through life. When it does, an expectation of what should be comes into conflict with what must be. The conflict creates change, priorities are quickly rearranged, and normalcy ceases.

The first of our many protective barriers under assault is how we felt about God. How do we reconcile pain and a good God? Or is it possible to embrace both? Regardless of how we were reared or prepared, darkness and pain can often lead to some manner of spiritual crisis, especially concerning our relationship with God. The 16th century Spanish mystic, St. John of the Cross, referred to it as the "dark night of the soul," which is a means of describing the spiritually fallow period that comes when life and faith are in conflict, and God seems absent. It is not a darkness and pain that displaces our security in a good God, rather it is a darkness and pain that take up residence within that trusting belief. One dynamic does not diminish the other, as grace allows for a patient embrace of our afflictions. The poet/prophet Khalil Gibran wrote: "Of your life, your pain would not seem less wondrous than your joy; and you would accept the seasons of your heart, even as you have always accepted the seasons that pass over your fields. And you would watch with serenity through the winters of your grief."[11] I understand that although St. John's dark night lasted decades, he eventually recovered. All are not so fortunate. Some can know pain and suffering throughout, even to the end of their time. And others find their walk with God strengthened and solidified in the center of pain and suffering. They are the noblest of all souls I know, and I have known many.

My father was in declining health because of Parkinson's disease several years before Gabe died. A group of eager Christians from an independent church paid him several visits. These were well-intentioned Christian people, and I mean no disrespect toward them or their doctrine and polity. Their intent was to displace Dad's sickness by filling him with faith. Their visits always included playing faith tapes, reading faith scriptures, and (of course) offering the prayer of faith for healing. They left a spiritual ultimatum after several visits and no visible signs of healing: Dad was told he had been healed by Jesus, but now it was up to him to believe and receive his healing. These fervent Christians exhibited a spiritual elitism that wounded more than it healed though they were well intentioned. It seemed a demonic thing to tell a sick person. They left their faith tapes, with an aspirin-like prescription to take one a day, and off they headed to the next sick person. I was furious when Dad told me this story. Don't misunderstand; I valued anyone who cared for my dad in his illness. I welcomed all prayers and petitions on his behalf. But suddenly, guilt, and a questioning of his own faith were added to his physical pain. "Dad," I challenged, "Does this even sound like something Jesus would do? When I was a boy, if I had my foot caught in a storm grate, and a truck was barreling in my direction, if I cried out to you for help, wouldn't you come and rescue me? Or would you demand I first ask in the proper way, and with more feeling? Would you demand a more positive spin on my cry for help? God doesn't work that way. God doesn't play games with our suffering. Jesus loves you." Dad, of course, already knew that, and over time he no longer believed his illness was due to a lack of faith.

But the story didn't end quite there. The well-intentioned but misinformed faith group told me later that my dad was healed, but I had placed a seed of doubt in him, and thus he lost his healing. I know—it seems incredible. My dad was an honest-to-a-fault man who had a simple and very honest faith, for which I held him in high esteem. Before Parkinson's disease robbed him of his considerable strength, my dad was the kind of guy who could handle any problem, at least from this son's perspective. But Parkinson's disease was stronger than even my dad. Nonetheless, I subjectively believe his real strength was his good heart and honest faith. Dad did die of his disease, but I believe he died with both his faith and heart intact, and I admire him for it.

Moments like these caused me to have a caustic attitude toward many overzealous pastors and parishioners. Soon after we lost Gabe, I walked into an office, finding there a self-appointed pastor I felt patronizing when it came to the doctrines and practices of the church. This fellow lacked any formal training, and often appeared to show a condescending posture toward lesser Christians, or at least that was my very judgmental view at the time. "How are you," he asked.

I was a bit stunned but pleasantly pleased that he would ask. "If you really want to know, I am terrible. I hurt. I am in deep grief" (If asked, I hid nothing in those days).

He offered me a knowing grin and responded, "Vincent, if you just knew Jesus like I know Jesus, you wouldn't feel this way."

"I do know Jesus," I responded, "and you haven't buried a son."

I hated moments and exchanges like this and didn't mind showing my contempt in the midst of them. Likewise, I was growing to hate the people associated with those moments and reasoned that a little pain would do their theology a world of good.

A Crisis of Faith

One of the matriarch's of my faith will forever be Mother Teresa. Few knew that despite her abundant and fruitful ministry to the poorest of the poor, she also suffered a mysterious interior woe and pain. Suffering became one of the key virtues of her life. At the urging of one of her confessors, Mother Teresa wrote a letter to Jesus confessing her pain and abandonment. *Time* columnist David Van Beima cites her stuggle:

Lord, my God, who am I that You should forsake me? The Child of your Love — and now become as the most hated one — the one — You have thrown away as unwanted — unloved. I call, I cling, I want — and there is no One to answer — no One on Whom I can cling — no, No One. — Alone ... Where is my Faith — even deep down right in there is nothing, but emptiness & darkness — My God — how painful is this unknown pain — I have no Faith — I dare not utter the words & thoughts that crowd in my heart — & make me suffer untold agony.

So many unanswered questions live within me afraid to uncover them — because of the blasphemy — If there be God — please forgive me — When I try to raise my thoughts to Heaven — there is such convicting emptiness that those very thoughts return like sharp knives & hurt my very soul. — I am told God loves me — and yet the reality of darkness & coldness & emptiness is so great that nothing touches my soul. Did I make a mistake in surrendering blindly to the Call of the Sacred Heart? — addressed to Jesus, at the suggestion of a confessor, undated.[12]

In part, the pain of which Mother Teresa spoke was entirely wrapped up in her faith. She served, but she served in poverty, solitude, sacrifice, and abandonment, and all the while, she felt estranged from Jesus. She often likened it to a bride abandoned by her groom. Still she served. On December 11, 1979, Mother Teresa received the world's ultimate accolade, the Nobel Peace Prize. In her acceptance speech she said, "It is not enough for us to say, 'I love God, but I do not love my neighbor, since in dying on the cross, God made (Jesus) the hungry one—the naked one—the homeless one.'" Jesus' hunger, she said, is what "you and I must find, and alleviate."[13]

All this came from someone who worked tirelessly among the world's rejected while struggling with her own spirituality. Darkness and pain, life in conflict with faith; it is a crisis. People like her are heroes and heroines in my book of saints. She lived her whole life for others, and through her deeds drew multiple hearts to Jesus, while at the same time feeling his painful absence herself. That's extraordinary. Her life and ministry would never make sense to many of the well-adorned preachers on television today. Surely she missed out on some part of the faith formula that gives some a pass on pain.

A bereaved mom once told me after the loss of her child, "I don't understand. We were good people, we raised our kids right, we went to church, and we played by all the rules." That's the rub; you can play by all the rules, and still, no guarantees. There must be middle ground here. Too many broken people have a foot in two worlds to ignore, and they are caught between grief and hope. They don't know what they've done wrong. The only compassionate and sensible response to suffering, pain, and faith is that they are as intimately linked as the Crucified One was to the cross that held him from the earth.

As far as I can tell, Mother Teresa never escaped her internal sorrows, but they never marginalized or diminished her mission or purpose. At her death in 1997 at age 87, she still maintained her virtues of charity, love, and compassion. Her suffering only served to paint those virtues with clearer, more colorful strokes. Stories like that of my dad, Mother Teresa, and a thousand others beg many questions:

- What if pain and suffering *aren't* enemies?

- What if they are rather a means of grace?

- What if they aren't something to be "gotten over," but something to be absorbed into the fiber of our being?

- What if they have the power to sharpen our focus in this brief life, and thus transform our vision?

All people will know pain, granted some more acutely than others. It is the nature of human existence. It will be what we do in the midst of that pain that will become the testament of our days. Deny it, contend with it, or be shaped by it; pain brutishly introduces itself into our lives without qualm or qualification, and pain brings change. It happens slowly, incrementally, in some people, and rarely does anyone notice. But people who suffer catastrophic pain are forced into change quickly. The old self dies, and a new one begins the painful labor of rebirth. Moreover, none among us would welcome a change like this. It would require a person of great internal integrity.

Running Toward the Darkness

Jerry Sittser was such a man, forced from a comfortable embryo of normalcy into the outer darkness of catastrophic pain. A religion professor at Whitworth College, Sittser had taken his wife, mother, and four children to a Native American reservation in rural Idaho to expose his children to Native American culture. While traveling home on a dark and lonely stretch of highway, a drunken driver coming at eighty-five miles per hour jumped his lane and smashed head-on into Sittser's minivan. In a vertigo-filled moment of shock and grief, a man watched his mother, his wife, and his four-year-old daughter die before his eyes, all while trying to comfort and calm his three surviving children. Days, weeks, months, and years of inescapable pain and darkness have filled this good man's life. Yet, what has drawn me deeper into his story is not his tragic loss, but his remarkable decision; a decision not to run from pain but toward it. Facing his anguish would lead on a journey where pain could be transforming rather than debilitating. This decision to face darkness gave courage and direction to my own obscure journey. In his very honest book, *A Grace Disguised*, Professor Sittser describes his incredible choice:

> My own catastrophic loss thus taught me the incredible power of choice—to enter the darkness and to feel sorrow, as I did after the accident, even as I continued to work and care for people, especially my children. I knew that running from the darkness would only lead to greater darkness later on. I also knew that my soul had the capacity to grow—to absorb evil and good, to die and live again, to suffer abandonment and find God. In choosing to face the night, I took my first steps toward the sunrise.[14]

If pain's power and place is not in just what it takes but what it gives, then could I find the courage to think of it as part gift as well?

Pain allows us to feel: passionately, deeply, fully, and completely. I've known men who I didn't think ever felt passionately about anything that wasn't in relationship to their careers or their sports teams. I have advised some to take what passion they can remember from their wedding night and apply it to everything else in life—and their world just might be a better place.

Ordinary days can be quite wonderful, but if they are the sum of our existence, they are an anathema to life itself. In the days following Gabe's death, I overheard several parents say among themselves, "I'm going to quit being so hard on my kids," "I'm going to give my kids a hug tonight," "I'm going to make a point to be home more," "I'm going to talk more to my kids." Shouldn't they be doing those things anyway?

> Why does it take something like a tragic death to motivate us to a life we should be already living? When something is truly understood to be vulnerable and impermanent, then the human response is to value it more, hold it closer, and cherish it deeper. That is what can happen to life when viewed through the lens of pain.

On one of Gabe's early teen birthdays, I gave him a box with several meaningless items inside, but each item had a moral attached. That, of course, was the real gift. One such item was an intact, blown-out egg shell. The message was that life is just like this egg shell. It is intentionally created for a purpose, but very fragile and temporary. As always, I advised him to make choices wisely and carefully. Of course, philosophies and eggshells were the last thing a teenage boy wanted for his birthday. I'm happy to report he was later appeased with a chocolate cake and the *Star Wars* trilogy. If we all carried our lives like an eggshell, then those things that pain remind us to practice and embrace would become our norms, not our exceptions.

Pain and Choice

If we have pain, we have the capacity to feel. When pain is absorbed into our being, it grants unexpected insights: hardened hearts begin to melt, compassion and empathy return, charity and benevolence become us, and we are given an immediate sixth sense toward others in acute pain. For myself, I know that I am much more sensitive toward others who are hurting, and am especially drawn to stories of untimely deaths. Are there suddenly more of them, or have I been given new eyes and ears to see and hear things to which I have been previously oblivious?

Everyone has a choice to make concerning his or her seasons of pain and loss. Either pain or loss will be dismissed as brief interludes in an otherwise healthy and happy life, or they will become moments of transformation, one after another—where life and death, darkness and light coexist. Pain and loss require us to live in the center of a game of *tug of war*. It is a pulling tension between rage and surrender, apathy and hope, doubt and belief, emptiness and fulfillment, and sorrow and joy—with each one being keenly felt and known. In that center, an epiphany occurs. Like the calm in the eye of a twister, you see something that's invisible outside the vortex of twisting destruction. It isn't the pain or tragedy that defines us. It can't be. Rather it is our response to suffering. Professor Sittser wrote that it is not what happens *to* us that matters. It is what happens *in* us.[15] Pain will invade every human life; that much is true. But to what end? Will pain and suffering abide as enmities and strife? Or will the eye of the storm draw us to a center, where there is a renewed quality of life, the capacity to feel, a new purpose, and even transformation?

In solitude, I have thought much regarding our great family tragedy, and where I was supposed to go from there. For so long, I simply wanted to die. I didn't feel as though I had any right to live when my son was gone. The unnatural order of all this didn't mesh with my concrete understanding of life. All my life, I've heard that *everything happens for a reason*, but now those words seemed so incredibly cruel. If there was any order to the universe that determined the untimely death of my son, I wanted to confront that order and stand in open rebellion to it. To disregard my life seemed the best way, and so I did, even to the point of contemplating the timing of my own mortality.

Only a couple months following our loss, Vicki and I kept a scheduled fishing trip with one of my best friends, Neil, and his wife Debbie. We traveled to Sheboygan, Wisconsin, to go salmon fishing on Lake Michigan. As we approached the pier to get on our chartered boat, I was overcome with guilt. How much Gabe would have loved this trip, I silently lamented. He should be going, not me. Why didn't I take him here when I could? The guilt and regret was suffocating. I could hardly compose myself, and when I looked at Vicki, I saw her flushed face and knew she had similar thoughts. But being good soldiers, we composed ourselves. I don't think Neil and Deb even noticed. I would not have wanted them to—and I began to despise my life. The pain only subsided when I slept, and when I awoke, grief and pain were waiting. They were relentless. I only knew one way out.

That fall I attended an event called "Mrs. Santa's Workshop," a brunch and crafts fund-raiser for the local Methodist ladies in my hometown. I saw a woman sitting alone, a noble woman of great faith and integrity, but a woman who had once lost a daughter, and then a grandson. With my coffee and cinnamon roll in hand, I headed her way. Few words need to be spoken when bereaved parents have a moment together. Regardless of how much time had passed or what the occasion, there would always be only one relevant issue. As we visited, this lady I had long admired said something that gave me great pause. She said in the center of her deepest grief she once drove out past a river bridge south of town, faster than safety allows. She contemplated a small, incremental turn of the steering wheel; just enough to take the car into the bridge piling—and the pain would stop. I was stunned. I didn't know others felt this way, too, especially not someone I had long admired as a bulwark of faith. Even though she never followed through with her contrivance, nor ever probably intended to, just the fact that she once contemplated it was enough for me. This must be normal, I reasoned. Drastic pain leads to drastic choices—life and death choices, and I began to seriously envision my end.

Then, one day, an intervention. While walking with my daughter Valerie up the sidewalk from my shop, she stopped me with a brittle question, "Dad, are you going to die?" I thought, "Does all this show?"

"No!" I emphatically answered, and it was a real no. In that moment, I knew even with Gabe gone, my life was still a heritage, and no way did I want to relinquish that gift, not for my sake or others. I discovered, as did my bereaved spiritual mother, that this was just another destructive link in the chain of parental grief. And as she did, it was time for me to move onto the next link. Maybe for the first time the sanctity and sacredness of human life was made clear to me, and I hallowed the gift. But I wondered how many other bereaved parents briefly considered such a traumatic end to their pain.

On the other hand, to attach any sense of purpose to our great pain seemed to devalue the pain and loss themselves. I would a million times rather forsake any sense of good or rightness that might be revealed, if in exchange we could have our son back. I would sign any agreement or bargain to that effect. Any contract would be agreeable if it meant undoing June 18, 2005.

Somewhere in my long search, a truth was uncovered, even unveiled. Purpose or reason does not replace pain and suffering. Rather, they are companions. Throughout the early months of our grief, I silently said over and over again (as if others were listening), "If you are waiting for the old Vince to reappear, you're in for a long wait." I am a bereaved father, and I will be shaped by this loss all of my days. Like an alcoholic, decades into his commitment to A.A., yet he still confesses, "I am an alcoholic," I will always be a bereaved father, but I will also be other things. I will not only be a bereaved father. My sorrow has not disappeared, but it is being integrated into my life and my ministry—and that is the difference.

> I am running toward the darkness, knowing it is the quickest way to find light again. In that life-long quest, my soul is enlarged and my purposes are prioritized. If pain has a gift to give, maybe purpose is part of the endowment.

A Tapestry of Light and Darkness

Vicki and I traveled to Alaska a couple years ago in honor of our thirty-fifth wedding anniversary. The scenery was breathtaking, the adventures were numerous, and the time spent just with her was romantic and joyful. But we encountered something I hadn't considered. It doesn't get dark there this time of the year. There is always daylight. Even though the sun sets just below the horizon for a few hours, it never gets completely dark. This is great stuff, I thought. Were it not for the necessary sleep, the vacation could have gone on unbroken.

However, Alaska also has a great curse. For every month of unending light is a month of unending darkness. That is what the early years of parental grief are like. The sun itself seems to have just died, and it is completely dark—all the time. I decided Iowa had a good thing going. A little light and a little dark in each day is a much better deal. I like life that way also, with a little light and a little dark every day. It makes me wonder: can light and darkness coexist? Or is displacement theory correct, with the presence of one creating the absence of another? I'm in something of a quandary over the matter. After all, when the daylight comes, the darkness doesn't disappear; it just moves on to spend time with our neighbors in China and Pakistan. It will come back to us at its appointed time. It is akin to a rolling tapestry of vistas united by twilight and dawn.

That has been our story as well, a weaving of darkness and light, sometimes existing in the same place at the same time—pain and purpose in the same life. I once thought life was manageable: home and hearth, babies and careers, happy beginnings and happy endings, and a theology on which I could put my finger. Then, darkness broke into our blissful light, and now I am learning how to live over again—in twilight.

Pain and Crosses

Christmas 2006 was an integral time for me in understanding this paradox of pain and purpose living together. It had been eighteen months since Gabe's death, and after having taken off the previous year's Christmas, I decided to give the season another shot. That first Christmas, younger daughter Tiffany, brave little Christmas junkie that she is, journeyed with me down to the local Kiwanis' tree stand, where we purchased a beautiful seven-foot Scotch Pine. Not daring to open up any wounds to be found inside the old family Christmas boxes, we traveled downtown to purchase new ornaments and lights. She picked red and silver, and we picked up every glitzy red or silver thing we could find. Then we decorated. Somehow, that tree was sad and beautiful at the same time, just like our lives. That was about all the "spirit" we could muster the first year. It is the only good memory I have of our initial *Gabe-less* Christmas—Tiffany and I putting up that shiny, glitzy tree.

By the next Christmas, I was better prepared to re-connect with the spiritual emotions that always overshadowed my holiday experience. My centerpiece, of course, in the holiday pageantry is the nativity. When the kids were little, I built a stable out of mahogany underlayment and lath. It looked like the kind of project a man whose talents lay elsewhere built in a freezing garage with cold hands and inadequate tools, and that's what it was. Nevertheless, the kids loved it, and so did I. With a little straw glued to the floor, and a seven-watt light bulb installed in the peak, we were ready for the lineup of shepherds, camels, wise men, and of course, the main characters—Mary, Joseph, and baby Jesus. Year after year, as the Holy Day itself approached, I would sit and simply stare at this gathering of plastic caricatures, mahogany wood, and glue, contemplating the mysteries behind the original production. At some point in time, my homemade manger gave way to a more polished production from China, but the mystery remained. But December 2006 found me looking deeper, longer, at the nativity, particularly the manger. Though always mesmerized by it, this year I found myself noticing something new—a shadow of the cross. I knew it wasn't real, yet I envisioned the wispy image of a cross shadowing the innocence of the baby's manger. Imagine, a king being born for such an end.

In the 17th century, an influential Christian woman lived in France, something of a prophetess, if you will. Her name, Jeanne Guyon, would later be analogous with many of the early saints. In a book, very instrumental to my Christian formative years, *Experiencing the Depths of Jesus Christ,* she contended there is the shadow of a cross over every life. In stunning language she proclaimed, "God gives us the cross, and then the cross gives us God." She encouraged her readers to receive, even desire, the crosses in their lives, fully embracing their pain. "Pain is an inescapable aspect of the cross," she wrote. "Without it, there has been no cross at all." And pain, the centerpiece of human suffering, is by its own nature and machinations somehow aligning our way with another, who chose the most extreme violence the cross could offer.[16]

But who wants crosses or pain? If given a choice, I prefer a blissful and happy story with an equally happy ending. I read an article once about the movie, *Pretty Woman*, starring Richard Gere and Julia Roberts. It seems the original ending was a bit sad. Richard Gere's character didn't climb the fire escape with a bouquet of flowers and take Julia Roberts away to a lavish life of romance and opulence. Rather, he drove off leaving the heroine behind, spurned, and alone. Test audiences booed and jeered. They hated it. So the director changed the ending—sad to happy, dark to light, and the movie became a monumental success. People *do* love happy endings.

Nevertheless, the most enduring drama in human history, the greatest story ever told, does not have a happy ending. The life of Jesus is book-ended by a manger and a cross. The epilogue which would occur three days later is a matter of faith. In real life happy endings are the exception. Apart from the movies, we identify more with mangers and crosses, life and death, light and darkness—and all by God's design. I knew whatever hope and peace I had for this life and the next I would find in that manger.

Pain Reveals Strength

Courage, character, determination, and will are often untested and unknown without being contested by grief, suffering, and pain. It's as if the great drama requires both dynamics. We are always hearing the gripping accounts of ordinary people who discover great strength when a great need arises. Long-time camping friends of my parents, C.G. and Eloise, knew a moment just like this. It was the year after I graduated high school, and we all went camping at Backbone State Park in Iowa. C.G., Eloise, their daughter Pat, my parents, and I spent that Saturday hiking the Backbone. It was the height of fall colors, and the view was stunning. The day after our camping trip ended, we all headed back to our collective responsibilities; they resuming their labors as farmers during a busy harvest. C.G. and Eloise were terrific people, and I remember them with great fondness. I know why my parents loved them so dearly. They were in the twilight of their careers, and neither gave the appearance of being capable of great physical acts, yet, they were. I never knew the entire story, but learned that Eloise's leg became caught in a piece of farm equipment, and C.G. somehow physically separated her from that machinery and carried her to safety. He probably saved his wife's life. The crisis revealed his strength. And Eloise, with one real and one prosthetic leg, has since had a hands-on participation in mission work on a global level, and, likewise, has shown great strength.

> Grief can be like that. Its pain can reveal things about you.
> It can unveil a person you have not yet known.

In a book that meant much to me following Gabe's death, *Lament for a Son,* author and professor, Nicholas Wolterstorff, tells of an emerging humanity coming out of his suffering:

> Suffering is the shout of "No" by one's whole existence to that over which one suffers—the shout of "No" by nerves and gut and gland and heart to pain, to death, to injustice, to depression, to hunger, to humiliation, to bondage, to abandonment. And sometimes, when the cry is intense, there emerges a radiance which elsewhere seldom appears: a glow of courage, of love, of insight, of selflessness, of faith. In that radiance we see best what humanity was meant to be.[17]

These insights are not by means of reconciliation or resignation, rather by experience and understanding. Wolterstorff wrote his book as a love song on behalf of his son Eric, who died in a mountain-climbing accident in his twenty-fifth year. Every love song is a lament, Wolterstorff reasons. With deep sorrow mixed with determination, he concludes that laments will always be part of life, but they also can help us determine our identity.

No one buries an immediate family member without being systematically changed. Something new emerges. If nothing is felt and nothing is changed, then that person is to be pitied most of all, for they are somehow dead, even though they live. People have asked me if it gets better over time. The answer is a simple no. It gets different. The night of weeping starts to see morning again, and the anguish is partly subdued, but many opponents are ahead. The pain is not as sharp, but it is just as real. Everything in our home reminds me of him. As long as Gabe is dead, it will not get better. But the difference that comes has the capacity to bring meaning, value, purpose, and dare I say, even a beauty to life. Those things sit side-by-side with our grief. As iron sharpens iron, each keeps the other in focus so neither is lost.

> Suffering is therefore as integral to life as breath is. If each moment is not holy, death already has occurred. Life is not in you if you do not feel compassion for another's sorrows. Pain is a prism whose parallel sides disperse a destiny and purpose, as well as a sorrow and suffering.

I came across a meaningful quotation by Chaim Potok shortly after Gabe died. I wrote it down and kept it close for some time. It read: "One learns of the pain of others by suffering one's own pain, by turning inside oneself, by finding one's own soul. And it is important to know of pain. It destroys our self pride, our arrogance, our indifference towards others."[18] Pain takes us outside our self-absorption, it displaces mundane, it creates perspective, it enlarges vision, and it reminds us of mortality. It is important.

I was in a large department store when an announcement was made that a young boy was lost. Kindly, the announcement went something like this, *Johnny Smith's mommy has gotten lost. She may find her son in the manager's office.* There was a truth to that announcement:

- The first step to being found is to admit to someone you are lost.

- The first step to finding an inner strength is when you admit you are weak alone.

- The first step to receiving forgiveness is when you confess you were wrong.

- The first taste of faith comes when you admit you have doubts.

- And your first sense of renewed purpose and place comes when you realize grief and pain do not have sole ownership of your life.

Pain can disguise purpose, but it can never extinguish it. After vacationing overseas a few years ago, we were making the long trip home from Dublin to Chicago, and I was anxious to land. The nine-hour flight had been turbulent from its initial moments. What gave me some measure of comfort, though, had been the amazing clear, blue, and sunny skies. You could see forever. I felt as if God were surely close by our side. As we finally neared O'Hare Airport, we began the long, slow, descent. Suddenly, the sun and blue skies disappeared into an ocean of gray fog. You could see nothing. Just before we landed, the clouds lifted, and there was Chicago—and it was snowing. Just minutes before I had been bathed in brilliant sunshine. Now I was covered in dark clouds and about to walk out to a snowy existence. My world had suddenly changed, but I knew the world hadn't really changed. I was simply in a place where my view of it had. The bright sun hadn't really disappeared. It was still there. The clouds just covered it now; and though my reality is now cold and dark, above me is still clarity and light. The presence of one does not negate the presence of the other. They coexist. Surely my faith journey through the pain and purpose of this often dark world is not dissimilar.

For those who find themselves still in the throes of grief, suffering, and pain, simple rhetoric offers little respite. Rhetoric must be tested before it can be trusted, and that takes time, experience, reason, and faith. To believe that something *is* does not make it so. There has to be a metamorphosis, where pain and purpose blend together like light and darkness at dawn. As the day progresses, light and life reestablish purpose and place, knowing for a while the darkness has moved on. The apostle John wrote, "The light shines in the darkness, and the darkness did not overcome it" (John 1:5, NRSV). That is the conviction that now guides my life. For what time I am given on this earth, I want it to be purpose-filled, to be given for good like a church offering is given—each moment being savored and treasured. I want to believe that what has separated me from life has also brought me to it. Pain is now part of my journey, and for mercy's sake—so is purpose.

CHAPTER 4

BITTERNESS: THE PARALYZING STING OF LOSS

The Heart Knoweth Its Own Brokenness

Though the stream of being floweth
Calmly to the sea of peace,
Though the weary pilgrim goeth
To his home of sleep and ease–
None, but he who suffers, knoweth
All a spirit's bitterness.

Thoughts there are with misery in them,
Sharper than the wintry wind:
Wounds there are, though none have seen them,
Rankling in the inner mind–
Woes, with not a joy between them,
Dark and vague and undefined.

Is there for a spirit broken,
Is there a balm of Gilead here?
Yes! The Lord–the Lord hath spoken,
Draw, ye sons of suffering, near
Christ, the Word–His cross the token–
See the cross–and banish fear.

John Bowring[19]

I FOUND MYSELF DRAWN into a conversation some time ago with a man who had likewise suffered a debilitating loss in his life. "How are you doing, Vince?" he queried. I responded with the generic, "Oh, you know, good days and bad days" kind of stuff, assuming he couldn't possibly understand my feelings. But, reluctantly, I had to reciprocate, "And you, how are you doing?" With half grimace and half plastic smile he answered, "I fight bitterness every day. How do we keep from becoming bitter?" I didn't respond because I didn't know. But there it was, what I had been feeling, but needing someone else to articulate, that feeling which was part friend and part foe to one in grief—bitterness! Like the swelling, burning, fiery pain that lingers long after the bee has left its stinger, so does bitterness stick tightly to one still trying to make sense of a life-altering loss.

James Rye, Director at Connections Counseling in Peterborough, United Kingdom, wrote, "Bitterness is loss frozen in resentment." Webster defines it as "hard to bear, grievous, causing sharp pain; characterized by intense hostility or resentment; experienced at great cost." Abraham Lincoln, who lost two sons during his lifetime, wrote, "In this sad world of ours, sorrow comes to all and it often comes with bitter agony."[20] I learned in our support group that twenty of our forty-four presidents were bereaved parents. I suspect they all knew some level of bitterness. John Kennedy lost two infant sons, one while President. George H.W. Bush lost a daughter, Robin, to leukemia at four years of age.

I know we are not alone in this, and not all grieve as bitterly as I did, but the cascade of rancor seemed inevitable for me. After having sat in my tears in grievous sorrow for nearly a year, followed by a seething anger that often bordered on rage, I found myself contending again with a most unwelcome emotional visitor— bitterness. In a Jekyll-and-Hyde way, I found myself morphing from social competence to brooding contempt and resentment in a

VincentD. Homan

heartbeat. There is nothing natural or humane about such thoughts and feelings, but neither is there anything natural or humane about a 29-year-old dropping over dead while out fishing with a friend on a sunny day. I don't know how he knew, but Rye was right: "bitterness is loss frozen in resentment."

I powerlessly began to resent many good people in my life, people I really loved and for whom I cared. What added to my emotional angst was that I knew these people loved and cared for me as well. I found myself secretly, but resolutely, resenting fathers with healthy sons with whom they continued to enjoy life. They were fathers who were just doing what fathers do, watching over the development of their sons from young adults to mature men with a paternal pride only fathers know—and I hated myself for resenting them. Yet Jekyll couldn't resist becoming Hyde; neither could I resist my dark side.

The Reasoning of Bitterness

Bitterness became me, as if I were the only one enduring loss, and this was my armor and shield. I began snapping at people everywhere I went. Vicki and I were out at the local pizza place one evening for supper. The restaurant had especially high dividers between the booths, which suited me well, as you could be almost invisible behind them. A nice woman who I have known for some time found me and put her hand on my shoulder. The minute I felt that hand, Hyde appeared. As she began to offer some words of consolation, trying to tell me she also had been victim to some sorrow—I snapped. I don't even remember what I said to her, but it was terse, mean, and loud. As other diners nearby looked our way, her stunned face became flush as she turned away and walked out the door. And I felt violated for her having intruded on my quiet supper. "How dare she," I thought.

This is the reasoning of bitterness. A few days later I did the same thing to someone who stopped me as I walked out of the local veterinarian's office. I began to wonder if I should even venture out in public, and to a greater extent—the church. I live near a small auto repair garage where I often go for a cup of coffee and some fluff conversation. It is a safe place, the folks there are welcoming and kind, and the conversation is usually benign. Once, however, a good man got talking about people who have died. I immediately became uneasy and began looking for an out. He is a fellow I like, though, and with whom I share some spiritual history. He began to share his own story, that he had lost an adult brother and how difficult that loss had been. I know it surely was. Then, with an unintended venomous bite, he turned to me and asked a pointless question, "Vince, you have lost a son, I have lost a brother. Which one do you think is worse?" His question took my breath away. I couldn't believe it. Why would you ask such a thing? If I said anything to him, it surely was hurtful. But I did literally bolt from the garage to the safety of solitude. Still, the remark set me back for days, and I found myself embittered toward that nice man.

Bitterness can grow from the literal loss of a loved one, or to differing degrees from the loss of a marriage, a job, a position, a reputation, your health, or a dozen other life disappointments. Regardless of the specific cause, bitterness often develops out of unreleased and unresolved loss. People whose pain directs them toward bitterness inherently know it to be taking them in an unhealthy direction, yet bitterness remains a safe and justifiable cause for all the malevolent expressions of loss. I thought it even seemed logical. Even rancor is rational when filtered through an embittered heart.

Tragic loss changes life. For those who suffer the death of a child, at any age, this loss is most injurious. It brutalizes with a sorrow for unending days, months, and years—and then it can harden and exacerbate you. Many good souls develop harshness as a defense mechanism to their wounded life. This may be different in men and women. I don't think Vicki ever passed a bitter or angry moment in her grief walk. It's not her nature. In some ways, her grief was more private than mine. I feared she might be internalizing it too much. I suspect she feared I might be externalizing it too much. She often commented that she hated seeing me hurt so much. But I knew she was hurting, too. I knew in the sanctuary of solitude she was looking, touching, and smelling things of Gabe's: clothes, boots, books, toys, pictures. While my grief covered my being like glove to hand, she rarely let her grief show outside the four walls of our home. Still, her grief has been just as vivid as mine, maybe more so. When we've lost a child, feelings become much more intense. Often, those acute feelings will be expressed to someone. For me, it was whoever got in my way.

Drs. Noel and Blair address the intensified emotions with which the bereaved often contend:

> Because loss of a child is such an unthinkable loss, everything is intensified, exaggerated and lengthened. Guilt and anger are almost always present in every significant loss, but these emotions are inordinate with grieving parents. Experts estimate that it takes anywhere from three to five years to reach renewal after a spouse dies, but parental grief might go on for ten to twenty years or maybe a lifetime …. It is just that the shock and severity of this kind of loss leaves us feeling completely helpless and full of dark despair.[21]

Changes Come

As I've said, when your child dies an imagined future dies also—a loss of weddings, grandchildren, and a lifetime of promise. We all know some things to expect after a loss, what we don't know and can't foresee is *if* or *how* our loss might change us. I have never been one who has adapted particularly well to any change. Apart from college and the first year of marriage, I've lived my whole life in two houses, one as a son and one as a dad. Even now, my mother lives in the house I grew up in, and when I visit, I can still walk back into my childhood bedroom, seeing the dings and dents in the baseboard from my endless wars with cowboys, bad guys, and dinosaurs. I drive cars a long time. I've been in the electrical business thirty-seven years, and am on only my third truck. The current one is also fit to be driven in Fourth of July parades, as a period car. I've been pastor of the same churches for more than twenty years. I like the same things now I liked as a child. I have supported one political party, one denomination, and one brand of vehicles most of my adult life—and I am married to the same person I wed over thirty-seven years ago. The point is I don't change easily. When asked by Maureen O'Hara in the western *Big Jake* if he had changed, John Wayne defiantly answers, "Not one bit!" I have been told I resemble that remark.

But loss forces change. You haven't changed your mind about someone or left him. He has left you and the void creates a change. You are left powerless against the intrusion. Something has left, but something is also coming. Clearly, my loss was changing me. I suspect it does most people. But would the coming change be a good thing or a bad thing? How much choice do we have in the process? Author and bereaved mom, Ann Hood, said when her child Grace died, a part of her also died. Out of that, she was forced to discover the new person she was becoming:

> Like most of us, I knew the common things: how hard each birthday and anniversary would be; how my husband Lorne and I might not sleep or eat very much; how we should try to talk about our pain. Grief brings emptiness with it, like someone punched a hole in you. My arms and my lap ached from the emptiness Grace had left behind. After the death of someone we love, we are forced to figure out who we are now.[22]

That is the question: who are we after tragic loss? Our humanity invites itself into its defensive positions of sullenness, guilt, chronic determination, isolation, sadness, reliance, or bitterness. They all change us, but bitterness perhaps affects us most. It, unlike the others, affects behavior *and* identity. Still, the Dr. Jekyll in me longs to look upward, higher, to the better angels of my nature, and there to wonder—if humanity can call us to such things in the face of loss, could divinity call us to more?

Old Testament characters often seem rampant with bitterness, strife, and woe. I am glad to feel more in the fold of New Testament saints. Still, sometimes I encounter Old Testament stories that feel akin to mine. Jeremiah was a prophet called by God while still in the womb. Prophets often had the unhappy task of telling God's people what they were doing wrong, warning them of judgment, and announcing their oft-following destruction. All of those dictums were in order after the Babylonians destroyed the temple in Jerusalem in 586 B.C., and Judah was captured. Jeremiah identified more with his exiled countrymen than his prophetic role, as he lamented… "Since my people are crushed, I am crushed; I mourn, and horror grips me. Is there no balm in Gilead? Is there no physician there? Why then is there no healing for the wound of my people?" (Jeremiah 8:21–22).

I think the prophet spoke more like a bereaved parent than a displaced holy man—for that is exactly how I felt. Gilead was a place where spices and medicinal herbs could be found, and a balm is anything that heals or eases pain. But there was no healing for what was wrong this time. Nothing could bring God's children back from exile—or our children back from the grave. An Afro-American spiritual in the *United Methodist Hymnal* recalls this lament—but in the context of faith and hope. Its refrain says "There is a balm in Gilead to make the wounded whole; There is a balm in Gilead to heal the sin-sick soul."[23] Whoever wrote this hymn saw something Jeremiah didn't. Rather than *is there a balm,* he saw *there is*; referring to Gilead's balm. The spiritualist saw a living Jesus who was present and able to heal the sin-sick soul. But how about an embittered, grieving soul—is there a balm for bitterness? Is there a balm for grief?

Job's Story—Patient *and* Bitter

Still, the character I am most intrigued by is Job. Most inside and outside the church know something of his story as an unwitting pawn in a celestial chess match between God and Satan. Job is portrayed as an upright and blameless man. Satan appeared and contended that the reason Job was such a good guy was because God had placed a hedge of protection around him and his family. Nothing bad could come to them as long as this protection endured. Furthermore, Satan suggested that should God remove the hedge and bad things happen, Job's righteousness would fade into bitterness, and he would curse God to his face. To prove his confidence in Job, God removed his protection, and Satan is allowed to do his worst, with one addendum—Satan is not allowed to kill Job. Of course the worse happened: Job lost his oxen, his donkeys, his sheep, his servants, his camels, and all of his children. Yet, despite all his tragedy, the Bible said Job did not blame God, and therefore did not sin. A famous Biblical quotation came from this defining moment. Job said "Naked I came from my mother's womb, and naked I depart. The Lord gave and the Lord has taken away; may the name of the Lord be praised" (Job 1:21). Some time ago a popular contemporary Christian song was based on this verse. "He gives and takes away; he gives and takes away," its refrain echoed. I couldn't even listen to it. It repulsed me. If God had taken our family away, how could this God be praised? I didn't understand. How could such a God be good? Yet, I have always believed God was good.

The other part of the story, as far as the public is concerned, is that Job had one great virtue—patience in the presence of suffering. I decided to find out for myself if this were true. It has long been my methodology when studying the scriptures to take a particular book of the Bible and settle in there, often journaling my thoughts and questions as I go. Ergo, a couple years after Gabe died, I took up residence in the book of Job. For over a year I spent a part of most mornings there, sometimes resigning myself to a single verse a day. What I found out was that for every time Job was remembered as faithful and patient, he was also embittered and broken, as I was embittered and broken. "Therefore I will not keep silent; I will speak out in the anguish of my spirit, I will complain in the bitterness of my soul" (Job 7:11), and I was grateful Job complained. It doesn't sound like patience was his only character trait. A broken Job believed what many broken people believe, that he was a recipient of God's injustice. "As surely as the Lord lives, who has denied me justice, the Almighty, who has made me taste bitterness of soul" (Job 27:2), he bemoaned. Job suffered without cause, and yes—Job was bitter.

I lay no fault upon Job. Whether this is good news or bad news for me, I don't know. But if a man like Job, blameless and upright, who feared God and shunned evil, could become so embittered against earth and heaven, what hope is there for me getting it together? I love the humanity of the biblical saints. They give me courage to dust myself off after an occasional fall. I have always been glad that angel wings and halos are the exception, and not the rule, concerning the scriptural heroes I have come to know and love. They are not that dissimilar from me. Their strengths and secrets are out there for the entire world to see, verse by verse. As I know their faults and foibles, I also know my own. And I know there is a fault line in the bedrock of every good person, cleverly hidden from all eyes but God's.

I cringe when a good and respected church member does wrong, and it becomes public. I cringe because I know what is coming. "How could they do that," others snipe. The media and the gossiper seem to especially enjoy feasting on the foibles of religious folks. But I know religious folks stumble all the time. Intentionally or not, they stumble. While I'd rather we all make better choices, I cannot hold bad choices against good people forever. Righteous and patient Job was embittered toward God, and I don't hold it against him either.

This book of the Bible often becomes a litany of helpful speeches by Job's *friends*, followed by Job's pointed and poignant responses. Many of these became markers for me, reminding me of my place and my path. "Yet man is born to trouble, as surely as sparks fly upward," Eliphaz reminded (Job 5:7). How true, I thought. It has always been my perspective that if you live long enough, no one escapes these short lives without a few scrapes and scratches. Job responded, "Then I would still have this consolation—my joy in unrelenting pain, that I had not denied the words of the Holy One" (Job 6:10).

What did you say Job? You would have joy in pain? It is your consolation? Not I. I felt inconsolable, and unlike Job, felt my pain making me wayward. "If I have sinned, what have I done to you, O watcher of men? Why have you made me your target? Have I become a burden to you?" (Job 7:20). Now we are getting somewhere, Job. Every shareholder in pain's portfolio has thought this, regardless of whether they have ever prayed it. *What have I done to deserve all of this?* I wrote it in the margin of my Bible. But secretly, I felt the ledger book would reveal ample sins in my life to deserve any punishment. Perhaps it was because over twenty years ago I reluctantly answered the call of ministry. Following my decision, I fully expected my behavior to be in line with St. Francis. I soon discovered, however, that my flesh was a formidable opponent. Nagging sins that I had contended with most of my life, repented for, moved on from, then repeated; continued their human cycle in my life. I could not reconcile my lack of righteous virtue with my sacred profession.

When Gabe died, one of the first and foremost devious thoughts that plagued me was that somehow, this was a punishment for my sins. I was haunted by the possibility. I knew about cause and effect. I knew that God punishes sin. Long ago I memorized a verse that terrorized me for years, "Yet he does not leave the guilty unpunished; he punishes the children and their children for the sin of the fathers to the third and fourth generations" (Exodus 34:7b). The implications of this old Hebrew text took my breath away. It seemed too much like *karma*. Could God really punish my children because I had sinned? The scripture said so, but I couldn't believe it. I could not embrace any such God. Nevertheless, I have always held the canon of scripture in high esteem, so I was unable to divorce myself from the possibility. It was that possibility that my waywardness had at least been complicit in my son's death, which tortured me.

I will never begin to convey the weight of guilt I carried in those days. But a moment came when even this was laid to rest. About a year after Gabe's death, we were at my daughter Valerie's house, and Vicki and Val had gone to do some shopping. I was alone, except for my thoughts. Again and again I asked myself, *Did my son die because of my sins?* Finally, that aching question was redirected to God. Over and over again, first silently, then aloud, then loud, I beckoned—"God, did my son die because of my sins? Was this somehow my fault?"

I am not a Pentecostal or a Full-Gospel Christian. I am not a mystic, a soothsayer, or a prophet. I am not given to expressive forms of worship or abstract experiences with God. Rather, I am a methodical Methodist, and a somewhat reserved one at that. I like my words from God in large, bold print—and from a reliable translation. Still, a word came to me. In an absolute moment of soul-searching anguish—a word came to me, and I believed then and now that it came from God. In my spirit (and perhaps even with my ears) I distinctly heard this answer to my aggrieved inquiry: "No, my son died for your sins." God said it, what my aching heart needed to hear. My son did not die because of my sins—but God's son did. Jesus died for my sins, mine—*and* Gabe's. Somehow, in that brief moment, I was able to bury the incredible guilt that was convicting me over my culpability in Gabe's death. Certainly, my sins were there, but they required Jesus' death—not Gabe's.

As with me, Job's life became a progression of angst, bitterness, resignation, and reconciliation. In what may be one of the most definitive verses in the Bible, Job valiantly placed his confidence in an invisible God, "Though he slay me, yet will I hope in him" (Job 13:15a). Despite all, I think I have always felt this way myself. Yet with his reconciliation came this request, "Only grant me these two things, O God, and then I will not hide from you: Withdraw your hand far from me, and stop frightening me with your terrors" (Job 13:20–21). In other words: *I have had enough, God. No more nightmares, real or imagined*, and I prayed in just that way. Having laid guilt and grief aside, Job enjoyed his defining moment. He reproved his *friends*, by affirming his faith: "I know that my Redeemer lives, and that in the end he will stand upon the earth" (Job 19:25). Somehow, reclamation of faith was invaluable in Job's ability to endure loss, and I knew it would be for me also. For all his venomous rants over the perceived injustices God had wrought, Job is shown in the story as faithful, penitent, and patient in his affliction.

People seem to get a pass in their funeral eulogy. Dirty laundry is always swept away, and only glowing reports of good character remain. They remind me of the story of a widow, who, after the funeral, asked for the casket to be reopened. When the funeral director asked why, she replied, "Because I want to see who's in there. I don't know who the preacher was talking about, but it sure wasn't my husband." I suspect the same wasn't true for Job. I think he genuinely was faithful, penitent, and patient. Was he embittered and broken? Of course. But that was not all he was. His bitterness was a season, but it did not endure. His faithfulness and patience did. It's as if Job's angst is a natural part of the carnal response to human suffering, even for one known for his patience and piety. In the end it didn't define him. His story is later tidied up with more children, grandchildren, and happy endings. Everyone is not so fortunate. Some must learn to move on from bitterness without happy endings.

> The execrable part of bitterness though, is that it not only afflicts its victim, but everyone with whom he comes in contact. It is a particularly unenviable attribute if one is a pastor.

Walking around with bitterness in your heart and mouth is like walking around with clay on your boots. It is heavy, cumbersome, and hard to remove. It leaves tracks everywhere you go. An old Charlie Brown cartoon shows Charlie lamenting over a spilled ice cream cone, upside down on a hot sidewalk. "A spilled ice cream cone is just like a misplaced word," he sighs. "It just lies there, and you can't pick it back up." Indeed.

We've all spilled words and wished we could pick them up again. But we can't. The minute they are spilled, they start doing their damage, often wreaking havoc for days and weeks to come. I spilled many bitter words, for sure. When addressing the Ephesian Christians, the apostle Paul wrote that one thing that makes the Spirit sad is when critical, cutting, embittered words come out of our mouth. It is a poor witness. Paul said to get rid of it (see Ephesians 4:25–32).

My season of bitterness was perhaps the most difficult to reconcile with professional ministry. It was overwhelmingly difficult some days to be inspiring, encouraging, and pleasing to others when I really wanted to scream at the world and everyone in it. I owe the good people of our parish a debt of gratitude for having been patient with me through those days. Nonetheless, the fact that the good apostle told the church to get rid of its bitterness must mean it was possible. I remember from the Christmas story the angel's message to Mary, "Nothing is impossible with God" (Luke 1:37), and I was encouraged by that possibility.

A Helpful Strategy

Basic Types of Pastoral Care and Counseling is a classic pastoral care book that I have often utilized when caring for others, but now found helpful in self-care. Author Howard Clinebell, Professor of Pastoral Psychology and Counseling, Emeritus at the Claremont School of Theology cites structured tasks intended to accommodate and encourage someone moving forward with/from grief. None are easy, and all require painful steps. He speaks first of accepting the loss, then experiencing, expressing, and working through our painful feelings. Third, the bereaved must eventually start putting his or her life back together again, minus what was lost. Fourth is to put one's loss in a wider context of meaning and faith. The final piece of advice is to reach out to others experiencing similar losses for mutual help. According to Clinebell, this process is unique to each person. Some may take months and years, depending on the significance of the loss.[24]

Though it seemed a beneficial strategy, the one caveat to such formalized means of recovery is the raging range of emotional duress which grieving people often feel—emotions over which they have no control. For me, nowhere was that more true than with my honest expressions of bitterness. That attitude alone made me despise even the idea of recovery. Recovery would seem to say either what was lost was not significant or could be buried in an irrelevant past. Yet, I clung to advice like Clinebell's, if for no other reason than to keep me busy and to give me hope.

I sometimes wonder if grief recovery is like a diet in that way. People who spend a lifetime contending with their weight often go through long seasons of dieting. With each new diet strategy or exercise machine, they have renewed hope and are immediately on board. Perhaps this will be the one they strategize, this will be the time when their war with weight is finally won. But, all along, the real culprits are simply metabolism, carbs, and discipline. Ab crunchers and fad diets rarely work long term. While we have some control over discipline and diet, our metabolism is what it is, and what it is, is beyond our control. That is what grief is like.

We seem to have influence over a part of grief, and part of it, we don't. I read many grief books, manuals, study guides, and sermons; I talked to many mentors and counselors. But in the end, grief often comes down to things we can control, and things we can't. I've watched people enter into lifetime struggles with weight, depression, addictions, greed, or any number of mortal foes. We all seem to have some silent idol or opponent that intrudes on our free will. Many find some semblance of success, usually between their own determination and their own abdication. My hope in moving past the embitterment which parental grief introduced me to would likely find its fruition in similar places. Attitude and time seem of great influence and position to one in grief. One (attitude), we have moderate control over. The other (time) operates independently. So we grieve: sadly, angrily, brokenly, and bitterly. Some of it is manageable. Some of it is not. But one thing we know for sure when providing care for those in grief, withhold all judgments (as previously stated, grieving people do and say irrational things), and never push them to *hurry up* and *get over it*. In fact, don't expect them to get over it at all. Some of the change is simply out of their hands. Tragic loss changes life forever.

Time has allowed me some sense of depth in how I view the changes that happened to us following our tragic loss. Like the seasons we experience so vividly and differently in Iowa, the seasons of bitterness and angst can give way to more productive ones that stand in absolute contrast to what has been. I have always loved talking about the weather. My Sabbath is Monday, and on each Monday morning, without fail, I meet a few fellows at the local coffee shop for breakfast and meaningless conversation. I greatly value these men and the time we spend together. Weather (along with sports, religion, politics, and the markets) is one of our big topics of discussion—and likely is for most men who gather in coffee shops in Iowa. Weather is particularly intriguing when it is extreme.

When I was a child, I heard older folks say of a hot summer or a particularly cold and snowy winter: *one extreme follows another.* They meant if summer was blistering hot, then the coming winter would be worse than normal, and vice versa. I wondered if the principle might apply to grief, whether the extreme season of bitterness I endured would give way to another season of extreme, yet with a more fruitful harvest.

Weeds of Bitterness

Bitterness can cause us to miss so much. Like a sty, bitterness swells and inflames and blots out acts of kindness, tenderness, grace, and comfort. It's not that those things are not happening; it's just that our ability to see them has been disabled. Even the scriptures warn how bitterness can overshadow the beauty in life, "Keep a sharp eye out for weeds of bitter discontent. A thistle or two gone to seed can ruin a whole garden in no time" (Hebrews 12:15, *The Message*). Clearly, seeds of bitter discontent are pregnant with malice and gall. But surely those seeds can be rooted out, the garden saved, and we discover resentment and malignity giving way to a higher calling.

My wife is a superb gardener. From the moment the first seed catalogs arrive in January, the garden plans are being made. It is a healing balm for Vicki. In spring, as she tills and turns the earth, the time for seeds and planting arrives. As spring segues into summer, the sprouts appear and stand at attention, all in a row, like soldiers. In those early weeks of summer, each plant is diligently guarded, and weeds and thistles stand little chance. But as the garden grows, so do the long days of summer grow. Even the fiercest of gardeners can grow weary of the battle. Mulching, tilling, hoeing, pulling—it has been a valiant effort. Weeds are relentless in their conquest of garden space. If they can grow victoriously through the tiny cracks in a sidewalk, how much more will they grow in the fertile, productive, soft earth of Vicki's garden?

Still, an amazing thing happens. For all their bravado, the garden's real purpose is unaffected. It's an illusion. By summer's end, though the garden may look a lost cause, yet it is not. The weeds have done no damage but to the eye. The earth is ripe with potatoes, squash, cucumbers, beans, zucchini, carrots, and more. I am always amazed at the seemingly unending bounty that comes out of that plot of land to grace our table. Last year, I think we ate our final potato from the garden in January—about the time the seed catalogues arrived, long after the weeds had been gone.

That is what I think bitterness is like. Though it seems to come effortlessly and flourish, it is only an illusion. It does not affect the real purpose. A renewed cycle of harvest, planting, and life is underway. The ebb and flow of it all remains undaunted. The timing and dominion of the seasons are out of our control, and we need to surrender to them. They will be what they will be. Our attitude and direction, however, are things we seek strength and counsel to contend with, yet often through tears. Like Jesus on the cross refusing the gall, we also must turn our face away from embitterment and trust in the Easter of a new life. Each of us is in the process of transformation. We are always changing—for good or ill. The process is painful and often bitter. But it doesn't have the power to endure. It can't. In the end, we just might discover it is better to be transformed by loss than by gain.

A Greater Light

French philosopher Albert Camus wrote, "In the midst of winter, I finally learned that there was in me an invincible summer."[25] It is in the darkest moment that light is discovered. As with pain, bitterness can serve its purpose. When we were raising our kids, we frequently took them to Lake Rathbun for a weekend of camping and boating. One of our favorite moments on those trips came at night. Always I would make a big campfire and light my gas-powered Coleman lantern. We would sit around the fire, roasting marshmallows and making s'mores, singing old songs, and playing our favorite word game, *Railroad*. But on clear nights, just before we'd crawl into our sleeping bags, we would stargaze. However, we couldn't see the stars as long as we were near the light of our Coleman lantern and campfire. We had to move away from our little light to see the greater light. We would pick up our lawn chairs and move out into the dew-covered grass, into the darkness, and look up. There, invisible before, was the Milky Way galaxy. Millions of stars appeared, previously all hidden when viewed by our little light. Newly revealed in majesty, we would seemingly sit for hours and marvel at them—satellites, stars, suns and moons, constellations, galaxies; the heavens themselves— all viewed best when in the dark.

Could viewing my life and loss through the darkness of bitterness and angst allow me to see something previously invisible? Pastoral counselor and author Bob Deits, in his very helpful book *Life after Loss*, tells the story of Alice, a person whose darkness allowed her to discover in herself that *invincible summer*:

> Alice was quiet and shy. She was a contented homemaker and mother of two sons until her husband got cancer. After his death, Alice went through a dark and dismal time that lasted for almost two years ... she refused to give in to her grief or to run from it. Alice is convinced that the Kleenex Company must have added an extra shift of workers to keep up with her need for tissues! Today, three years after her loss, she works as a doctor's receptionist. She meets people easily, is considerably more forceful and dressed in brighter, bolder colors. Alice says, "It's hard to admit I'm a better person today, because it sounds like I'm glad Larry died. Nothing could be further from the truth. I'd give anything to have him back. But I do like the me that is emerging as a result of getting through my grief. I look back and I just can't believe I really did it."[26]

No one can believe it, Alice. We all want an invincible summer to emerge in us, but not at the expense of a hard winter. Something good came to Alice's life, not because of her loss but because of the transformation that occurred while going through her loss. A million times over I have thought I would forfeit any opportunity for character, idealism, or virtuous living if I could have my son back, but I can't. The weeds have overtaken the garden. They are relentless. So I move out into the darkness, willingly, in hopes of a greater and more just harvest.

It is a law of physics that when you move toward something, you move away from something else. I never would have mustered the courage or fortitude to move away from the dubious cycles of sadness, anger, and bitterness that plagued my first years of grief. Therefore, I began, slowly, incrementally, moving toward something. As the proximity to one neared, the other lengthened. Professor Sittser who lost his family in a car wreck discovered running toward darkness remained the shortest route to light.

Likewise, moving toward comfort, counsel, hope and faith—was the quickest way to distance myself from rage and bitterness.

The Drop Zone

Jekyll hated the Hyde within him. I'm convinced most people who struggle through life with a dark side do. Years ago we had a mid-week outreach at one of our churches to children and youth of the community. In a moment of divine inspiration, I dubbed the group *The Drop Zone*. For many years, forty to fifty children and youth attended. *Drop Zone* presented a more holistic approach to children's ministry. This was in direct correlation to the demographics of the community. With a disproportional amount of at-risk and high-needs children, we sought to care for more than just their spiritual needs. Through no fault of their own, life had dealt many of these children an unfair hand. Several had poor social skills, poor hygiene, learning disabilities, low-functioning homes, lacked proper nutrition and healthcare, and were often ridiculed in school. My heart effortlessly endears itself to this type of ministry. Certainly, many of the youth and children from the community who attended were not in this category, but the ones who were dominated the energy, patience, and attention of the staff. They are the ones that come to mind the most. In order to best meet their diverse needs, we offered a multipurpose program that included a hot nutritious meal, help with homework, recreation, life application skills, and devotions. Despite occasional conflicts occurring between kids (and occasionally staff), everything was covered with a self-affirming love.

Though we were a faith-based institution, when it came to instilling values; worth was as important as faith. Of all those years, I recall one family especially. With several siblings, each one seemed often to struggle with a dark side. They attended for years, and we loved them and did our best to help them. Sometimes, though, that meant we had to send them home. In a heartbeat, Hyde would show up in one of them, causing them to become uncontrollable. They would vandalize the building, start fights with other children, throw rocks at cars, curse the staff, and become utterly defiant. The next week when they would all come to *Drop Zone*, we held our collective breath, wondering if something might set one off, triggering his or her personal Hyde. The youngest boy, however, was at first, an angel. He rarely misbehaved. It wouldn't be until later that we discovered he was being medicated for some manner of social or emotional disorder. I have always been somewhat suspect at the perceived over-medication of children, but what a difference *meds* made in this youngster. When he was on them, he was very likable and compliant. But on the occasional meeting he showed up un-medicated, he was out of control. I will never know how much of that family's behavior disorders were a matter of environment and choice, or how much were simply out of their control. Perhaps it was both. Regardless, it became clear to me that one little boy could be two persons—like Jekyll and Hyde.

As the good Dr. Jekyll despised his dark alter ego in the Stevenson classic, I don't think that little boy liked his Hyde either. The family moved away about the time *Drop Zone* ended. I have often wondered what happened to them, and if their struggles continued. But I didn't judge them then, and I don't judge them now because I know the power of Hyde. For over two years, he was manifested in my life. Anger and bitterness bid him welcome. Though I didn't like him, I fully became him, and he became me. I could see no life without him.

I like it when loose endings get tidied up, when all the toys are put back in the box. It gives me great satisfaction. Many people who endure the bitter winter of grief do find in themselves an invincible summer. Resentment gives way, and loss thaws out. For them, there is a *Balm In Gilead*. In Alice's story, she came through her grief, seeing herself as a better person for her trial. Job certainly found a happy and tidy ending to his story. The Bible says the Lord blessed the latter days of Job more than his beginnings. In addition to thousands in his flocks, Job had seven more sons and three more daughters. He died an old man who was full of days.

But it is not so for me. I will have no more sons (as if more sons would restore the one lost). Happy endings are elusive. It's not because the bereaved don't want to find a new, happy, productive normalcy to bring sorrowful abnormal reality to a merciful end (in fact, they would love to). It's just not all up to them. Wounds don't heal by telling them to or by employing faith and conviction. Rather, grieving people stumble in their quest for a return to happy normalcy because they are still grieving people—and no other answer is needed.

Yet, even creation tells us winter doesn't last. Earth has been changed by winter's dark blast, but in return there is a full embrace of summer. On the south side of my home is a concrete block foundation that stands a couple feet tall, acting as a backdrop for Vicki's flowerbed. By late January, the south sun warms the block, and the warmth radiates into the earth. It is not a direct warming, but a reflected one. Because of it, snow and frost prematurely leave the flowerbed. About the end of the month, I start looking. You have to look hard, sometimes even moving a remaining fall leaf. I look every day. Then, one day, it is there, just barely there, coming up from the earth, the tiniest green shoot. Is it a daffodil? A crocus? A tulip? It doesn't matter. It is a sign that summer is coming, and winter is going. Many dark and cold nights are still to be endured. Snows and slick roads must be contended with and conquered. But summer is coming, invincible. Winter will not last, and neither will bitterness. It will change those who endure its frosty blasts, but in return the change will allow a full embrace of a new life. It is a life that will be missing something much loved. But it is also a life that will have found something, dare I say, even something beautiful.

Chapter 5

HIS EYE IS ON
THE SPARROW

A SPARROW'S SONG

It's only a sparrow, an ordinary bird;
After all, there are so many.
Others with ease take their place in the trees.
Matthew says, "Two for a penny."

And children are sometimes like sparrows,
Most common, of little renown.
They soon leave the tree, they go—*c'est la vie,*
Unnoticed by all but their own.

But sparrows evolve to a steely resolve,
Not given to whimper or whim.
A sparrow can tweet on its own two feet,
Far out at the end of a limb.

Should it break, will anyone answer?
Will there be a reply when they call?
Will a weary land do its plodding unplanned?
As it does when a lone sparrow falls.

For the song of the tree has diminished,
By a single, unnoticed trill.
Yet the change in the song resounds all along
To the One who hears in the still.

And sparrows will fall—like children,
And go where the angels have trod.
They've taken their mirth from the sons of the earth,
And they sing in the hands of their God.

Vincent D. Homan

T HE EYE OF GOD is on every sparrow, every time it falls to the ground. This image tells me something wonderfully endearing about the heart of God. Jesus said, "Are not two sparrows sold for a penny? Yet not one of them will fall to the ground apart from your Father. Even the very hairs of your head are all counted. So do not be afraid; you are of more value than many sparrows" (Matthew 10:29–31, NRSV).

A sparrow is a small, unremarkable, colorless, throwaway bird, yet it is precisely this bird that has caught the eye of God. It wasn't eagles with their independent bravado or cardinals with their scarlet hues and magnificent song or toucans with their rainbow-like colors and distinctive bill or flamingos that embody elegance and grace or even the swift and powerful condor that captured the eye of God. It was the sparrow. It isn't because God doesn't care for and watch over flamingos and toucans; it's just that God's eye is especially on the sparrow, like a parent's eye is on the child who needs it most. Perhaps the sparrow is God's favorite.

Over the years, I've stumbled on a number of versions of the tale of the favorite child, but my preference is attributed to columnist, Erma Bombeck. She perfectly captured the heart of a favorite child:

> My favorite child is the one who was too sick to eat ice cream at his birthday party, who had measles at Christmas, who wore leg braces to bed because he toed in, who had a fever in the middle of the night, the asthma attack, the child in my arms at the emergency ward. My favorite child spent Christmas alone away from the family, was stranded after the game with a gas tank on E, lost the money for his class ring. My favorite child is the one who messed up the piano recital, misspelled 'committee' in a spelling bee, ran the wrong way with the football, and had his bike stolen because he was careless. My favorite child is the one I punished for lying, grounded for insensitivity to other people's feelings,

and informed he was a royal pain to the entire family. My favorite child slammed doors in frustration, cried when she didn't think I saw her, withdrew and said she could not talk to me. My favorite child always needed a haircut, had hair that wouldn't curl, had no date for Saturday night, and a car that cost $600 to fix. My favorite child was selfish, immature, bad-tempered and self-centered. He was vulnerable, lonely; unsure of what he was doing in this world—and quite wonderful. All mothers have their favorite child. It is always the same one: the one who needs you at the moment. Who needs you for whatever reason—to cling to, to shout at, to hurt, to hug, to flatter, to reverse charges to, to unload on—
but mostly just to be there.[27]

Every parent has known that favorite child. Frustrating—indeed! Wonderful, you bet. Favorite children evoke a parental love of which you didn't know you were capable. Perhaps that is the sparrow in the Bible. Perhaps that is why God has his eye on them. Maybe it was because God had a child that was somewhat *sparrow-like*. Jesus was not born in the palaces of royalty but in a stable surrounded by animals and shepherds. The prophet Isaiah said he was not a handsome man; there was nothing about him that would draw others to him, rather, he was despised and rejected (see Isaiah 53:2–3). He did not call the Scribe or Pharisee to discipleship, but called fishermen and tax gatherers. He did not do his ministry in the great cities of Athens, Corinth, or Rome, but among the small seaside villages of Galilee. He was mostly ignored by the elite and powerful but was welcomed by the poor and abandoned. His friends were not priests, Levites, or Caesars, but prostitutes, lepers, and sinners. His life did not end with either the respect of his foes or the support of his friends—but alone, crucified between two thieves. But God's eye is on the sparrow.

A Sparrow's Life

In the wake of Gabe's death, I took great solace from this scripture, this idea that God loved sparrows, and kept a parental eye on their lives. Like Jesus, Gabe's life was often sparrow-like. Many days it was three steps forward, two back. If anyone was to be assigned blame for anything, it was usually Gabe. A memory that became a microcosm of this took place in our garden during the innocence of Gabe's childhood. Elmer, an old wheelchair-bound man, lived in a ramshackle house just west of our garden. Elmer was a nice old man to whom Vicki and I extended our neighborly best on many occasions. One spring afternoon, Gabe and two of his neighborhood friends were just sitting by the garden being boys. Of course, boys like to pick up any nearby projectiles and flip them in some direction. So, three little arms began excavating clods of garden and projecting them in all four directions, one clump breaking a window of Elmer's house. Of course, when the time came for reparations, it was Gabe who took the full blame. The other boys were nowhere to be found. Being a responsible dad and wanting to raise a responsible son, I took Gabe with me, and we repaired the window. I don't remember if I subtracted the expense from his allowance, as I felt he had gotten the point. He was the one blamed. Though three little arms were winging clods of our garden, Gabe was the offender. And that pattern often followed his sparrow-like life.

Whatever the reason, life wasn't always sunshine and roses for him, and there didn't seem to be one damn thing I could do to change it or make a difference. Often unnoticed and unappreciated in the tree of life, Gabe had to find his own niche—a sparrow's niche. He sometimes had a hard time fitting in, many times finding himself on the periphery of the clubs and cliques. Fathers quickly recognize through their children that schools can have a way of separating into two groups: the *in* and the *out* kids. Gabe and I would soon become aware that sparrows must find their own niche, even in schools. They don't always fit the predetermined mold.

Like many schools, sports played a significant role where Gabe attended. Young men and women trained tirelessly to achieve victory on the gridiron, field, and court—which they often did. With victory came recognition, and with recognition came value. It is the natural progression of life. It was that way when I attended school (in a different school system), and it's that way now. I never begrudged any merit attached to victories; in fact, I did a fair bit of applauding in the bleachers myself. School-spirit was a virtuous thing to watch and support. I knew those students worked hard for what they earned. But prestige and value were a bit harder to come by when boys and girls didn't fit this pattern. Sometimes a lack of recognition bordered on ostracism. And Gabe did not fit the preordained formula for status or recognition. His worth came from another place.

I suspect wherever people of any age gather, some will always be outside the mainstream. It is a great unspoken criteria which determines a person's worth and social status, and it's prevalent in adolescence, quite an achievement for thirteen-year-olds to recognize it. Still, Gabe usually seemed quite content wherever he found himself. It was all a matter of perspective. Sparrows don't recognize or regard social status. They are just as happy being sparrows as robins are being robins. But Gabe attracted many friends that were also sparrows. If you watch closely, you'll see that sparrows appear to enjoy each other's company. So do boys. I found myself becoming Dad to quite a number of sparrow-like boys; some who had no active dad in their lives, some who weren't athletic, some who didn't feel like they fit in, boys with time on their hands and no one with whom to spend it. They, like Gabe, were happy being sparrows, and I loved being their surrogate dad. Many times I took several of them camping, swimming, fishing, hiking, and sledding. We would take off down the river in our little boat filled with sleeping bags, hot dogs, and fishing poles for a great adventure. These little memories are entrenched in my heart. I taught these boys how to clean a fish, keep the dew off the sleeping bags, make a fire, catch a ball, and swim in a river. They taught me to never forget the value of seeing the world through a boy's eyes.

Gabe loved being a boy, and I relished boyhood again through him. Though my daughters always had me firmly wrapped around all ten of their fingers, there is something special about dads and their boys. Gabe and I wrestled; threw balls, sticks, rocks, and anything else we found. We lined up his plastic army guys and systematically mowed them down with the B-B gun. We played endless games of "H-O-R-S-E" down at the shop where the basketball hoop was set up (though for us it was always a game of "H-O-M-A-N"). But Gabe preferred a game called "Around the World" because he could sink the basketball from a great distance. We loved to watch monster movies together. We went swimming. We camped. Often we set the tent up in the back yard for a home camp-out. Gabe's friends joined in on his little adventure many times. They wanted Dad to scare them during the night, and, of course, I always did. Some of our most cherished times, however, came when we jumped in our old pickup truck and headed out to the country. Occasionally we stopped and jumped out, running through fields, for no other reason except that's the kind of stuff boys do. We picked up coffee cans of night crawlers after summer rains. This was as much an adventure and good time as fishing with them, which we did more times than I can count (but more on that later). Regardless, Gabe loved being a boy, just like his dad. How I cherish those years.

Creating a Memory

When the boys were about twelve, I took Gabe and a couple of his buddies on an overnighter. We traveled a few miles down a nearby river and found a perfect white sandbar on which to spend the night. While Gabe and I stored our gear, the other boys rolled their sleeping bags out on the ground. I told them not to, but I only told them once. They were big boys and knew better. We set our ditty poles in strategic places in our quest for the elusive catfish, and then we came back to camp to gather firewood and prepare for the night. As we relished in moments of roasting hotdogs and marshmallows, tossing in our fishing lines and telling tales, darkness quickly fell. With it came the thickest fog and mist I have ever encountered on the river. It was a chilly night, and the water was warm, which results in air you could cut with a knife. It was so dark you couldn't tell one boy from another away from the fire's light. With the darkness, fog, and a growing chill in the air, I decided it best to just get the lads in their sleeping bags and wait for morning. Gabe and I rolled ours out and crawled in our warm, dry beds. However, the other boys, who had already unrolled their bags, found them completely soaked by the dew and mist, so they lay down close to the fire and close to me. But rivers have a way of getting your attention at night. The heavy mist made it seem like we were extras in a remake of *The Wolfman*. A large fish had gotten hooked on one of our nearby pole sets and was thrashing about in the water. Owls hooted unmercifully. When a couple beavers began to clap to each other down the river a ways, the boys came to attention and weren't so sure about their wilderness machismo.

Each boy had brought his B-B gun for this adventure, I guess just in case we had to defend ourselves against Bigfoot. By this time each had their B-B guns loaded and ready for action. They were later glad they did. Even a B-B gun gives a twelve-year-old boy some comfort in the dark. Somewhere around 2 a.m., a pack of coyotes decided they liked the smell of our camp. They came right up to the timber's edge, stopping just short of the sandbar, some twenty feet from where we were lying—and they began to howl. There is something about a pack of coyotes howling and yelping at each other in the middle of the night, in a pea-soup fog that makes a person take notice. Even I had a few hairs on my neck stand at attention. And the boys—they were coming out of their skins. They quickly discovered that B-B guns were of little practical value when it comes to motivating a bunch of coyotes. "Get me *outtahere!*"—I believe was the boy's common call. No one slept much after that, except me. Evening finally surrendered to daylight, morning came, and with it a great harvest of catfish. We roasted hotdogs for breakfast, and then jumped in the river because we could. By the time I got everything loaded up, hauled home, put away, fish cleaned, me cleaned, I was bushed—but I had the time of my life, and wouldn't take a million dollars for that night. Precious moments like these are treasure-troves in our family story. It is imperative that parents build memories with their children—while they can.

During Gabe's upbringing we had dozens of similar night adventures. I was very privileged to have those times with Gabe, but also with other wonderful young men. Truly, some of these boys became like sons. In recent years, following Gabe's death, a couple of them have told me I was the only father they had known. The halls of Congress couldn't give me a higher honor. Sparrows are precious things indeed. The world misses so much when it doesn't recognize their song amidst its clamor.

A Sparrow's Value

Matthew's gospel said two sparrows are sold for a single penny (Matthew 10:29). Luke told us five sparrows are sold for two pennies (Luke 12:6). The point is that two sparrows could be purchased for a penny, but if the buyer had two pennies to spend, he got not four sparrows, but five. The fifth sparrow was thrown in as part of the bargain because it had no value. I have known children who were like the fifth sparrow. I have done enough living now and have encountered enough people to know the ground isn't level on this earth. It isn't an even playing field, and everyone is not dealt the same hand of cards.

So many things can put a sparrow on a branch by itself: some little physical defect, a lack of esteem, poverty, learning disabilities, poor athleticism, single-parent homes, and speech impediments. Sigh. When I was a kid, one boy was ostracized at school for having pimples. And should some little sparrow fall into trouble or mischief, well, communities can have notoriously long memories. My conviction, though, is that God's point of view on all this is quite different than the cultures, and I long ago made it my life's mission to get that point across as succinctly as possible.

In Jesus' day, society's crème de la crème were scribes, rabbis, and Pharisees. These groups were often renowned for their judgment of others as much as for their self-piety. Jesus offered them this chilling rebuke: "Woe to you, teachers of the law and Pharisees, you hypocrites! You are like whitewashed tombs, which look beautiful on the outside, but on the inside are full of dead men's bones and everything unclean" (Matthew 23:27). Appearance and status may derive a few advantages in this short life, but they don't carry much weight with our creator. An internal integrity must be sought and lived out. Clearly, heaven and earth view us differently. Prestige can be gained by others' perceptions. Yet, a greater value is given, one inherent to our birth. Every life is sacred to the One who gave it. Though cemeteries have many unmarked, forgotten graves, every life comes with purpose and reverence. The world's eyes may be on red carpets and those who walk them, but God's eye is on the sparrow.

God's eye is not just on the sparrow. It is especially with the sparrow that falls. New Testament commentaries and dictionaries are not all of one mind regarding what it means to fall. Though often only associated with death, some commentaries suggest it may mean something more. Perhaps the fallen sparrow is also the wounded one, the hurt one, the alone one. Perhaps God is even grieved by the fallen sparrow. This is an image of God that draws me near.

A God, who watched as his own sparrow, Jesus, fell to the ground, watches all sparrows with compassion. It almost makes God seem vulnerable. Yet, if God is a parent, then God would surely be vulnerable. Jesus felt abandoned by God on the cross, as if God could not look while his son suffered. I have heard preachers say the reason for this was the world's sin fell upon Jesus, and the penalty for sin is separation from God. The Bible does say that God made Jesus, who knew no sin to become sin for us, so that we could be right with God (see 2 Corinthians 5:21). God cannot look upon sin, they reason; therefore, God could not look at Jesus.

I don't know if God can look upon sin or not. I have always suspected God has caught me misbehaving a time or two. But I am a father, and believe something more is at work in this text. Many times Jesus called God his Father, and no father or mother wants to look upon the death of his or her son or daughter. Perhaps even God turned away. As a bereaved father, I could approach that kind of God. God's wounded heart would understand my wounded heart. A God who knows no pain cannot minister to my pain. However, a God who has known some vulnerability, some sorrow, some affliction, that God would be welcome in my grievous world.

Theologian, pastor, and Christian martyr Dietrich Bonhoeffer wrote, "God is weak and powerless in the world, and that is precisely the way, the only way, in which he is with us and helps us …. Only the suffering God can help."[28] This God doesn't have the same look and feel of the God I first encountered in the little United Methodist Church of my youth. That God had the *whole world in his hands*. That God walked on water, shut the mouths of lions, slew giants, and kept prophets alive in the belly of a whale. But a God who suffers? Who is this God? Yet that is precisely the God I welcome today. The world around me will continue to do what it's always done: reward appearance, achievement, and behavior. It will line up for award shows, victory parades, and first-place finishes, while lauding both heroes and victors. But God's eye will be on the sparrow.

Picking out Funeral Music

I was not prepared to pick out music for my son's funeral. Recalling those moments still brings a chill and an ache to my bones. We were all into the contemporary hymn *I Can Only Imagine* at that time. Recorded by the Christian band, *Mercy Me*, and written by their founder, Bart Millard, it is a hopeful piece that contemplates a day when we are all on the other side, walking and talking with Jesus. We wondered if using the piece at Gabe's funeral would mark it and make it unlistenable in the future. It did for me. Regardless, we decided it to be a good choice. What a thing to have to decide. The opening stanza beckoned us to sing along, and on that dreadful day, we did.

> I can only imagine, what it will be like—
> when I walk by Your side.
> I can only imagine, what my eyes will see—
> when Your face is before me.
> I can only imagine, I can only imagine.[29]

Every good funeral has two songs (or so I have observed), and I didn't want to breach protocol. I had only one request for the second song, the classic gospel hymn: *His Eye Is on the Sparrow.* Gabe likely never heard this song nor knew it existed. I'm sure he would have preferred Dad picking something from *Pearl Jam* or *Metallica*. Maybe someday I'll get to apologize to him for the music selections. But as I was taught, funerals are for grieving families. On the day we buried him, I needed to be reminded that God's eyes are on the sparrows. We asked my dear friends Terry and LaVonne to sing, and Jan to play, which they did impeccably.

This wonderful song, a staple in African-American worship services, was written by two white people in 1905. The lyricist, Civilla D. Martin, said this about her inspiration to write the song:

> Early in the spring of 1905, my husband and I were sojourning in Elmira, New York. We contracted a deep friendship for a couple by the name of Mr. and Mrs. Doolittle—true saints of God. Mrs. Doolittle had been bedridden for nigh twenty years. Her husband was an incurable cripple who had to propel himself to and from his business in a wheel chair. Despite their afflictions, they lived happy Christian lives, bringing inspiration and comfort to all who knew them. One day while we were visiting with the Doolittles, my husband commented on their bright hopefulness and asked them for the secret of it. Mrs. Doolittle's reply was simple: 'His eye is on the sparrow, and I know He watches me.' The beauty of this simple expression of boundless faith gripped the hearts and fired the imagination of Dr. Martin and me. The hymn 'His Eye Is on the Sparrow' was the outcome of
> that experience.

The day after she wrote this, Martin mailed the poem to composer Charles H. Gabriel who wrote the music. Gabriel, the name seems kind of fitting. As Martin had written, and Terry and LaVonne sang, the poem unfolded. As my ears strove to hear its hopeful message, my soul sank in utter despair and complete brokenness. It was a place of death that somehow carried a message of life—like the cross. Nevertheless, the lyrics brought a sense of something good.

> Why should I feel discouraged,
> why should the shadows come,
> Why should my heart be lonely,
> and long for heaven and home,
> When Jesus is my portion? My constant friend is He:
> His eye is on the sparrow, and I know He watches me;
> His eye is on the sparrow, and I know He watches me.

Refrain

> I sing because I'm happy, I sing because I'm free,
> For His eye is on the sparrow, and I know He watches me.

> "Let not your heart be troubled," His tender word I hear,
> And resting on His goodness, I lose my doubts and fears;

Though by the path He leadeth, but one step I may see;
His eye is on the sparrow, and I know He watches me;
His eye is on the sparrow, and I know He watches me.

Whenever I am tempted, whenever clouds arise,
When songs give place to sighing,
when hope within me dies,
I draw the closer to Him, from care He sets me free;
His eye is on the sparrow, and I know He watches me;
His eye is on the sparrow, and I know He watches me.

Refrain[30]

In my memory, I revisited this song many times. I can still see Terry and LaVonne standing before that single microphone offering us their gift. It was true compassion. As I have replayed the song again and again in my mind, I realized that I, too, was a sparrow of God. All these images from the song I knew and would know again: discouragement, shadows, loneliness, longing, trouble, doubts, fears, temptations, clouds, sighing, and death.

But God's eye is on the sparrow, and I knew God was watching me as well.

Life Matters

I grew up in the tiny town of Webster, which afforded my childhood many great adventures. I often took my B-B gun out with a few buddies in search of some great trophy. That usually meant we ended up down at the local elevator. In the center of that community of grain bins was a taller building (it seemed a tower to me as a child); a place where trucks dumped their load of corn and beans. It is long gone now. Then it was a beehive of activity for sparrows. It was fun to line one up in our sights and fire away. Rarely did any of us actually hit one or do enough damage to bring one down. I don't think I really wanted to anyway. I just enjoyed the hunt. Still, occasionally, someone would get lucky, and a sparrow would fall.

It would lie there—dead. There was no putting it back. I figured out long ago that I wouldn't make a good hunter. I have never exactly wanted to hurt anything. Young boys are very impressionable, and the sight of a dead bird in the place of one that had been happily singing and flying around has something significant to say, at least it did to me. I am fully aware most are not overly concerned with the mortality rate of sparrows. Maybe it was life itself that I recognized as being so precious. If God cares about a single sparrow, I wonder how much more God cares about us. Regardless, I don't think I ever ended many sparrows' lives. I kept my best shots for my plastic cowboys in my unending *Gunfights at the OK Corral*.

I once took a class on world religion. The instructor was a wonderful and gifted fellow who never let his religious preference show. He knew I was a Christian, and it made for good debate. I remember writing on a paper that I would love to see Lao Tzu, Solomon, and (then) Senator Biden play Jeopardy. I truly enjoyed this man's class. With a natural ability for teaching, he allowed me to sort out some of my myths and prejudices from religion's orthodoxies. His wife was Hindu. Hindus see all of life as sacred, in part to their understanding of a "spark of the divine" being in all life, and in part to their doctrine of reincarnation. Regardless, an orthodox Hindu would never shoot a sparrow for sport. I doubt a market for B-B guns exists in the East. Our instructor told us some disciplines of his wife's family. They took great measures to safeguard all life. Even a gnat's life mattered. I don't know if all Hindus are this orthodox, but I was impressed by their fidelity. I knew early on I would never be tempted to convert to Hinduism. However, their utter respect for all life left me captivated. I have always enjoyed a hamburger too much to allow for the possibility of a cow being sacred. Still, in our ever-violent world, where even human life seems disposable, Hindus might be on to something: life *does* matter.

But it matters for the whole of the journey, not just at its end. I've sometimes suspected my evangelical brethren of becoming a bit wayward here. Jesus wasn't only interested in the sweet bye-and-bye. He was interested in people's todays; how they were in the given moment. I sometimes think if we treated each other with as much dignity as Hindus do an ant, this world would surely be a better place.

Death is simply everywhere. The news is full of it. I am frightened and disillusioned by accounts of women and children sent into classrooms and markets with bombs strapped under their clothes. I do not understand torture. When planes full of innocent people were hijacked and flown into buildings filled with more innocent people, something seemed to systematically change in our world. Death seemed to become more palatable, and I am bewildered. I don't understand why there isn't more lamenting in this country for the millions of pre-born children who are never allowed to see daylight or for thirty thousand plus who die daily from malnutrition and preventable diseases. I wonder if we are becoming desensitized by the sheer number of people who have died in our ever-growing list of natural disasters. I don't understand gang or ethnic violence and the spray of bullets throughout residential neighborhoods, which often claim the innocent. Domestic violence, abduction, rape, and molestation are sadly a part of our every-day language and fill the evening news. Death even reigns here in the pastoral, rural landscape of Iowa. It is a rare day that the evening news does not report a shooting, a fire, an accident, a drowning, or any other means that a life ended. And I think, if a single sane word could be given this world, it would be this: not a single sparrow falls to the ground outside God's watchful eye, and people are of much more value than sparrows. Life matters!

Office Visits

The "Life-Matters" mantra has shaped much of my professional ministry. Years ago I walked into my own pastor's office to sort out a problem. He was busy tinkering away at his computer. I am more gracious in this memory today than I was at one time as I think of how much time I am forced to tinker with my computer. How did the kingdom survive before we had them? Regardless, I walked in hoping for this man's attention, but he clearly didn't want to talk to me at that moment. He turned partially toward me, still keeping an eye on his work. Nevertheless, I gave it a shot. I began to make myself quite vulnerable by opening up regarding some things troubling my life. A few minutes into the one-sided conversation, I noticed he glanced up at his clock, as if to measure how much time I would be allotted. I got the hint. I quickly terminated the conversation and left. And I vowed if I were ever a pastor, should someone enter my office, I don't care if only to talk about the weather, I would give that person the time they deserve—and it wouldn't matter what I was doing. I saw a plaque on another pastor's wall that read, "Interruptions don't keep me from my business. Interruptions are my business." I liked that saying then, and I like it today. Anyone, for anything, will always take a higher priority than an administrative task, because— life matters.

Now I am a pastor, and have been for over two decades. That lofty goal of giving full attention has been put to the test many, many times, and I know a few things now I didn't that day. I know deadlines, and endless reports, and sermon preparation, and newsletters, and mail, and correspondence, and committee work, and evaluations, and profiles, and continuing education, and small groups, and bulletins, and audits, and budgets, and nominations, and a hundred other tasks all tie you to a computer. And I know many good folks wander into a small church pastor's office. Some have troubles to sort out, while others have time on their hands, with nowhere to go and nothing to do. I have tried to always give them my respectful attention, because after all, interruptions are my business and life matters. But I confess that my body language probably demonstrated my busy schedule more often than I should. God forgive me. There is a place, however, where I try to draw a proverbial line in the sand. I know the difference between someone passing the time of day, and a lost sparrow looking for a place to light. Several of those sparrows have come throughout the years, some more wounded than others. As any pastor can tell you, he has seen life-and-death moments in that office. I have felt sometimes like I was just keeping my finger in the hole of many leaky dikes.

I will always think about one young man. He has been singing with the sparrows. Knowing how deeply I appreciated any little kindness people showed my children, I have tried my best to show kindness to him. He is now a young man, and a good man—but he is still singing with the sparrows. Through no fault of his own, he was born into layers of poverty and problems. An absent dad, loss of income, trouble at school, bad decisions, lack of opportunity, no mentor, no money; all these add up to one thing—a sparrow's life. And the world is so unforgiving to sparrows. Apart from the occasional meal we share, and the times we have provided some practical help for the family, I have been unable to offer this fine young man any real help or promise. Once I found him a real job possibility. Unfortunately, he didn't have a car, he couldn't get insurance, he didn't even have a license, and he had no money to pursue any of them. He needed a job to get the money to move forward with life, but he first needed money to get the job to get the money. Poverty is so destructive.

We should not judge the *have-nots* so easily. We should not assume they are all lazy or dysfunctional. We have not walked in their shoes. This young man comes into my office once or twice every week, and spends considerable time. That is my good fortune. God help me to never look up at the clock when he is there. I had him fold the bulletins a few times. It's amazing, I live in a place where some people have the ability to give $10,000 for an acre of ground, and some people don't have $3 for a gallon of gas. I have to remind myself occasionally that God's eye is on the sparrow—and I have to guard myself to ensure that my eye is also sparrow-focused.

A Flood of Compassion

Are we to be the eyes of God to the sparrows among us? Or are we the sparrows ourselves? My practical mind beckons the question, what does this look like in real life? How does God watch, and how are people valued? Too often I believe, the church offers over-simplistic answers to the life-long traumas that sometimes happen to fallen sparrows. With a prayer, a memory verse, and a positive confession, we send our fallen sparrows on their way. Being the eyes of God upon the fallen, the lonely, the sick, and the grieving can require more hours and honesty than our busy lives can sometimes afford. Even in the church, it is often only those who have been broken under the wheels of life themselves who have the servitude to be the eyes of God upon a world of fallen sparrows. I have no interest in the doctrine or practice of a church if it doesn't pour out of its heart compassion, mercy, and love for the sparrow that falls. The great illusion of religion is that it often tries to lead where it has never been itself. Still, with compassionate hearts, churches could become communities of wounded healers, offering sanctuary to fallen sparrows, near and far.

Former television news personality Edward R. Murrow in his book, *This I Believe,* recounted the experience of a great American actress who lost her young daughter:

> When my daughter died of polio, everybody stretched out a hand to help me, but at first I couldn't seem to bear the touch of anything, even the love of friends; no support seemed strong enough. While Mary was still sick, I used to go early in the morning to a little church near the hospital to pray. I had rather cut God out of my life, and I didn't have the nerve at the time to ask God to make my daughter well—I only asked God to help me understand …. I kept looking for a revelation, but nothing happened. And then, much later, I discovered that it had happened, right there in the church. I could recall vividly, one by one, the people I had seen there …. Here was my revelation: Suddenly I had realized that I was one of them. In my need I gained strength from the knowledge that they too had needs, and I felt interdependence with them …. I experienced a flood of compassion for people. I was learning the meaning of "Love thy neighbor."[31]

Herein lays the secret of the church. Fallen sparrows do not need our pity or advice. They need compassion in life and in death. Come; take your place beside them. No judgments, no condemnation—rather compassionate hearts going out as equals in the sharing of feelings and bearing of burdens.

Pastor and radio preacher, Professor Ralph Sockman (1889–1970) wrote: "Compassion does not flow like a stream from a higher to a lower level. Compassion moves as the tide moves across the ocean, that is, on the level drawn by the attraction of a power above."[32] What an amazing metaphor, compassion is like the tides. When we were in Maine on a family vacation, we walked out to a small island to get an up-close view of a magnificent lighthouse. Of course, the tide was out. We walked across slime-covered rocks, and I marveled at the power of the tides. A sign warned us to head back before the tide returned. Even if the water was only ankle deep, don't start out, the sign read, because before you could get back to the mainland, you would be overwhelmed by its force. I made sure we were safely back long before the water came trickling in from the sea. The power and speed that the ocean asserted upon its return was an amazing testimony to nature's prowess. I was certainly glad I wasn't hobbling across that rocky and slick bottom when that happened.

Compassion is like a tide coming in from the ocean. When a sparrow falls, compassion seems completely absent, like when the tide's out. Grief can be an incredibly isolating thing. The perception is that you are completely alone because no one can fully enter into your experience. Then it comes, a trickle here and a trickle there; suddenly, it is ankle deep, then up to the knees, and then a flood. We have that power. If we don't faint or fail, we have the capacity to bring compassionate care to the wounded and hurting sparrow, like a tide brings the sea back into the harbor. It may be the primary mission of the church.

Churches that would be the eyes of God to a fallen world must have compassionate hearts.

As I have reflected on our painful loss, we first watched our little sparrow fall; then we became fallen sparrows ourselves. I've begun to understand the treasure of a compassionate heart. It is to know that when we fall, someone is watching, not to critique or give advice, but to hold and help pick up the pieces. It is said that every pew holds a broken heart, or a fallen sparrow, hoping this might be the service, this might be the day when someone shows his or her care. If we would be the eyes of God, we must be that someone. Our lives before God must be both vertical and horizontal. Worship may draw us upward, but compassion sends us outward. Ralph Williams' prayerful hymn *When the Church of Jesus* reminds us that worship and compassion go hand-in-hand. Its memorable second verse states this sentiment:

> If our hearts are lifted where devotion soars
> High above this hungry, suffering world of ours;
> Lest our hymns should drug us to forget its needs,
> Forge our Christian worship into Christian deeds.[33]

Perhaps you, also, are a fallen sparrow. Life has become unraveled, and you have lost your hope. Knowing someone cares can provide strength and courage for the day. Even in my darkest days following Gabe's death, when I despised the world the most, I knew that someone cared. Friends and caregivers kept showing it until I could finally see it for myself. In one mysterious Psalm, the psalmist appears jealous over a sparrows' apparent unhindered access to the temple and the altar. There, they are even able to build nests for their young. Psalm 84:3 says, "Even the sparrow has found a home, and the swallow a nest for herself, where she may have her young—a place near your altar." Though this probably has something to do with Israel's place with God, I would tell the psalmist there is no need for jealousy. If they knew the whole story, they would know that God and sparrows have a unique relationship. Sparrows are always welcome in the presence of God.

Jesus said if God watches when a sparrow falls, God will watch over our lives even more.

I believe one way God does that is by having us watch over each other. After other bereaved parents visited us in those first dark days, I told Vicki we must follow in their footsteps. I said, "The next time someone's child dies, and there will be a next time, we must go and let them know they are not alone. Someone cares." We must resolve ourselves to be people of compassionate hearts. The world will always be full of fallen sparrows. We must help God keep watch.

CHAPTER 6

IN SEARCH OF SIGNIFICANCE

LIFE

Let me but live my life from year to year,
With forward face and un-reluctant soul;
Not hurrying to, nor turning from the goal;
Not mourning for the things that disappear
In the dim past, nor holding back in fear
From what the future veils, but with a whole
And happy heart, that pays its toll
To Youth and Age, and travels on with cheer.

So let the way wind up the hill or down,
O'er rough or smooth, the journey will be joy:
Still seeking what I sought when but a boy,
New friendship, high adventure, and a crown,
My heart will keep the courage of the quest,
And hope the road's last turn will be the best.

Henry Van Dyke[34]

Certain things in life are lost by being kept—
and certain things are saved by being used.

IT SEEMS AS THOUGH God gave us these lives to be spent, not saved. Recently, I visited a nice man in a nursing home. He has spent all his life practicing a profoundly frugal standard of living and is known by that lifestyle which I've heard called: "tight as the bark on a tree." But he was also frugal because he farmed during some tough years. As agriculture became a more prosperous way of life, many of the old-timers kept their business and their checkbooks close to the vest, as if it were still the 1930's or the 80's. This man was like that and remained fiscally entrenched in those decades. He likely prospered, but it never showed. I saw him around the community many times in an old pickup, well-worn overall bibs, and a free, much-stained, seed corn cap. When the local coffee shop raised the price of coffee by a dime, he left for the convenience store (refills weren't free there, but it was a matter of principle). This man probably could have driven new pickups and worn new overalls his whole life. He likely could have drunk *Starbucks*, but he didn't. He was frozen in an ethic, birthed during a tough time. But he is a warmhearted man, and I have always enjoyed his company, visiting him many times over the years.

One day, as we sat on white wooden seats under the overhang at the nursing home, he offered a small lament, "I'll never go home again. I can't take care of myself anymore." Then he asked, "Do you know what it costs me a year to live here?" Even though my dad had been in that very home for five years, I had no idea. When he choked out the sizeable amount, he concluded, "All the money I have saved is just going here." I razzed him a bit, saying he should have driven those new pickups all along. But I got the message. I could see it in his face. We keep nothing. Nothing outside our own humanity will travel with us. All who think their significance is in their land, their reputation, their bank accounts, their businesses, or their assets, are fooling themselves. This man had to fit his whole life into two dresser drawers and a small closet. Time will force the issue on us as well. Our undeniable end will beg the question: are we saving or living our lives?

It's Not About You

Our inevitable mortality seems to scream its lessons and mores with great fervor and persistence. The death of my son has allowed me to hear them again.

- If we live carefully, thinking always of our own profit and status, solely concerned with what we'll have left;

- If we're mindful of only our ease, comfort, and security;

- If our sole aim in life is to make our days as long and trouble free as possible; and

- If we make no real effort except for ourselves—then we are losing *real* life all the time.

Preacher and successful author Rick Warren was exactly right when he wrote, "It's not about you."[35] I have always believed we were created for a higher purpose than our own. I speak with no unmerited piety, as I also desire worldly things. I suspect the fading flowers of this earth hold some attraction for all of us. Regardless, the lives we live are not for our sole benefit and wellbeing. Until we understand that, life will never make sense.

People mistake self-fulfillment and success for significance. As mentioned, Vicki and I took a wonderful vacation to Alaska. Vicki had planned every detail of this trip. Not me, I'm an impulsive planner—and packer. Not many days into our two-week stay, I realized I made a strategic mistake. I seriously over-packed, taking more clothes than I needed. The thing about traveling is, whatever you pack you have to drag all over: at airports, on trains and buses, at lodges, etc.—whether you use it or not. Most seasoned travelers know this rule: when traveling, always pack a few days in advance of the trip, then, just before you leave, take out a third of what you've packed. I apparently didn't get that memo in time, as I had to drag a lot of unworn clothes all over Alaska. I was *stuck* with possessions I didn't need, but was compelled to hang on to for the duration of my journey.

Life can be like that. We are now trying to get rid of the extra stuff we spent the first half of our lives working hard to acquire. It seems like extra baggage now, heavy, unneeded, and in our way. I've discovered it's as rewarding getting rid of stuff now as it was acquiring it then. Like on vacation, we're only visitors here. Whatever we acquire will just be stuff to move around and store. We won't need it where we're headed.

Years ago I read an account of a Western traveler visiting a historic monastery in the East. Entering the Abbot's quarters, the visitor was stunned at its simplicity: a small table and washbasin, a straight-backed chair, little clothing, a single bed, and a lamp. Suddenly, the Abbot entered the room. With a thousand intended questions prepared, what surged out of his mouth was, "Father Abbot, where are your things?"

"What things," the old Abbot meekly replied. "Your stuff, your property, your possessions; where are your things?" At that, the wise priest seized a moment. "Where are your things," he asked the Westerner. "My things, you're asking about my things?" "Yes, your stuff, your property, your possessions. Where are your things?" Father Abbot continued. "Why would I need things," said the tourist. "I'm just a visitor here, I'm just passing through. I won't be here long. I don't need a bunch of stuff just to visit. It would only clutter up the journey and cause me to miss why I'm here." And the Abbot said, "And I'm just a visitor here, I'm just passing through. I won't be here long. I don't need a bunch of stuff just to visit. It would only clutter up the journey and cause me to miss why I'm here."

I have learned none of us are here very long. It is a shame spending it acquiring, storing, moving around, and getting rid of possessions. The circle of life being learned these days has less to do with conception, birth, life, and death, and more to do with attraction, purchase, debt, payments, and garage sales. Many men and women are driven in their quest for more, always more, as if they get to keep it or achieve some kind of power from it. Debt created by acquiring unnecessary possessions is a leading cause of family/marital stress. Marriages that end in divorce can spend half their money hiring lawyers hoping to retain what cannot be kept. In our driven quest to acquire the temporal, we are losing something of the eternal.

Self-Help or Self-Sacrifice

We learn a subtle and deceptive white lie in this life: significance is found in things extrinsic to our inner beings. What we have, who we know, what we do, or who we are become our aspirations. Messages line bookshelves and bulletin boards directing us to be the best we can be. They offer many weary and predictable steps toward self-improvement: Set goals. Aim high. Be a leader. Believe in yourself. Never give up. Be disciplined. To be clear, I am not diminishing the value or merit in achieving self-betterment. I tend to admire those disciplined souls among us who stick to their regimented diets and exercise programs; in fact, I'm married to one of them. I am reminded that it would do this body of mine some good to adopt similar aspirations. I applaud those who achieve their goals of higher education, running a marathon, or climbing Everest. However, I would kindly remind them that they are the same people after accomplishing their goals as they were before. And both of them are beautiful.

Goals and dreams are wonderful, but "motivational speak" should not be our mantra. A self-gratifying smugness and an anti-humility ethic could be trending upward, as if to say the world is becoming about us. When many reach their motivational mountaintop, achieve their worldview of success, and take home their trophy, they can still discover they're missing the significant life for which they were intended. Life requires more than "self," and self-help advice. Jesus cautioned, "Self-help is no help at all. Self-sacrifice is the way, my way, to finding yourself, your true self" (Matthew 16:25, *The Message*).

My significance does not come from my acquisitiveness. And I will not forget the Abbot's advice: "Remember, you're just a visitor here. Don't over-pack. You'll only clutter up the journey, and cause you to miss why you're here."

Packing up Memories

When one is thrust into the whirling debris that follows sudden death, life's priority list quickly gets rearranged. Some things suddenly matter less. Some things suddenly matter more; much more. It was an unexpected and additional sorrow and angst for me when we had to suddenly retrieve and store all of Gabe's possessions. Gabe had been living with a couple close friends in a small town near his place of employment. The building didn't make this a great home, but the friends surely did. Gabe truly loved those folks, and it would soon become clear that they also loved him. And now, we had to walk into his home and pack up what he had spent his life acquiring. It was as if his whole life was suddenly being put away in boxes. How difficult it was to be forced into sorting through and boxing up his clothes, DVDs, stereo, tools, personal items, furniture, dishes, etc.

In the middle of the task, I went outside and fell apart by a tree. The tears and anguish poured out of me. I anticipated a demanding day, knowing my heart would be parceled out with Gabe's things. I didn't anticipate a blistering return to my *Ground Zero*. I had only cried three times in my adult life before Gabe died. But now, I was all too familiar with its wretched emotion—and I hated the experience. Yet here, behind a tree, weeping raged. I know the psalmist said, "Weeping may remain for a night, but rejoicing comes in the morning" (Psalm 30:5b), but it seemed my night was to be interminable. So I cried. And when the moment subsided, I went back inside and packed up some of his CDs.

I was somewhat amazed at how much stuff he had acquired, and how he had managed to get all of it in his relatively small living quarters. I also *grinned* a fatherly grin over some of the boy stuff in his stash. In his heart, he still loved much of the same stuff his father did: fishing stuff, music, movies, toys, and tools. Some of his things we gave to his roommates and friends. It seemed the right thing to do. But most items we brought back home. Much of it we stored upstairs in his old room. The rest went into plastic totes and put in the basement. I didn't really know what to do with his things. I knew we couldn't keep them forever, but how does one throw away something that belonged to your only son? I couldn't conceive of it. Those who have not traveled this wretched valley cannot imagine the horror of discovering all you have left of your son or daughter is memories and full plastic storage boxes.

Is this all that is left of us after we die?

About a year after Gabe's death, Vicki pulled his tennis shoes from the kitchen closet. They were all spread out like his feet and carried the muddy stain of a pond's edge. "Are you okay with throwing these away?" she asked. The moment caught me off-guard. I had to think about it for a while—but I was. It was time. So that day, his tennis shoes went into a yellow garbage bag, and into the garbage truck. In the years that have followed, we have taken more and more of his items to Goodwill: his vacuum cleaner, movies, furniture, clothing, etc. Some things did not endure the years spent in my wet basement and were disposed of elsewhere. I am currently seeking a good home for his *Holy Grail*: his stereo—and the gargantuan Cerwin Vega speakers that accompanied it. Something inside of me says I am shipping out a part of Gabe each time we part with an item. Perhaps we are. Though it's getting easier, it is still a riveting experience to see one of his prized possessions go out the door for the final time. It requires a few deep breaths. But then, all of our prized possessions will ultimately go out the door for the final time. It's just a matter of when. Maybe the people deserving empathy are the ones who don't seem to understand that. Gabe's significance was not in his CDs, speakers, or even his beloved fishing poles. And neither is ours.

A Model of Self-Sacrifice

Beulah is a lovely lady in our church. One thing I love about little rural United Methodist churches are the ladies (affectionately known as *church basement ladies*)—and each one is a saint. Beulah is a saint who serves her church by example. She teaches the Bible's morals by living them. Through a very modest, unassuming life, Beulah never draws attention to herself. But her significance is as authentic as it is anonymous. Beulah has a compassionate heart and is a selfless giver. When she gives, it is for the right reasons. She got this value honestly. At a Bible study, years ago, Beulah told a terrific tale of her grandmother's generosity. I was so moved by the story I approached her about writing a definitive account and submitting it for publication to the church devotional magazine, *The Upper Room*. So Beulah and I met to work out the details, and we submitted her heart-warming narrative. It was accepted and became the day's devotion for September 7, 2003. The text and devotion was entitled, *A Giving Spirit*:

> Command them to do good, to be rich in good works, to be generous and ready to share with others. In this way they will store up for themselves a treasure which will be a solid foundation for the future. –1 Timothy 6:18–19 (GNB)

> Whenever I give a gift, I think of my grandmother. She loved to knit, crochet, and make quilts. She won many blue ribbons showing her handiwork at the fair. She was a generous person and gave away many of her handmade creations as gifts. Early one morning, Grandma and Grandpa awoke to find their house on fire. They barely escaped with their lives. A neighbor asked Grandma if she had saved any of her fancy work. She replied, "Only what I gave away!" Later, when a friend told my grandmother that she sympathized with her because of losing everything in the fire, Grandma responded, "I've got something far better, something the world and certainly a fire cannot take from me." Indeed it could not. My grandmother's giving spirit demonstrated her abundant faith, which endured beyond this loss.
> – Beulah Green (Iowa)[36]

It's an amazing story. The only thing Beulah's Grandmother could keep was what she had already given away. Then it came back to her. Like most homeowners, I have often thought of what I would try to save first should the house ever be on fire. And like most homeowners, I've thought of how I could quickly save the photo albums, the family videos, and the pictures on the wall. These *real* treasures are the things that remind us of the people and times that have made our lives what they are. Everything else is a throwaway and replaceable item. Beulah has no children; nonetheless, she has real treasures. Like her beloved Grandmother, she has given away her best gift—herself. In the end, that which she ultimately keeps will be the very thing she has given away. And she is much beloved for it. "If you insist on saving your life, you will lose it," Jesus said. "Only those who throw away their lives for my sake and for the sake of the Good News will ever know what it means to really live" (Mark 8:35, TLB). Beulah doesn't have to worry about losing her fortune in the stock market crash or her house in the mortgage crisis. Nobody outside her family, church, and community knows who she is. But Beulah knows what it means to *really* live. She has found significance.

The Significance of One

Many years ago, I stumbled across the noted "I am only one" quotation by Edward Everett Hale. I typed it up on my old Tandy HX1000 computer and printed it in bold on my dot matrix printer. For a long time, I kept it in my old study Bible (where important things are kept). It might still be there. I deemed it worth a place among the pages of holy script because it pointed out something I always thought to be important, the significance of a single person. Hale said, "I am only one, but I am one. I can't do everything, but I can do something. The something I ought to do, I can do. And by the grace of God I will."[37] It affirmed what I suspected: every person has uniqueness to his or her life and purpose, and significance flows from that.

Years later I found a similar quotation attributed to Helen Keller. It seemed to fine-tune the Hale quotation for me. She said, "I am only one, but still I am one. I cannot do everything, but still I can do something; and because I cannot do everything, I will not refuse to do something I can do."[38] If there is such a thing as a significant life, Hale and Keller's quotations are pointing in that direction. Author

Mitch Albom wisely states "The way you get meaning into your life is to devote yourself to serving others, devote yourself to your community around you, and devote yourself to creating something that gives you purpose and meaning."[39] We may think ourselves as only one, invisible in the universe, yet we are undaunted. If there is only one thing we are to be about, then let us do it with all our hearts. The world is not here for us; we are here for it. Now and then it takes someone or something to remind us of that.

A preacher told of a visit he'd had with a member of his parish who was in a wheelchair, living in a nursing home. She was resigned to the apparent fact that her life no longer mattered. She told her pastor how she had once been able to do much for the church. She taught Sunday School, sang in the choir, served in the woman's society, served on the board, prepared many meals for church functions, and cleaned up afterward. Now she could do nothing, and it saddened her greatly. But the pastor was a wise fellow and seized a good moment. He quickly told her that he was overwhelmed by a part of his job, prayer requests. He said he simply was unable to remember all the needs of the parish in his daily prayers. Then he asked this willing lady if she would serve as the church's prayer intercessor. Wherever she was prayers may be offered, whether at home, in a church, or even in a wheelchair. The job requirements included faithfulness, time, and compassion, with no age requirement or mandatory retirement. She met all three requisites and was thrilled with the prospect of being needed again. The pastor would deliver her a list of prayer needs every couple weeks, and she would do the praying. Her life suddenly seemed significant again.

Perhaps there is no place or time in our lives where we are exempt from the possibility of usefulness. If significance is found in meaning, in purpose, in place, in mattering, then we all have that latent trait. It is different from being important. Important people know who they are. Significant people often escape the public eye, living below the level of recognition and attention. Sometimes no one but God knows they are significant.

In the United States, more than 750 *Halls of Fame* and more than 450 *Who's Who* publications exist. Television regularly host award shows honoring their industry. Ribbons, medals, and trophies can be more endearing treasures than Christian charity or marriage vows. We love being important. Achieving status can feel like an American ideal. I have always held people who achieve or accomplish great goals in high regard. Mother Teresa said if you are successful you will win some false friends and some true enemies. Succeed anyway, she advised. I just don't think status or success makes a person more than he or she already is, or than other people are. Sometimes adults can think it's accomplished through affluence, position, and achievement. Sometimes kids can think it's accomplished through affirmation, appearance, and popularity. These things may satisfy our considerable egos and impress our neighbors, but they are a poor substitute for a life of significance. Jesus warned, "Take care! Don't do your good deeds publicly, to be admired, for then you will lose the reward from your Father in heaven" (Matthew 6:1, TLB). Only one person is in line for glory if we are Christians, and it's not us. Significance is only found when life is lived for a cause greater than self. If there is a greater cause; if there is such a thing as significance; it is surely found in life-experiences that focus on others first, while simultaneously crucifying our secret and selfish idols.

I've talked to many bereaved parents since Gabe died, telling them how helpful it was to keep my focus on others, rather than myself. Henri Nouwen wrote, "In order to be of service to others we have to die to them, that is, we have to give up measuring our meaning and value with the yardstick of others ... thus we become free to be compassionate."[40] To live a significant life, we must live free of the expectations of others. From childhood, we are shaped by a westernized ideal and expectation. Anything less than success and prosperity is almost considered failure. It's a "he who dies with the most toys wins," kind of thing. But we all know that he who dies with the most toys is still dead. I see nothing wrong with success or affluence. I would have preferred more prosperity in life. At this point, however, these things no longer hold the same luster for me. All of that changed June 18, 2005. In matters of life and death, my importance means nothing to me—but my significance means all the more. A cultural prestige is inconsequential compared to things that are really sacred. I would much rather hold my child and be thought a scoundrel than to bury them and be thought important.

Our Trip to London

Our daughter Tiffany attended the first semester of her senior year of college in London the fall after we lost Gabe. It was terribly difficult for her to keep this goal, so far from home and family, and so soon after her brother's death. In early November, Vicki and I traveled to London to spend a couple weeks with her. When she met us in Heathrow Airport, my heart soared. It was euphoric. Losing one child makes the others *seem* more vulnerable. Having her on another continent, knowing the depth of her grief, somehow magnified mine. When we walked into the terminal, and I saw her sitting on a bench waiting for us, no family reunion could be more meaningful. If it is true that we again meet our loved ones on the day of resurrection, I can't see how that day could be of greater joy than the one we knew in Heathrow. Vicki, Tiff, and I shared the kind of hug that transcends words. Our time in England was simply transforming as we traveled through centuries of history.

Seeing Buckingham Palace, the London Bridge, Parliament, Westminster Abby (where we worshiped), the Tower of London, and much more through Tiff's eyes, gave them an indispensable grandeur. And being both a Methodist and a Beatle's fan, I had ample opportunity to catch up with each. I'm still not sure if *Wesley's Chapel* or *Abbey Road* was my burning bush. But also of interest to me was contrasting the things that *seemed* important to the Brits against what *seems* important to us. Granted, two weeks doesn't make one much of an expert on culture. Yet I could tell something was different. Many of our social mores concerning what it is to be *significant* here seemed *insignificant* there: things like achievement, ego, abundance, prestige, competition (with the notable exception of their beloved football), and advancement. I know all things are not equal, and mine was a small sampling, but pace and priority had a distinctively different feel there. Perhaps it was just that I was on vacation, but I welcomed the relaxed and less-hurried tempo.

I had the good fortune to visit a pub one afternoon rather than going shopping with the girls in *Notting Hill*. Though I remember their shopping trip being successful, so was my visit. It was the middle of the afternoon, and the pub was filled with what appeared to be good-natured folks enjoying darts, cards, each other, and a good Porter. I'm sure many of them had more important places to be, but in that exact moment in my life, this pub seemed like a perfect place to spend a nice afternoon. I thought that churches might learn a thing or two about hospitality here. I wouldn't want to make a habit out of it, but for this afternoon, at least, work could wait. As Tiffany traveled throughout Europe, the natives often challenged her about why we *Yanks* spend so much of our lives working. They just couldn't get that forty-hour thing; it seemed a poor exchange for so much of our lives, regardless of the return. And frankly, knowing how brief this little life is, I sometimes don't get it myself. Any amount of baubles or trinkets acquired in exchange for precious hours of our lives would be deficit spending in my book. As the old adage warned, "No one on their death bed ever wished they'd spent more time in the office." Though personal responsibility is an ethic dear to my heart, a nice day spent in the boat or with the grandbabies can be more cherished in the end than meeting some goal at work. I greatly valued my time in England and certainly don't want to leave the impression the British people were not hardworking and self-motivated. All these things existed there; they just didn't seem to be the impetus for their signification. And it did not feel wrong.

A Significant Moment

I believe significant lives are lived in the shadow of no one's expectations, at least no one's earthly expectations. But I must allow for the possibility that what we offer this world is subservient to heaven's expectancies. An interesting story comes from a side trip Jesus took while on the way to the cross. I think about little moments like these in the Bible, easily skimmed over, yet they hold some of the real meat of the story. In Bethany, Jesus stopped at the home of Simon, a leper by Matthew's gospel, to share a meal. A woman entered the house. In the East, homes rarely had doors to keep out visitors. She simply walked in. John's gospel said the woman was none other than Mary, a friend of Jesus and sister to Martha and Lazarus. Regardless of her identity, she did an amazing thing. She poured a bottle of costly perfume over Jesus' head, enraging Jesus' band of followers. "What a waste of good money," they said. "Why, she could have sold it for a fortune and given it to the poor." Two of the three gospels that carry this story note that the perfume could have been sold for three hundred *denarii*, which meant it represented nearly a year's salary. This was a huge gift she gave but had poured out. Jesus tersely responded to the disciple's criticism by saying she had done a good thing and that she would always be remembered for what she had done throughout the whole world (see Matthew 26:6–13).

The point is Jesus and the twelve viewed this woman's gift differently. They called it a waste. He called it significant. I've known many men and women like her. They are people who gathered up the courage to volunteer, give, serve, participate, or offer a suggestion, only to have someone in power dismiss their idea or offer. That's why most suggestion boxes are anonymous. People can be quickly taught to keep to themselves. Sadly, I've seen this happen in churches many times. But, like Mary, I suspect Jesus considers people's suggestions in more favorable ways than do their peers. When we live in a way that calls attention to our service, not to ourselves, it is never wasted, regardless of the criticism of the crowd.

Years ago I attended a women's meeting, where the speaker was a nun who served at a mission house. She told how she had sought a significant role there but found herself in charge of janitorial services. She was a scrubwoman wearing a nun's habit. One day, in the heat of summer, she was dispatched to clean the attic, where no one wants to be on a hot day. As she knelt by a window, scrubbing the sill, she had a moment. She admonished herself, "This is God's house. It must be clean. What I do here, I do it for God!" With the right attitude, even scrubbing a windowsill becomes significant. The apostle Paul told a church, "Whatever you do, whether in word or deed, do it all in the name of the Lord Jesus" (Colossians 3:17a). Little things can matter so much. Others may never notice, but yet they matter. I don't always know how movers and shakers become movers and shakers. I've never thought there should be such a thing as *power people* anywhere, much less in the church. But if we all saw people's offerings through the same eyes as Jesus saw Mary's, more suggestions would be in the box—and they'd be signed.

Forty years ago when I graduated high school, we graduates were given a yearbook to commemorate all our happy and formative years. I assume they still do that. I have kept mine all these years and sometimes take a look back at a different world and a different Vince Homan. Near the back of the book is a section called *Senior Brag List*. This is where we get to brag about all our many achievements through our four years and perhaps attach some significance to our lives in the process. A quick glance reveals the successful students, with some having more than eight lines of accomplishments (one girl even had twelve; she was *so* cool). However, a few poor schmucks mustered only one line. I, as usual, fell just south of the median with three lines in the book (though one of my achievements was fabricated). We really didn't have a Ping-Pong Team, though my Ping-Pong ability was renowned during the noontime matches up on the stage. Though I had little athletic ability, I could really play Ping-Pong. I routinely beat jocks and teachers alike. I recently gave this brag list a closer look, partly to see what I missed out on, and partly to see where I fell in the pecking order. And there they were: Class Vice-President, Class Secretary, Letter Club, Bearometer (school paper) Staff, Football, Prom Queen, National Honor Society et al. Again, I am in the front row cheering on achievement, and am glad there are people who are capable and willing to serve in such noble capacities. But everyone knew then that the significant people in school were the ones with the most lines in the Senior Brag List. And people assume that to be true today.

Beautiful People with a Terrible Problem

Is it a realistic goal to suggest to a self-made society that the significant life is the selfless one? Probably not. With the exception of a few insightful souls, most stumble onto significance by life experience, and they may not even know it is happening. They don't offer classes in significance in school, and few would pursue it for a career. Rather, our goals consist of betterment, achievement, and advancement; and the only measuring stick we have for that is others. As long as we have more lines in our brag list than our peers, we must be doing something right.

Author Donald Miller gave an alternate point of view to contrast with our human version of significance based on comparisons. He wondered what an alien might think of our race. I liked the idea. Miller suggested that the visiting alien, after taking a long and lasting look at humans, returned to his alien planet where the head alien asked him, "… what the people on this planet were like." Miller responded with a great alien impression:

> Humans, as a species, are constantly, and in every way, comparing themselves to one another, which, given the brief nature of their existence, seems an oddity and, for that matter, a waste. Nevertheless, this is the driving influence behind every human's social development, their emotional health and sense of joy, and, sadly, their greatest tragedies. It is as though something that helped them function and live well has gone missing, and they are pining for that missing thing in all sorts of odd methods, none of which are working. The greater tragedy is that very few people understand they have the disease. This seems strange because it is so obvious. To be sure, it is killing them, and yet sustaining their social and economic systems. They are an entirely beautiful people with a terrible problem.[41]

No doubt the head alien wondered if the earth was worth the gas to get there. For a race created a little lower than the angels, we could do better than finding our significance in the number of lines in a brag list or in comparing ourselves with others. We wouldn't want the aliens getting the wrong idea about us.

So, is significance found in *doing* or in *being*? A mentor of mine told me there was more in the middle of the road than a dead skunk or a yellow stripe, and I suggest that is true here. Perhaps our significance lies with our doing and our being, with one augmenting the other. Daughter Tiffany and I share a deed that I think is significant—

we've each saved a life. I saved my sister's life on one of our many trips to Rathbun Lake. We'd just beached the boat and gone up to the campsite to eat. Cindy, my sister, noticed the boat had drifted offshore and was getting away. Being a good swimmer, she took off to catch the boat—without a life jacket. But the boat was drifting away quicker than Cindy could swim. Soon the realization set in; she was far from the shore and from the boat, and she was quickly getting in real trouble. Fortunately, we had left the ski tube on the shoreline. I ran down to it, plopped in it, and paddled as hard as I could in Cindy's direction. I think I got to her just in time. She would surely have died if that tube wasn't left on the shore. And I thought about how fragile life can be.

Tiffany, likewise, saved a person from drowning. She was a lifeguard at the Sigourney pool. It was time to take her shift on the chair from where lifeguards kept a watchful eye. She had just replaced the guard who had been on the chair, when she noticed a shadow on the floor of the ten-foot deep end. Immediately, Tiff dove in and swam to the bottom, finding a motionless young boy in a very grim situation. Tiff, petite as she is, brought him to the top, as others assisted getting him out of the water. The lifeguards did life support until the professionals arrived. The boy's life was saved, with no harm done. And for Tiff, there was no thank you, no recognition, no name was put in the paper, and no award for a job well done. In fact, I think the mother of the boy threatened a lawsuit over negligence. No one noticed, and today no one remembers. But I do, and I know that Tiffany did something very significant!

In the years following Gabe's death, I have witnessed many examples of significance in ordinary people who do extraordinary things. I see them in the selfless service of many in our churches and communities, and I see them in my family. Daughter Valerie, and her husband Alan, are wonderful parents to their children: Lily, Kain, and Sutton. Valerie teaches first graders, and Alan provides for his family as an insurance representative—significant accomplishments indeed. Tiffany, also, has started her family. She and her husband Ryan are raising their son Graham. Tiffany works for an organization that provides housing and housing services to working-poor families.

Ryan is a police officer. To be sure, these are significant lives. But my family's true signification is the same as that of every person; it is God given and begins with the first heartbeat.

Everyone wants his or her life to matter. Somehow it validates our existence. We all approach our living with some sense of predetermination about us. Baby boomers are often credited with the idea of destiny, but it has long existed. It stirs our collective conscience to consider that we are here for a purpose, and that we each have our place. It can become a middle-age thing to start some type of quest to discover it. Careers and communities have been exchanged. And sometimes, regrettably, spouses have been exchanged in search of it. I am a proud baby boomer, and it's safe to say that most of us are now clearly on the downhill side of our mid-life crises. A speaker I heard at a conference said of the moment that baby boomers are now getting out of bed in the morning and looking at themselves in a full-length mirror. They spread their arms out wide and find things aren't where they used to be. In one hand they see their birth and in the other their death; and they are headed in an irreversible direction.

As every baby boomer knows, growing old and having instant gratification are not easily compatible. Things we used to find our significance in become less and less important and less and less achievable. There must be something more fulfilling. I have known many people who change their focus in life when they begin to seriously contemplate its inevitable end. If there is a reason for our being here, our time is running out to find it. So we volunteer, we come back to church, we travel, we study, we change jobs and friends, we downsize, we upsize. Life itself becomes a moral responsibility when each day is viewed as significant. Things that used to matter to our families when we were children suddenly become important again: home, family, responsibility, work ethic, personal faith, charity. And as Mary and Beulah's stories have reminded us, it doesn't take a noteworthy thing to create something significant.

Christian author and former professor Tex Sample spoke of life's inalienable value:

... life is intrinsically valuable. That means that life is good in and of itself, and the one thing you don't do is make the mistake of sacrificing life for the sake of something else. Life is supposed to be lived fully and deeply. Don't throw it away![42]

My conviction is the little things life presents us on a daily basis become our primary opportunities for significance. I would rather spend these days at a lake or with friends than save them in hopes of a lavish old age, dining on prime rib with my dentures. What we do, have, or know, do not make us more than we already are.

Gabe's Significance

After Gabe died, I had the distinct privilege of meeting many people whom he had touched and been a part of—and to my surprise most I did not know. One fellow, also named Vince, told me that his uncle had died, and the uncle had been a father figure to him. He told me that he couldn't go to the funeral by himself, so Gabe took a day off work to go with him. I had no idea. Another lady told me what Gabe had done for her. She had lost her job and was moving to where her family was, halfway across the state. She had no way to move her things. But Gabe volunteered. Over two weekends, he drove his pickup hundreds of miles and helped her move.

Many, many people who worked at his side in the plastics factory said Gabe helped them get through their day. Gabe had a terrific sense of humor and could make others laugh, despite the day. Sometimes I chagrined over his method of inducing chuckles, but I guess Dad was just getting old. It was clear that his friends cherished him in part because he was always able to brighten their days. Several coworkers said he was a true friend who never judged others and would always be there if needed. Again and again these wonderful people told me stories of what Gabe had done for them or of a time they shared with him. I thought I knew my son, but I didn't know this. It was clear to me that Gabe was living a significant life.

I find truly significant people rarely get their name in the paper. They don't have poster boards detailing their awards and ribbons.

Often their names are unknown outside their own family and friends. But they are gifts to this world. Where would we be without them? Ernest Hemingway once said, "Every man's life ends the same way. It is only the details of how he lived and how he died that distinguish one man from another."[43] But the significance is in those details. You and I have known many people who have given their lives to their careers, with some never getting to enjoy the fruits of their labors.

One baby boomer said she used to watch her dad as he spent his life working for a corporation. She said he used to promise her, "Dear, when I retire I'm going to have the kind of pension that we are going to be able to do all of the things we haven't done before. I just want you to hang on with me because we are going to really live." So she hung on, forty years until he retired. And he got the great pension and gold watch, but six months later, he was dead. She said, "There were medical reasons for why my father died, but they aren't the real reasons. My dad died because he could not live without putting off life. And that's not going to happen to me."[44] I read of a man in New Hampshire who took his own life because he lost his retirement money in the scandal-driven stock market fall. It is a sad commentary on misplaced securities and significance. We all will lose everything; it's just a matter of timing. Nursing homes, funeral parlors, taxes, crashes, illness—there are plenty of opportunities. I will not risk my significance along such fragile fault lines.

In as much as I have wanted my own life to be significant, I have wanted the same for my children, yet even more so. But not in the way that clouds the real issues or leads them down a seductive path toward fulfillment that is mostly a façade. I don't want them to exhaust their days in pursuit of a goal, which when reached, leaves a void. We have more than one way to have life end too soon. We have more significant things on which to center our lives. Mother Teresa was once asked, "How do you measure the success of your work?" She looked puzzled for a moment and then answered, "I don't remember that the Lord ever spoke of success. He only spoke of faithfulness in love. This is the only success that really counts."[45]

I believe it is infused in the heart of every person to live a life that matters and to finish their course knowing the world is a better place because they came along. It is a comforting thing indeed to believe that your life mattered for good on this earth.

Sometimes I read a certain piece at funerals because I have seen it comfort many families and because it is true. Grieving families want to know that their lost loved one lived a memorable life. Whether people have or haven't accomplished any great or noble deed, it doesn't negate the fact that each life mattered. An unknown poet penned this piece that I've kept in my funeral folder for many years. It is called "Success," but it could have also been called "Significance."

> That man is a success who has lived well,
> laughed often and loved much;
> Who has gained the respect of intelligent
> men and the love of children,
> Who has filled his niche and accomplished his task;
> Who leaves the world better than he found it,
> Whether by an improved poppy,
> a perfect poem or a rescued soul,
> Who never lacked appreciation for earth's
> beauty or failed to express it;
> Who looked for the best in others
> and gave the best he had.[46]

I am only one, and a day may come when I, too, will have to fit my world into two dresser drawers and a small closet like my aged farmer friend. But that time has not yet come. I am still here, I have time, and I am one. I cannot do everything nor do I need to. But I can do something, something significant. And even though I cannot do everything, I will not refuse to do the one thing I can do. These brief lives we live demand it. Even small things become significant when they're done in love with the right attitude. Just ask Beulah Green and Mother Teresa.

CHAPTER 7

REGRET AND CONTRITION

REGRET

It's deep within me, the sinner;
More than sorrow—or shame,
A binding tie, calling me backward,
To ravage again and again.
It knows no sleep or slumber,
No rest and no defeat.
Like thread woven throughout,
Its pattern is complete.
If only I were guilty,
If only there was a crime,
There would then be liberation,
For I have done my time.
But this enemy is cunning,
It strikes with no remorse.
It leaves a harsh resentment,
And keeps me on its course.
Guilt would be a simpler foe,
Repent and then be free.
Regret demands a gift from God,
A peace from mercy's tree.

Vincent D. Homan

REGRET HAS BECOME WOVEN throughout the intricacies of my life and my grief. It, unlike all other manifestations of grief, seems to have no parameters or season. It is a random thing, dipping down to extract a good moment or to interrupt my sleep. Regret may be the cancer of grief; it diminishes life and replaces it with hopelessness. Regardless, it certainly is a most loathsome manifestation. Like rust, regret systematically, incrementally, and relentlessly erodes at our humanity and our attempts to reclaim normalcy. When everything has been taken, and we have no means or ways of remuneration, regret offers its demonic taunt that you have failed, and have no chance of ever making it right. Regret and death seem made for each other. They are bedfellows, justifying and giving credence to each other's purpose. And they can strike in an instant.

Our family has been long-time boaters. Time on the water has been a great sanctuary. Seemingly endless are the memories of our times zooming around the lake with a boatload of kids and friends. A favorite thing we often did was to simply anchor up in a cove, strap life jackets on the kids, and toss them overboard. Those were maybe the best moments in our family story. I did this as a kid with my parents. I did it innumerable times as a parent with my children. I am now doing it with my grandchildren. There is something so wonderfully innocent and jubilant about an anchored boat in the center of God's beauty and a cannonball off the swim platform at the boat's stern, preferably making a significant splash in the direction of another. When my children have talked about what made their childhoods so rich and wonderful, three things always stand out: simple Christmases at home, long vacations in the van eating bologna sandwiches from a cooler, and boating. I'll take boating. I have loved being on the water since I first got in a boat. It is my happy place. I learned long ago, a boat didn't have to cost a fortune to give a family much joy. My dad bought a beautiful 18-foot blue Starcraft boat in, I think, 1965. That boat became a major player in our family history. Mom and Dad, and a host of good friends enjoyed endless trips in "Ol' Blue."

At some point, Vicki and I kind of inherited it. It gave me great satisfaction to drive my kids around lakes in the same boat as my dad had driven me. Though it wasn't very user-friendly, we had great fun in that boat. Back then boats didn't have open bows, swim decks, or boarding ladders. It didn't matter. I could pull myself up over the side without any ladder. I was a young dad full of vigor. I could lift the outboard motor up with ease and jump over the windshield to board or debark. That was the boat Gabe knew and loved. I have dozens of wonderful pictures of him, along with family and friends, passing many happy, sunny days in that old boat. I finally sold her for a $1,000. It was over forty years old, and the trailer its senior by an additional decade. At some point, things we love and have treasured go away. I may not have ever sold "Ol' Blue" but for a chance conversation I overheard.

Vicki and I were down at the lake alone. Our family was intending to join us the next day. I had taken "Ol' Blue" out by myself, parking over some shallows to do a little fishing. Sitting in this old friend, hearing the water rise and fall beneath her hull, I lazily watched my worm harness drift over the sandy bottom. And after the right amount of sea and sun, I gently pulled her up to the shore near the boat ramp. Tied there was a magnificent yellow twenty-foot bow rider. Sitting up on the bolsters were a couple young chaps, tans and abs aglow, feeling ever bit their youth. I had to listen closely and use my peripheral vision, but sure as shootin', they were checking out "Ol Blue" and me. I gave a little grin to the sun as I realized these boys recognized a classic boat and boater when they saw them. I should have stopped there. A closer listen revealed this exchange, "Look at that old blue boat," said one. "Yeah, it's really cool," said the other. "Yeah," countered the first, "My grandpa once had a boat like that." The next spring I replaced "Ol' Blue" with a Larson inboard/outboard with an open bow, swim deck, and a 4.3 Mercruiser motor.

In any case, we loved boating, regardless of the boat, and everything attached to it. A novel sight we were occasionally treated to when cruising across the lake was when gulls followed our boat. They come in a flurry, so close you think they'll land on the stern. You can take this personally and think they are following you or chasing you, depending on your mood for the day. Regardless, they are an amazing sight. Whatever the speed of the boat, they systematically keep time. But they are up to something. Their interest has been peaked by more than our boat. In the flotsam and jetsam of our wake are little shad—a wonderful delicacy for a hungry gull. On occasion you'll see one dip down, extend his beak or claws, and snatch his prey.

That is what regret does to me. Something in me is suddenly snatched away. In a fleeting moment, out of nowhere, comes a talon or a beak that robs me of a good mood or a good day—or even a good moment. Like the gulls, regret seems to systematically be keeping time with my grief journey. But unlike the gulls, I never see it coming. Pictures trigger it. So do random discussions, reading the scriptures, walking around the house, watching another dad with his son, a fishing boat, a yellow lifejacket, or seeing a green Dodge Dakota pickup. Sigh. A thousand traps await one like me who is plagued by regret. Lament, rue, sorrow, shame, remorse, guilt, bemoan; whatever name it is given, its effect is the same, and we are left awash in a sea of sadness—with a great *incompleteness* to our lives.

Human Regrets

I hunch many people find they line up in the trenches against regret at some point in their lives. It is a common human experience. We regret where we live, how we live, what we do, who we married, what we've done, what we've said, where we've gone; ad infinitum. Like grief, regret surely must have varying degrees. And, as in grief, each person's regret seems the worst to him or her. Someone who speaks an ill-advised word about another often regrets it as soon as the words are off his tongue, wishing he could take the words back, but he cannot. He fears the repercussions, should his words ever get back to him. I've known people near the end of their career who deeply regretted what they had done with their working life.

They wish they had done something more fulfilling, better paying, or more prestigious. I've known people who didn't want children during their childbearing years. And I've wondered later, when in middle age, do they deeply regret being alone?

I've known several good people who had affairs. Common sense succumbed to an adventurous passion—and even adultery had a sense of *rightness* to it. But when light came to his or her darkness, and secrets were revealed, guilt and regret reigned. As the family anguished over the betrayal, he or she was filled with remorse. He or she rued the day that decision was made. I've known people who have burned bridges with parents or children. Somehow things got out of control, beyond repair, things were said, people moved out, and years later, the poison of that separation still stung. He or she longed for a healing of the relationship. Separation, longing, and betrayal—all are indeed regrettable.

Sometimes I fill in downtime at the office with a game of computer Solitaire. Not one prone to reading instructions, I've simply played the game as I have known it. One day, on impulse, I clicked on the file Options and found the *undo* option. What a marvelous option. If you make a mistake, if you don't like the choice you made, if you see something better—just hit undo. Your bad move is immediately removed from the game. You are free to make a better move, even a good move. Games are won and lost with this option. Had I known about it earlier, I would have certainly accumulated a better won/lost record in Solitaire.

I wish life had an undo button. I wish when I erred, made a bad choice, and did something I regretted—I could hit the Option file and click on undo. A number of things in my life could stand an undo option. As a means of confession, a significant part of my parenting could also stand an undo button. Perhaps many parents feel this way. They regret things they said to their children, decisions they made, rules that were excessive, being absent from key moments, poor leadership, or any other parental blemish.

But when you lose one of your children, those things magnify.
All grief magnifies regret, but parental grief landslides it.

When your children are still living, you have this sense that there is yet time to fix things or get them right. I've known men who were especially harsh and demanding with their sons when growing up. They had great expectations and tried to fit them into a certain mold, even if the sons had no desire to fit that mold. The damage can be excessive. But a balance comes back to the relationship as life goes on. Mistakes that were made can yet be corrected. The father and son become more equals, rather than one being subservient to the other. Sometimes a parent can try too hard to impose values, ethics, or even faith on children. And the children can grow a crusty resentment to the parent for it. But as time elapses, the parent mellows a bit, the child grows more mature, and both the parent's and the child's value/faith system dovetails into a harmonious future.

Sometimes parents are over-protective or controlling with their children. This was me. Rebellion can grow out of such things. Children roll into puberty, adolescence, and young adulthood with such fervor that independence—not parental control—becomes their value system of choice. Kids can feel that their parents don't trust them. But if you're given time, protectiveness and control melt away, and rebellion transforms into self-determination. The parent and the child are better for it all. The turbulent things are over, and all those battles now become jovial memories bantered about over the Thanksgiving meal. It is a lesson for us all—parent, child, spouse, adult child, and friend.

The Importance of Each Moment

But the Homan parents weren't given more time for one of our children. Our time suddenly, irrevocably ended. Just like that. Whatever had been said remained. The final discussions, times together, conflicts, and joys remained—forever, everything now frozen in time. I have often thought about the last things I said to Gabe, the last time I saw him, lying on the couch in the back room. I had no idea it was the final time my eyes would rest on my boy.

> Perhaps it is why I am careful today what
> I say to others or how I treat a moment.
> I never know when it will be the last one.

We would all chose our words and actions more carefully if we thought they might be the final ones. Once I was highly anticipating hearing a popular Christian author and pastor who was scheduled to speak in a nearby community. I had read one of his books and was very excited to hear him in person. However, about a month before his scheduled speaking engagement, he died of a heart attack. Remarkably, his widow fulfilled his commitments and kept every engagement on his schedule. I went that night to hear her but with less enthusiasm than was originally reserved for her husband. Now, all these years later, I doubt I would have recalled anything that good man might have said. But I do think about something his wife said. She said every day that her husband left for the office, they embraced and told each other "I love you," even on the days when they might have bickered about some little thing. And so it was that on the final morning she saw her husband, they embraced and told each other "I love you." She remarked that she was glad today that they never parted with a mean or unkind word.

I was upset with Gabe about something the last night I saw him. But I didn't say anything about it. There had been a time in our relationship when I couldn't have let it drop. I would have brought it up. I am glad today that my last conversations with him weren't a meaningless argument. Rather, our final words were about Valerie's upcoming wedding, how sleepy I was, and we also talked about a movie. It wasn't Hamlet's soliloquy toward Ophelia, mind you, but much preferred over some trivial dispute. There is a lesson to be learned here, and I am paying attention to it. These days, I never let Vicki, my daughters, sons-in-law, grandchildren, or my mom, out of my sight without telling them how much I love them. I have seen up close death's power to separate. It is a ghoulish thing, indeed. I will not add a regrettable parting to such a ghastly moment.

About a week after the funeral, Gabe's good friend Russell offered to go fishing with me. I didn't know if I ever wanted to go fishing again, but I know Russell meant the offer as a kind gesture. Since

I didn't have Gabe to go fishing with, he would go. Reluctantly, I agreed, though it took incredible effort, and each moment of the trip is forever etched in my memory as a painful experience. I wept all the time we were getting the boat ready to go. After launching it at the dock, Russell held the rope as I parked the pickup, but I was quickly coming undone. I walked into the restroom and broke down. I recall being so broken I could hardly reopen the door or get my breath. I know it was a short fishing trip, and probably an ill-advised one. We each caught a couple of bass using Gabe's patterned method of letting a weightless worm sink slowly amidst brush and cover.

But something significant did happen on this trip. When a loved one dies, you try to find out every little detail about what they thought and did, from anyone who was close to them. Russ was as close to Gabe as anyone, and I wanted to know something very personal. I found myself asking Russ if Gabe really knew how much I loved him—how much I cared. Repeatedly, he assured me that Gabe did, and that he deeply loved me as well. Though I knew this, I asked Russ again, "Are you sure? Did Gabe know how deeply I loved him; how much he meant to me?" And with much conviction, Russ reiterated that he did.

I know I have always told my kids that I loved them. But I didn't know I was about to run out of those opportunities with Gabe. And I found myself deeply regretting not telling him I love you, even more.

Guilt and Regret

I think people confuse guilt and regret. Guilt is more of a cause-and-effect thing. If we have wronged another, committed some crime, or offended some virtue or sensibility, we are guilty. Whether charged or not, we are guilty. Guilt also has the potential of being personal and collective. Not only are we guilty for our own offences, but those of society, by association. By simply living in the West, we are now guilty by connotation of many of the world's woes: global warming, the energy crisis, world hunger, etc. And guilt can fester and grow like a boil on the conscience. But in the end, its cruelest blows are those we inflict upon ourselves. The very cognizance of our wrongdoing can become a self-imposed life sentence to us. It's as if our constant berating and self-flagellation becomes an ointment to our seared scruples.

Author and theologian Frederick Buechner, in his book, *Wishful Thinking*, said this of the guilty:

> We steer clear of setting things right with the people we have wronged since their very presence is a thorn in our flesh. Our desire to be clobbered for our guilt and thus rid of it tempts us to do things we will be clobbered for. The dismal variations are endless. More often than not, guilt is not merely the consequence of wrongdoing but the extension of it. It is about as hard to absolve yourself of your own guilt as it is to sit in your own lap.[47]

I am guilty of many things in my life. When the apostle Paul told the church at Rome that all have sinned and fallen short of the glory of God (see Romans 3:23), this was not news to me. By thought, word, and deed—I am guilty. But I also believe in grace and mercy. These things I have embraced and believed by faith and reckoned them as complete works in my life. I know a certain man very well who feels guilty all the time. I think he enjoys it. Whether as means of confession or penalization, he willingly beats himself up. It is a penance kind of thing for him. I know he also believes in mercy, but as a partner with guilt—not an anecdote for it.

There is a remedy for guilt, but I have not found one for regret. Guilt I can do. Regret suffocates me. I regret things for which there is no moral sense of right and wrong. Some of them are just little moments. They happened as quickly as a breath. Then they were over. They broke no rules or laws. And still, they trouble my soul.

A Regrettable Moment

In the center of my parenting golden years, we took the kids to Florida. Tiffany was a little tyke, barely tall enough to clear the height hurdle for Disney World's Space Mountain. Valerie was a budding adolescent, mature beyond her years. As George Baily's father told him in the Frank Capra classic, *It's a Wonderful Life*, "You were born older, George"—Valerie was *born older.* And Gabe was now a young teenager: pimples, awkwardness, changing voice, and all that goes with it. To help us keep track of our beloved little brood, Vicki had made matching Iowa Hawkeye shorts for them all. Wonderful! But a moment intruded on our lovely little vacation. It was only a moment, and it happened at the Epcot Center. Gabe, who had always loved sporty cars, stumbled across a little red number. It was a futuristic looking thing, with something of a retractable plastic rooftop—sort of like the *Jetson's* car. It looked like it could fly as well as drive. Gabe loved it and jumped right into the driver's seat. Putting his hands on the wheel, I could tell he was having a wonderful moment. No doubt he was going a hundred miles an hour down the *Autobahn.* After a few minutes, Valerie wanted her turn. Quicker than a toll on the turnpike, those two got quarreling.

A father has a number of acceptable ways to handle such a moment—ways that would have allowed for both kids to enjoy that car, and each other. But I didn't choose one of those ways, not me. In a mood-killing moment, I grabbed Gabe by the arm and yanked him out of that red sports car he was enjoying so much. Then I stuck Valerie in it. There, I fixed the problem. But I didn't. My ire shook both of the kids, and I ruined a terrific opportunity. I have regretted that moment for over two decades. I just can't forget it. I broke no laws, but I violated something more sacred. I took something from Gabe and Val that day, and I can't put it back. If Gabe was alive today, then perhaps, but he is not—and I cannot. It is things like this that strike at the heart of what regret can do. Even though it was many, many years ago, I am still troubled by my parental protocol of that day. Many times when I've seen some sporty little car, I think of that time, as if it had just happened.

All these things have a tendency to add up to becoming an unconquerable opponent when your child dies. You wish you could have done so many things differently. Each little indiscretion piles upon another, until you think all your parental choices must have been like them. It can make you doubt the validity of your place in the institution of fatherhood. Objectively, I know I was a good father to my children. I did many of the right things. I was there, I held a job, I told them I loved them, I took them to Sunday School, I was faithful to their mother, I read them stories at night, I took them to the lake. But in my collective memory, I am tormented by moments I deeply regret. And they are right—one bad apple *does* spoil the whole bunch. For all the good I did as a parent, every little regrettable moment that is woven in between seems to taint the whole. I wonder if I would have felt this way if Gabe had lived. Or is this yet some other devilish manifestation of grief?

The Wheel of Regret

I recently picked up a book on prayer at our church's Annual Conference. Entitled *Sister Wendy on Prayer*, its author is Sister Wendy Beckett, affectionately known as the *Art Critic Nun*. Sworn to a life of silence and contemplation, Sister Wendy began to study art following an illness. Her study led to writing a book and then contributing to magazines about paintings. Soon, she was taking part in a documentary on the BBC, which led to her having her own series. It seemed strange for a woman who had answered a call to solitude and contemplation to be suddenly thrust into the media's spotlight, but Sister Wendy saw it as a call to teach spirituality to the secular world through classical art.[48] Her spiritual insights into art brought me vignettes of grace and gospel not previously seen.

One episode from her book took me to a crossing in the road that linked regret with whatever recovery my life would find. She separated—then connected—regret and contrition, with peace and prayer being the binding ties. "Guilt and remorse go round and round on a treadmill of regret, whereas prayer sets us free from any treadmill and takes us into the peace of being loved," she wrote.[49] Sister Wendy reasoned that regret is like a potter's wheel or treadmill, things that move but don't go anywhere. But life is shaped on those things. Much of what unfolds throughout our day-to-day living comes from our time spent on that wheel, for good or ill. When regret is the track moving beneath our feet, we live with the fruit of that. Perhaps it is an emotional thing more than an objective one. All that rage, brokenness, guilt, bitterness, and self-pity, maybe it is all birthed out of our emotional center and that center is tied closely to our *wheel of regret*. I don't know. But I do know that during the tough days: Christmas, Halloween (which he loved), his birthday, his death day, on those days regret fills my life, and with it, an emotional onslaught.

Whether regret is an act of self-importance, I do not know. Certainly, when one is lost in its fog, self becomes iconic. It is truly a moment when all attention is inwardly directed. But then it has to be, if it is really regret. I once asked a group of fine women at a Bible study what kinds of things caused them to worry or fret. One of them rightly said she was worried about past mistakes and things she wishes she could have done differently. I loved her response. It was so very human and so very me.

Perhaps it is within the heart of every man and woman to live with some regrets, some sense of being sorry. I have cried out to an invisible Gabe a thousand times that I was sorry: sorry for the times I got angry with him, sorry for the times I didn't listen to him, sorry for the times I wasn't there for him, sorry for the times I didn't or couldn't help him. But as John Wayne told Dean Martin in *Rio Bravo*, "Sorry don't get it done, Dude." And it doesn't. Being sorry when your loved one is dead is a helpless feeling indeed. The past cannot be changed. We must start again. That meant contrition for Sister Wendy. "Contrition is healing," she wrote. "It is a trustful sorrow for our sins that looks at God and knows that He will heal us. Any real act of contrition offers us to God for Him to restore us."[50] Nowhere is restoration more needed than in the ravaged, regret-ridden heart of a bereaved parent. Is God capable of such a thing?

A Man After God's Own Heart

David is one of my favorite Bible characters. I have felt a kinship with this man a long time. He has been called a man after God's own heart. Secretly, I always thought I was too. Something deep within me hungered for God even from childhood. That hunger sparked and shaped my life long before I gained any sense of doctrine or application. But I have also learned that *feet of clay* and *hearts after God* are not mutually exclusive traits. That was the primary reason I resisted professional ministry for so long. I simply couldn't separate or reconcile my spirituality and my physicality. So David's story became endearing to me. God picked this man to be king of his people, not based upon his stature, skill, or strength, but upon his heart.

I was never very athletically inclined growing up. My three lines in the Senior Brag List didn't include one athletic achievement (except for the fabricated Ping Pong Team). I couldn't punt, pass, or kick. We often practiced this devilish little system of prosecuting and persecuting youngsters starting in middle school and junior high. Whether the game was kick ball, volleyball, or basketball, the coach/teacher would pick two team captains (usually the most popular or athletic kids), and they would, in turn, pick their teams. Game-challenged kids like me watched all other kids get picked in this unwelcome popularity contest, just hoping someone, anyone, would be picked after them. Everyone watched while this sordid little drama unfolded, and value was quickly attached to pecking order. I never minded being picked next-to-last. Just, please God, don't let me be the last one standing—unpicked. The last one was clearly unwanted, and considered more of a liability than an asset. Victories always mattered more than people back then, and I suspect the same is sadly true today.

So it was good news to me that God has a different system for picking his team. You don't need to be able to throw or catch a ball to be number one on God's team. It is the heart that God considers first when picking a lineup. And I knew my heart was after God's as well. We would make a good team.

But good hearts often make bad choices. David just couldn't be content with a good thing. It was in the spring of the year, when kings go off to war—but not this king. Though the whole army of Israel was on the battlefield, David stayed behind in Jerusalem. There his good heart was powerless against his flesh. The scripture reveals, "One evening David got up from his bed and walked around on the roof of the palace. From the roof he saw a woman bathing. The woman was very beautiful, and David sent someone to find out about her" (2 Samuel 11:2–3a). And the trap was set. It is a trap we know all too well because we continue to see it unfold in the lives of men and women with good hearts. And we say, "How could they do such a thing?" "They teach Sunday School." "They are our neighbors, our co-workers, and our friends." I don't know why bad things happen to good people, and I don't know why good people do bad things. But they do.

A Broken and Contrite Heart

David slept with the married Bathsheba, impregnated her, and plotted the murder of her faithful husband, Uriah the Hittite, to cover up his sin. When the prophet Nathan finally pointed his boney finger of judgment at David, he knew his secrets were no longer secret. Even the king of Israel cannot keep things hidden from God. In rebuke for despising God's word, Nathan pronounced a series of judgments to come to David's house. He said the sword will never depart from David's house, calamity will befall them, a friend will sleep with David's wives in broad daylight, and because David's sin made the enemies of the Lord show contempt, the son born to David would die (see 2 Samuel 12:7–14).

And in the middle of the night, when terror can stalk a human heart, I have wondered if I was like David in this also. Unlike David, I have never broken my marriage vow or committed murder, but my mind has taken me to places it should not have. A wayward thought can compromise even a God-like heart. I have never understood why God required the death of that child as atonement for David's sin. Perhaps David didn't either. In the 103rd Psalm he wrote, "He will not always accuse, nor will he harbor his anger forever; he does not treat us as our sins deserve or repay us according to our iniquities …" (Psalm 103:9–10). Regardless, David's loathsome sin and deadly consequence brought him to an incredible place—contrition. Every penitent sinner has prayed through tears these words of David:

> Create in me a pure heart, O God, and renew a steadfast
> spirit within me. Do not cast me from your presence or
> take your Holy Spirit from me.
> Restore to me the joy of your salvation and grant me a
> willing spirit, to sustain me.

> You do not delight in sacrifice, or I would bring it;
> You do not take pleasure in burnt offerings.
> The sacrifices of God are a broken spirit;
> a broken and contrite heart,
> O God you will not despise.
> Psalm 51:10–12, 16–17

A broken and contrite heart, O God you will not despise. I have carefully and thoughtfully prayed these words for years, but especially since Gabe's death. If my heart was not broken and contrite before, it certainly is now. I must allow for the possibility that this is where God desires hearts to be. I do not need to be healed from the perpetual wound of regret—I need to be *liberated* from it. I need to be *delivered* from it. And if a broken and contrite heart is my deliverer, then let it take its prayerful place in my life. If this means turning to God a thousand times a day, I will turn to God a thousand times a day.

A story is told about a master gardener who always took great pride in the state of his lawn. However, one year dandelions showed up in the yard. They soon spread their yellow hue over and among the rich green. This good gardener tried everything to get rid of them: spraying, fertilizing, and picking. Nothing worked. Finally, exasperated, he contacted the Department of Agriculture explaining all he had done. "What else shall I try?" he wrote. The reply came, "Get used to them, and start appreciating their beauty."

I doubt any of the self-help books in my local bookstore will give any hints or tips on the best way to achieve being broken and contrite. But I am getting used to both, considering them friends, and appreciating their beauty.

To be delivered from something does not mean it has ceased to be. If it was a part of our past, then it will be a part of our present and our future. My regrets, amplified so deeply, are not displaced by contrition.

> Stepping into the land of milk and honey did not make the Hebrews forget four hundred years of bitter bondage to the Egyptians. Rather, contrition takes us to a place where we are less likely to feel the sting of the taskmaster's whip.

Contrition fills in some of the potholes, and lowers some of the inclines to make the journey more palatable.

An Offering of Hurts, Concerns, Sins, and Pride

My religious practices are fairly predictable. I have always had a rhyme and meter to my Christianity. Whoever initiated the Christian calendar did me a favor. To me, the designated seasons are comforting, their dates and times being signposts in my journey. Though the Christian year begins in *Advent, Lent* has become my spiritual *New Year,* particularly *Ash Wednesday*. In our post-Christian world, where Christianity is no longer the dominant civil religion, it saddens me a bit to realize most people don't even know that Ash Wednesday exists, much less observe it as day of penitence and grace.

But Ash Wednesday is a big day for this sojourner. It's not because I walk away with the image of the cross, made with ashes, on my forehead. But because of something very real I experience. Taken from a practice I observed in a youth meeting years ago, I incorporate an activity in our Ash Wednesday services called *An Offering of Our Hurts, Our Concerns, Our Sins, and Our Pride*. Every attendee, including me, receives a small slip of paper entering the service. After the right amount of liturgical prayer and praise, we are invited to write a short note to God. It is a note of contrition. Those things that plague us most are offered on that slip of paper, which are then carefully placed in the offering plates. One by one I burn them, as part of the service, with only God and the penitent knowing what was written.

When all that is left of our sins and sorrows is ashes, I blend in the ashes of the previous year's palm branches. It is that hybrid of residual promise and sorrow that we place in

When the soul has laid down its faults at the feet of God, it feels as though it had wings.

– Eugenie De Guerin

the form of a cross on the forehead of each worshiper, and a symbol of death becomes a sign of a contrite heart. It is an act of faith. Nothing in the burning of a note and the wearing of ashes eliminates regret unless a broken and contrite heart accompanies it.

I somehow leave those services feeling as though I have a jump-start on Easter morning. Something seems to come back to life in me. My dirty little secrets that I burned up on paper will likely run their due course in my life. I will still feel culpable in my sins, but they are less weighty hanging over my head. There is a sense of mercy about Ash Wednesday. Like the fabled Phoenix that burns itself to death and rises from the ashes, there is a rising in me, a rising that invites me upward.

Jesus told a story about two men who went up to pray, but only one man knew about contrition. Luke said he told this story specifically to some people who were confident in their own goodness and liked to look down on others. In the story, one man prayed in such a way that drew attention to him, while discounting lesser men. "I thank you that I am not like other men ..." he said. But his companion stood in absolute contrast to this prayer. He was the other man. He couldn't even look up at God or out at others. He simply beat his breast and confessed, "God, have mercy on me, a sinner" (Luke 18:9–14). I have sometimes thought the righteous man in this story is probably not a bad guy, and he most likely gets a bad rap. He is a person who has lived right, accomplished much, and now wants to make sure God knows it. I sometimes have to guard myself lest I tell God I'm glad I'm not like that man. But the other fellow, a tax collector, was full of regret. He had lived his life in such a way that he despised it.

People who suffer regret know it often is a self-inflicted thing. Maybe that is why regret can be so despicable because we feel we have done it to ourselves. Nobody sets out to ruin their marriage, alienate their children, become addicted to some narcotic or compulsive behavior, bankrupt their family, or lose their faith. It is in a series of small, neglectful, self-centered choices that we ultimately build toward disaster—and regret. I have seen it, and I have known it. But *would haves* and *could haves* don't do a regret-ridden soul much good. We need more, much more. I can see this man who is praying, slumped in the shadows, tear-stained face cradled in calloused hands, closer to earth than heaven. He barely whispers his words. Still, his words echo who he is and what he desires most.

"Have mercy on me, a sinner." This is contrition. I know because I have been there. Jesus said only one of those men, the contrite one, went home that day forgiven.

Consequence and Regret

Many years ago I was involved in counseling a married couple that was in deep distress. For years the wife had felt taken for granted by her husband. She fulfilled her understanding of *wifely duties*, while feeling emotionally and personally neglected. Though married, she saw herself living a lonely life. Finally she began going to bars with a friend, where she quickly met fellows very willing to pay attention to her. Soon the inevitable affair erupted. When her husband found out, he presently got a better view of his marriage. He regretted his choices more than hers and longed to make things right, which he remarkably did. After several sessions, where we planned techniques and strategies intended to strengthen commitment and trust, he made the necessary changes to be a good husband. The problem was the wife had gotten a taste of the nightlife and all the adventure and excitement that can accompany it. Forbidden fruit is hard to put down. Though she had promised God, her husband, and me that she would be faithful if he would change, she was unable to keep her word. Her life had become a collective lie, deceiving even her. And as the affair again became known, her husband decided to end the marriage. He loved his wife with all his heart, but he couldn't go through the heart-rending process of betrayal, confession, forgiveness, and reconciliation again.

What I remember about this sad story is what happened next. In a late-night final attempt to save the marriage, we met together in my office. When it soon became apparent that the husband was not going to change his mind, his broken wife fell at his feet and wept. Like the woman who washed Jesus' feet with her tears and dried them with her hair, she wept. I can still hear the cries of regret and apology, accompanied by the promise to change. I will never forget the image of this broken woman lying prostrate on the floor of my office at the feet of her deceived husband, clutching the hem of his jeans, begging forgiveness. But it was too late; he was undeterred.

These were good people, people who started off with high ideals. They were people I cared about. But they ended with a pot full of regret. Her broken and contrite heart had no power to sway the conviction of her betrayed husband.

My role and place in the center of that impassioned evening has stayed with me. I have wondered if my regrets concerning Gabe's life and death were like those of that woman, who lamented them so. Will tears, and desire, and remorsefulness make any difference? Are they all for naught? Or will I be like the penitent man in Jesus' story, who by beating his breast and confessing his sinfulness, found mercy and healing? I have to believe it is different with God.

We cannot take back past times. We cannot take back our words or choices after the fact. We do not have an undo option on our lives. We can sometimes change our image, but not our past. We will live with the effects and consequences of our lifestyles, marital commitments, fiscal choices, parenting styles, behaviors, and faith walk (or lack of it). Galatians is right that we "reap what we sow." The apostle Paul warned, "The person who plants selfishness, ignoring the needs of others—ignoring God—harvests a crop of weeds. All he'll have to show for his life is weeds. But the one who plants in response to God, letting God's Spirit do the growth work in him, harvests a crop of real life, eternal life" (Galatians 6:8, *The Message*).

Though many can count their sins easier than their blessings, others simply wonder what kind of crop they have sown to reap such a painful harvest. For me, to lose an immediate member of your family can force one to live with a regrettable sense that things could have been done better, or at least differently. Logical or not, this is my reality. Something I loved is gone, and I cannot fix the things I broke. But David's words haunt me. "A broken and contrite heart, God will not despise." The unbearable pain of parental bereavement can taint any promise, but that is a powerful image. If the Gospel is good news at all, then it is good news to those who erred and strayed most.

Nearly every churchgoer knows something of the story of the prodigal son. It is a masterpiece in storytelling. Jesus portrays a young man who comes to deeply regret his choices. Dissatisfied with his father's plan for him, he demands his share of the inheritance and then goes off to the city in pursuit of his own life. His was a worldview that focused on self and the here-and-now. He squandered his new wealth on what the *King James Bible* calls "riotous living." I've done a little of that myself. And finding himself in life's pigpen, quite literally, he was forced to come face-to-face with his choices, and he deeply regretted them. With no resources left, he decided to go home, face the wrath of his father, and expect the worst. But that was not the father's intent. Instead of the worst, the father gave him the best. Before this wayward son arrived home, his father saw and ran to meet him, kissing him, hugging him, and throwing a huge festive party in celebration (see Luke 19:11–32). Any parent of a wayward child can understand this moment. We all know the story. The prodigal, because of the role of the loving father, was not to be defined by his waywardness. He was received back, despite himself. Regrettable choices that had been made gave way to an unbelievable flood of grace and acceptance.

I know Jesus told that story to tell us about God's nature and abounding love. And I know who the prodigal was in the story. I see him every morning when I shave. Nevertheless, I am persuaded that regrets of the darkest kind, like mine, may still give way to a flood of grace and acceptance.

So I move forward with my life. I am thankful for the good and bad times with my son. Time, penitence, and perspective have allowed me to find value in each. Though regrets can force memories of mistakes and turmoil, a contrite heart can help refocus that past, reminding me that the good far outweighed the bad. But my future is also shaped here. I am utterly determined to be the finest husband to Vicki and the best father that I am capable of to my remaining children, Valerie and Tiffany. And I am now a grandfather—*Papa*, among the inner circle. Like becoming a parent, becoming a grandparent is something you know only by being one. I treasure my grandchildren as I did my own children. And I am absolutely committed to living a regret-free life with these wonderful gifts of God. In this upwardly mobile and fragmented society, children and grandchildren need roots, heritage, and family more than ever. With God's grace and help, I am devoted to making sure they have those gifts.

As with so many of grief's manifestations, regret probably isn't done with me or me with it. Writing this book or living more years will not totally diminish regrettable moments in my past. Nevertheless, I am resolved to face forward, knowing prodigals are always welcomed back. I will trust that brokenness and contrition in God's world are sufficient to bring liberty to the inner prison of regret. And I am assured, a broken and contrite heart, God will not despise.

CHAPTER 8

HOPE–A MOURNER'S MANIFESTO

Brown Grass

All the grass has turned brown,
Crackling underfoot—when I walk,
But I walk through it anyway.
It's in my way, brown and asleep,
Yet I walk on—crunching as I go.

Sometimes life is like brown grass.
Trampled on and cut down.
Still, it's expected to carpet the earth,
To look manicured and neat; even when it's brown.

Is it an arid taunt from the skies?
Living water has ceased to be. It is a drought!
And droughts give birth to brown grass,
To crunch underfoot where I walk.

But brown doesn't abide. It's just a façade,
An imposter, an actor.
There will be a reckoning—dye for die!
The green blade will rise again.

Sometimes life is like brown grass.

Vincent D. Homan

I F HOPE REALLY EXISTS, then it must surely exist for the bereaved. It is one of the three great gifts Paul offered us, "And now these three remain: faith, hope, and love" (1 Corinthians 13:13a). Though he would conclude that the greatest of the three was love, broken hearts know that not to be true. The greatest gift is hope. Natural hope is defined as a wish to get something, or for something to be true, especially if that hope seems possible or likely. But that hope won't do. It isn't enough. Natural hope is of no good in matters of death. You must have a supernatural hope—a God hope. And a God hope is a wish to get something, or for something to be true, even if that hope seems impossible or unlikely. That hope alone shepherds us from a valley of tears to a horizon of burgeoning life. It is, perhaps, God's own antidote to loss of the most profound and overwhelming kind.

I couldn't bear the prospect of it in the first years after Gabe died. I didn't want hope. There seemed to be nothing but the contemptible sneering of the grave, and any inference to the alternatives seemed an insult to my pain. Loss is like a dark song, a dirge, which echoes sorrow and disillusionment throughout our beings, and the death of a young person is the most mournful sound on the earth. How dare anyone attempt to lessen its pangs with a hopeful song? And yet, I have found within myself an opening. It has been a small one, yet it persists and through it is a glimmer of hope.

There is a very sad story in the Bible—at least for me. An angel warned Joseph in a dream to flee Bethlehem in favor of Egypt because Herod was intending to kill the newborn Jesus. Herod the Great, a man I have studied often, was a brutal soul with no love except that of self. He even ordered the death of his own wife and several of his sons,

In all things it is better to hope than to despair.

–Johann Wolfgang Von Goethe

179

suspecting them of usurping his kingdom. It was said at the time it is safer to be Herod's pig than Herod's son. Herod was very devious when the Magi inquired about the new king. He suggested they report back when they found the child-king, so he could likewise pay homage. Then a heavenly intercession came; an angel gave a warning to the Magi, and they redirected their path toward home, bypassing Jerusalem. Herod became furious when the Magi didn't return; fearing a rival to the throne might survive. What he did next seemed inhuman. Herod arbitrarily ordered the death of every boy under the age of two in Bethlehem and its vicinity (see Matthew 2:1-16).

A Voice of Mourning

It is in response to this deathly siege that Matthew's gospel records an amazing ancient text. Quoting the Old Testament prophet Jeremiah, he wrote, "A voice is heard in Ramah, weeping and great mourning, Rachel weeping for her children and refusing to be comforted, because they are no more" (Matthew 2:18). I know that voice. I have sung it, and I have heard it sung, *weeping and great mourning, refusing to be comforted because their children are no more.* Where is the hope here? In its Old Testament context, Ramah is a town through which Jerusalem's people passed on their way to their Babylonian exile. It was a trail of tears. Many died along the way. Rachel was Jacob's favorite wife and matriarch to the two most powerful tribes in the northern kingdom. Those tribes buried their children on this march. Rachael came to represent every mother who has ever suffered or wept for a child.

Sadly, this world has had many of those marches, many "trails of tears." Native American nations were forced to relocate following the Indian Removal Act of 1830, moving them from their homelands to Indian Territory in present-day Oklahoma. Many died from exposure, starvation, and disease, including thousands of children.

Between 1944–1945 thousands of prisoners (mostly Jewish) were forcibly moved from German concentration camps near the war front to camps inside Germany. Thousands died during these infamous death marches and in the camps. Children were buried with their parents in mass graves.

Recently, a million Somalis had to flee their homes because of war, drought, and famine. Over half of them were at a refugee camp in Kenya. The journey became a death march for multiple families and their children. Alas, there are many trails of tears: Rachael's voice is weeping still, and Ramah is not far away.

However, a response existed in the prophet Jeremiah's words to these (and our) tragic tales. To the weeping voice of Rachael, he proclaimed this hopeful promise, "This is what the Lord says: 'Restrain your voice from weeping and your eyes from tears, for your work will be rewarded,' declares the Lord. 'They will return from the land of the enemy. So there is hope for your future,' declares the Lord. 'Your children will return to their own land'" (Jeremiah 31:16–17). Jeremiah declared something that seemed inconceivable: hope in the wake of unjust and untimely death. Hope for the future. That prospect became my opening. Hope seemed distant to me after Gabe's death, something I couldn't see, and perhaps even resented. But hope is also persistent, and it was beckoning me with its song.

I have seen hope in others who have suffered. It is a most noble ideal. Something about it lifts us, as though our very nature was being redeemed in the process. A man I knew whose wife had left him would not let go of the hope that she would return. I had told him that she, in all likelihood, was not coming back, and he would do himself a favor if he would just let it go and move on. But he was undaunted. He had hope, and he frantically clung to it. Or maybe it clung to him, I don't know. Regardless, I was not able to talk him out of his hope of a future reconciliation, and rightfully so, because after a time, they did reunite.

Over the years, various people I've known have lost hope. One lady, who was an exacting, yet cherished friend, was dying of cancer. I had been close to her and her wonderful husband for years, even playing my guitar at their wedding. Though she was a valiant fighter and explored all options for a cure, barring a miracle, her death was becoming more and more a reality. One day, while I was sitting with her in her living room, she suddenly had a change in demeanor to that of despair and defeat. "I have lost all hope," she said. Her face, filled with terror, said it clearer than her words. I have never forgotten the look on her face that day, and I wondered what it was like to lose all hope. I secretly prayed that such a fate would never befall me.

Losing hope is a devastating sentence. I have always known hope was central to our existence. We must believe something better is ahead. Hope is a key ingredient in every sermon I give. Humanity must have an optimistic attitude, an attitude that helps us embrace the future. Humanity must have hope. The death of my son caused me to lose my hope, and I had to find it again.

Balancing Grief and Hope

Central to allowing hope back into my life was the realization that it need not displace my grief. I think I felt that if I dared to hope again, I could no longer grieve. Perhaps it is our own instinct that suffering of any kind and recovery of any kind must be an either/or thing—like the marriage vows: better or worse, richer or poorer. But that does not always serve us well. I found that hope and grief *can* comfortably co-exist. In fact, they must!

A certain verse is oddly comforting concerning this. In a somewhat cryptic passage, Paul introduced a concept concerning what has happened to the dead, and what will happen to those who are still living at the coming of the Lord. He began with these words, "Brothers, we do not want you to be ignorant about those who fall asleep, or to grieve like the rest of men, who have no hope" (1 Thessalonians 4:13). There it is, grieve, but not like those who have no hope. The Bible paraphrase, *The Message,* rephrased it this way, "And regarding the question, friends, that has come up about what happens to those already dead and buried, we don't want you in the dark any longer. First off, you must not carry on over them like people who have nothing to look forward to, as if the grave were the last word." What an ostentatious thing to say, and I wondered if Paul ever lost anyone close to him.

Sometimes I think the writers of the Bible had some kind of privileged look into things that trouble the rest of us. They were in the know; we are in the dark. But this strange little text seems to invite us close to one of God's big secrets: death and hope are uniquely linked. As I have said before, grief has become part friend to me. Like an annoying family member who moves into your home for a while; grief is at first unwelcome, irksome, and cumbersome, and getting used to it takes time. Wishing the visit would mercifully end, you put on your brave face while silently resenting the intrusion. But after a season, the guest seems to belong. He has found his own niche—as if he has always been there.

I have now walked with grief so long that I no longer can imagine my life without it. It is like my scoliosis. I do not need to be reminded that I have a double spinal curvature. It has always given me days and seasons of pain. For many years, the pain would intermittently dissipate, and I would forget the shape of my spine, but no more. Now it is constant. It works itself into my sleep. It affects how I sit, how I walk, how I move; it is in every piece of my life. I cannot recall the last time I have gotten in or out of a bed or a chair or my car without wincing. Back pain has moved into my world, not to leave until my death. And so has grief.

But it takes more than familiarity to make a guest a friend. Simply because grief has moved in doesn't qualify it for inclusion into my inner circle. To be a friend you must have some give and take, some *quid pro quo*. And also a measure of commonality is needed. I know what grief has taken. I am learning what it gives. A foggy notion, but I have known this common-law relationship long enough to recognize that I have received something in kind from my inalienable life-mate—grief.

Sociability and Grief

I am not a deliberate man. Affability and easy-going seems a better fit, or maybe in the *Peanuts* lexicon: *wishy washy*. It takes me some time to process things. I was not a good umpire when my kids played ball. I didn't have what it takes to make those sudden, snap decisions: *safe or out, strike or ball*. Shudder! Let me have time to think it over, and I'll get back to you. Once while I was umpiring first base at a men's slow-pitch game, with a guy already on first, a grounder was hit up the middle. I watched as intently as I was capable of watching as one *bang-bang* play followed another. Though I saw them both, I had no idea if either runner was safe or out. And since I didn't have time to think it over, I allowed my affable nature to make the call: *one safe, one out.* There, that was fair. And both teams were upset with me.

Truth is that God gave me a mind and comportment that requires a little *boot-up* time. Just ask Vicki. The first few years of our marriage was certainly an adjustment, as I slowly learned to transition from singleness to partnership. I regrettably confess I was more committed to my *buddies* than my dear wife, at least for a while. What a patient and committed soul she was in those days. Yes, it takes me some time to get accustomed to changes.

Then, one day, out of a beautiful sun-kissed June afternoon came these words, "Gabe collapsed while fishing, and there is no pulse." If I couldn't process strikes and balls, I sure couldn't process this. The world stood still, and I entered a shock-filled panic, one where words, expressions, breaths, and emotions all cumbersomely unfold as they do as if you are coming out of anesthesia. To move from that demonic day to a day when hope is again a possibility requires a friend. It requires grief.

Grief is a binding tie, a hinge, a missing link between sorrow and hope. Like a new parent potty training a two-year-old, grief patiently takes us through a needed process, though we are completely unaware of our need for it. And grief is patient. One author who understood grief spoke of it as being a demon, only sleeping when we did. As soon as we awoke, the demon was there—ready to meet us. That was how I saw grief in the first years after Gabe died. I hated how grief made me feel:

- I felt almost inhuman, like I should be kept somewhere, as in a leper's colony.

- I felt capable of self-harm and was empowered to be insensitive toward others.

- I didn't know grief was functioning with a perfect timeliness.

- I didn't know it was accomplishing its ordained task.

- I didn't see the deterministic end.

- I didn't know a one-time enemy could become an arms-length friend.

Indeed, grief has earned its acrimonious reputation well. Some never survive the betrothal. But grief does its work, whether we participate or not, until finally, the darkness relinquishes its dreadful hold, and we are given something that enables us to reclaim a measure of life. For me, that something was hope, and my patient friend grief brought me to the place I could see it. Yes, Paul, we grieve, but not like those who have no hope.

Funerals and Christian Hope

When I first started officiating at funerals, though having been trained, I had much to learn. I was told in pastor's school that one thing mattered most at a funeral—the family. It would be good counsel. At many funerals I had earlier attended, I felt the pastor hadn't bothered to learn much about the deceased. One particular funeral was for two young adults who died in a car wreck. The church was packed, and the hour was dreadful. No, it was more than that. It was hellish. The parents came in and sat in those front pews with the look that only parents of dead children know. Then the service happened, twenty minutes from start to finish, with little said about the ones who had died. Guilt, regret, injustice, sorrows, and suffering; much could have been dealt with here. Did they play basketball? What kind of music did they like? What was their favorite holiday? Tell me about their families. We did have time for *Amazing Grace*, the 23rd Psalm, the obituary, and a few kind words, but that was about it. Perhaps it was intended that way, perhaps the family had requested a short service, but it felt particularly egregious, so very wrong to me. The pastor was a compassionate man who, I know, intended well. He was a good caregiver to his people and I certainly didn't harbor any ill will toward him, nor would I have wanted his job.

But the funeral felt so comfortless, and seemed so hopeless. As I looked at those caskets, I longed for something to hold onto, something to trust in, some way to make sense of this tragedy. Maybe that was too much to ask for, regardless of the size and shape of the service. Maybe some words of comfort and assurance *were* spoken, but my broken spirit couldn't hear them. Perhaps hope is too lofty a goal for such a dreadful moment. Maybe it's right to get in and out of that nightmare as soon as possible, but I don't think so. And I resolved that day to never do a funeral without an intentional infusing of Christian hope into my message and the service.

In school, a pastor-in-training asked the instructor what to do if we had a funeral for someone we didn't know. He said, "I hate to disillusion you, but nine out of ten funerals you do will be for someone you don't know." And now, after having done hundreds of funerals, I suspect his ratio was low. So God invented legal pads, ink pens, and computers so pastors could interview families in order to develop a meaningful eulogy. One pastor told me he had several *canned* funeral messages, and he just rotated them. Appalling, I thought. I think even more so today. I feel it is my responsibility as a pastor to get to know the person in death, even if I hadn't known him or her in life. A human life is such a gift from God. Long or short, rich or poor, easy or hard—life is to be celebrated.

And I know from sitting in the family section at funerals that talking about the person who died isn't painful—it's comforting.

We are also at funerals to grieve. I don't like funerals that are church services. I don't mean funerals should happen at the expense of theology (and I'll speak more to that later), but I've been to some where the tone has been more of a crusade than a lament. I've known pastors who see them as an opportunity to accrue converts. "We have a captive audience," they boast to any who will listen. It is an attitude I'll never understand. A family's sorrow is a poor choice of intrusions to satisfy a preacher's whims and personal agendas. Funerals are about families. And a personal bias, I'm not fond of some of the *show-biz* performances I've witnessed at a few funerals. Funerals are about comfort, not entertainment. At a funeral I officiated for a good man, the person doing the special music likely had the most noble and modest of intentions as he offered his gift, but it seemed we had all just been transported from a sanctuary to a theater.

I understand everybody's musical taste is not in sync, but to me, a service without some sacred music seems most hollow. But funeral music can tastefully speak to a person's life, spiritual or not. At Dad's service we did a couple country gospel songs that well represented his life: *Life's Railway to Heaven* and *The Great Speckled Bird*. I expect *Let It Be* to be played at mine, the album version with the guitar solo. And I would not be opposed to having the congregants whistle the theme song to *The Andy Griffith Show* as a postlude. *Holy, Holy, Holy* will be the congregational hymn.

Finally, I hold a small prejudice toward people who use funeral settings to catch up on *table conversation* with folks they haven't seen for a while. It is an uncomfortable and awkward intrusion. Perhaps there are acceptable moments for "coffee shop talk" at visitations or funerals, but they aren't normally social occasions. They are a time for grief. It is a bereaved community. It is a sad time. Grief has an important role to play here. At Gabe's visitation, a woman standing in line to *comfort* us was laughing. She really was. We were so broken we could barely breathe. I was sitting on a stool, as I didn't have the strength to stand. I suppose she was chatting with a friend and heard something amusing. But she laughed. And in that moment I hated her for it. Tiffany asked, "Dad, why is that person laughing? "I don't know, honey," I answered. "I don't know."

> Pastors that don't allow for grief at a funeral service have missed an important opportunity and are sorely lacking in protocol.

But funerals are also a time for hope, perhaps most importantly— for hope. It is hope that allows us to sit in the presence of our loved one in a casket. In truth, all who mourn long for hope. Many of the families I have been with during times of death were not church-affiliated, and many not of any personal faith at all. It didn't matter. They feasted on the prayers and scriptures that offered hope. Everyone hungers for it. It isn't a temporal hope they hunger for, but one that lingers into eternity. "If only for this life we have hope in Christ, we are to be pitied more than all men," said the apostle Paul (1 Corinthians 15:19). But grief has work to do to bring us to that place. The preacher who can tie the two together has done the bereaved a great service.

Hope and the Afterlife

A stunning thing happens also at the graveside that is a signpost of hope. All caskets are laid west to east, with the head facing the sunrise. This is so the dead can rise to meet the Lord when he returns. Through the eighteenth century, many of the tombstones and memorials were inscribed with the word *resurgam*, which in Latin means, "I shall arise." The belief was that the now-dead person, though in some intermediate state with Christ, would be resurrected to a new bodily life at the second coming.[51] Traditionally, the Christian conviction is believed to say that after death, the saved go to heaven and the damned to hell. But when the trumpet sounds and Christ returns, the saved are resurrected and body and soul are again complete. Paul wrote, "We believe that Jesus died and rose again and so we believe that God will bring with Jesus those who have fallen asleep in him" (1 Thessalonians 4:14).

While at school I argued that text with an instructor. He reasoned that no disembodied spirit floats around heaven until the apocalypse. Rather, he said what we are waiting for is the final resurrection. He insisted the creeds attest to that. He might be right. But I like the idea of being consciously with a loving God until that final day. It *seems* to give us the best of all options. Still, death has not allowed me to simply take the option that comforts me or agrees with me most. The death of my son has pushed my theological side to force the issue. I want a hope I can put my finger on, one I can trust.

As stated, every mourner hungers for hope. It is our manifesto. If I were to parade about with a sandwich billboard over my shoulders to tell the world who I've become, the front would simply say: Grief; the back: Hope. It is my doctrine, my dogma, my testimony, my philosophy; it is who I am. I will always be shaped by both. My grief will keep me connected to the earth and those who walk it. My hope will lift my eyes to heaven and to those who dwell there. All matters of personal belief are tested throughout our lives. Mercy is tested by inhumanity, love by malice, generosity by greed, faith by doubt, goodness by evil, compassion by contempt, joy by sadness, and hope by death. I am here to tell you that my hope has been tested. In the years that have followed Gabe's death, it has become my higher calling to rest in it again.

It seems a partisan thing to trust one's hereafter to such a narrow way of thinking. I was taught not to put all my eggs in one basket. Surely it would be a better thing to embrace at least two or three of the world's religions—and a televangelist or two. Legend says that W. C. Fields was found reading a Bible on his deathbed. When asked why he would bother looking at the Bible now, he is said to have replied, "I'm looking for loopholes." My rational, practical side says 'tis better to face death *after* having covered all the bases. Yet, the savior with whom I have cast my lot said, "I am the way, the truth, and the life, no one comes to the Father except through me" (John 14:6). And to our pluralistic planet he said, "Enter through the narrow gate. For wide is the gate and broad is the road that leads to destruction, and many enter through it. But small is the gate and narrow the road that leads to life, and only a few find it" (Matthew 7:13–14). With Christ, covering all our bases may mean we are missing the only essential one. It appears to be a rather exclusive club. What does a seeker do with this?

Biblical scholar and author, Bishop N.T. Wright, speaks to the confusion:

> Beliefs about death and what lies beyond come in all shapes and sorts and sizes. Even a quick glance at the classic views of the major religious traditions gives the lie to the old idea that all religions are basically the same. There is a world of difference between the Muslim who believes that a Palestinian boy killed by Israeli soldiers goes straight to

heaven and the Hindu for whom the rigorous outworking of karma means that one must return in a different body to pursue the next stage of one's destiny. There is a world of difference between the Orthodox Jew who believes that all the righteous will be raised to new individual bodily life in the resurrection and the Buddhist who hopes after death to disappear like a drop in the ocean, losing one's own identity in the great nameless and formless Beyond.[52]

But knowing and understanding these belief systems are not compatible ideals. Who am I to think that just because I have believed it, it is so? I have not always chosen correctly. I changed my formidable baseball allegiance from the Boston Red Sox to the Chicago Cubs some years *before* the Red Sox won their two World Series championships. This year the Cubs will be at 103 years and counting since their last world championship. There is always next year, right? But then, isn't this the essence of hope? If I could somehow know, it would no longer be hope. Something would be lost—something important. Paul said to the Romans, "For in this hope we were saved. But hope that is seen is no hope at all. Who hopes for what he already has? But if we hope for what we do not yet have, we wait for it patiently" (Romans 8:24–25). And so I wait, with a forced patience—in hope.

Faces of Hope

But hope is also a fragile thing. It always teeters on the edge of a frightening void. *Palm Beach Post* staff writer Susan Salisbury tells the story of *Faces of Hope*, a book published in 2002. In it were the faces of fifty children, one from each state, who were born on one of America's darkest days: *9–11*. The author, Christine Pisera Naman, gave birth to a son, Trevor, that day. Asked what made her compile the book, she commented, "I was like most people in the country, looking to find a bit of hope on that day … I did the book as an offering of hope. I wanted it to be a dedication to the people who were lost as well as their loved ones. Then I wanted it to be a little bit of inspiration to the babies born on that day to go out and do good."[53] An offering of hope, it is a beautiful image. I love things like this, a book of fifty children, each one a face of hope. But as stated, hope is a fragile thing, always seemingly teetering on the edge of a frightening abyss. In January 2011, a man with a lost soul sprayed a clip of bullets into a political town hall meeting in Arizona, hitting nineteen people. Of those shot, six died. Of those six, one had been a face of hope. If part of the reason for *Faces of Hope* was to inspire babies born on that day to go out and do well, then surely nine-year-old Christina Green heard that call, because that is exactly what she was doing there that day. And then, just like that, she was gone. I wonder; did the hope that was Christina extinguish the same day as her life? Because that is how it felt.

I have prayed for my children nearly every day since I first became a parent. The prayers were fairly simple: asking God to help them with homework, bullies, dating, health, school, but mostly, keep them safe and alive. That was my hope, and I had great confidence in God to do just that. Though precariously bordering on mysticism, I marked scriptures in my Bible that I felt were signals from God to those ends. But my prayers were not answered. The thing I feared most came upon me. I had prayed relentlessly, uncompromisingly, and passionately for Gabe—and yet he died. Did my hope die the same day as my son? It felt like it. One of the first scriptures I stumbled upon after Gabe's death was in Job, "For what I fear comes upon me, and what I dread befalls me" (Job 3:25). A lifetime investment in faith suddenly felt fragile and tenuous, perhaps on the brink of leaving my life forever. Suddenly I distrusted God and put little confidence in prayer. Can hope withstand such abandonment? Or can something that has always been, still remain, despite the assault? That debate became my contemplative quest.

Funerals should be a hybrid of eulogy and theology, a commemoration of life and a witness of faith. Having said how much I cherish the celebration of each human life, if the eulogy is the "end all" of a funeral, our hope seems finite and temporal. If it is an invitation to doctrine, then it is open-ended, and so are the possibilities for hope. Central to that hope (for me) is the bodily resurrection of Jesus. This cannot be something up for debate. It is the centerpiece of all Christian hope and points to the final resurrection and whatever intermediate state may lead up to it.[54] It is a prelude to our own translation from what we were to what we shall be. The anticipation of it thrills me.

I never thought we would ever have to pick out a cemetery plot for our son. What a ghastly thing. But it forced another issue. I picked out my own spot. I will lay right next to my son, and Vicki by me. It's a lovely spot, really (if such a thing can exist within the boundaries of a cemetery). It's just north of our home, about two blocks away, down an asphalt lane just outside the city limits. The nearby pond is stocked with bass, bluegill, and crappie. Stately oak trees stand tall, and if you look south by southeast, you can see the roof of our house. I sometimes think that I can never leave this place because I feel I would be leaving Gabe. And I have this vision of the day of resurrection, the final day when all things are made new. I can see us rise together, out of the graves that held us. I see us looking at each other, embracing, and knowing the long nightmare is over. And death will be no more. Everything I have wanted to tell Gabe about my life, my mistakes, my choices, my parenting, and my regrets will no longer matter. They won't be relevant. We will be children of the new creation together. Our past will be as useless as the graves we have abandoned. That truly is my hope.

An Easter Memory

I have a fond memory of my youth. While in United Methodist Youth Fellowship (UMYF), we had a wonderful pastor who took great interest in us. I don't remember much of what he said in sermons and lessons, but his *ministry of presence* spoke volumes and has influenced my own ministry. One year, as Easter was approaching, Rev. Roy (as we called him) suggested we build three crosses for a sunrise service. Another member of our youth group was my aforementioned lifetime friend, Neil. Neil's dad had a woodworking shop in an older building on his farm. We had earlier made a worship center for the concrete-block room in the back of the church basement where the youth met. I didn't know what a worship center was, but I recall the project, and Neil's dad doing most of the work. I suspect that shop was also the birthplace for this project, and where the crosses were assembled. Regardless, we fashioned three crosses, which we placed in anticipation on the east shore of Earnest Sturdevant's farm pond, two miles north of the church.

On Holy Saturday, Neil and I, Rev. Roy, and probably others from our group, set up the crosses. I had a child-like wonder, debating whether this was what it was like when they placed the three crosses for Jesus and the two thieves in their stands. The crosses were strategically placed so the sunrise would cause them to reflect in the pond. I could hardly wait for the morning. It was like Christmas Eve. I'm still amazed when I think about the depth of my religious intrigue at that age. And on Easter morning, while it was still dark, our youth group went out to the pond, and sat, waiting on the sun to do its thing. I have distinct memories of crawling over a fence, being chilly in the morning air, wading through brush and weeds, and feeling the dew creep through my shoes. Then it happened. The sun rose behind the crosses, and they perfectly reflected in the quiet pond—just as we had planned. It was breathtaking for a young theologian like me. I have never forgotten the moment. I think it was the first time I felt true hope. Somehow an empty cross by a farm pond on Easter morning was as telling as an empty tomb was to Mary, Johanna, and Magdalene. Even today I am reminded of the words of the angel, "Why do you look for the living among the dead? He is not here; he has risen!"(Luke 24:5). Though I am still victim to the tireless sieges of bereavement, I cannot abandon this part of me. For each day I am swept over by waves of disillusionment, bitterness, anger, sadness, and regret—I am also lifted up by hope. But it is a specific hope. It is a God hope. And it is my choice to dwell there as often as I can.

What Kind of Person Are You?

I was intrigued by the movie *Signs*. The script communicated genuine mystique and a contrast of choices. Starring Mel Gibson, *Signs* is fashioned after many of the horror movies of the 40's and 50's. Much of the horror is left to the imagination. Aliens are invading the earth, communicating with each other by crop circles, one of which was in Graham Hess' field.

Played by Gibson, Hess is a former clergyman who had abandoned his clerical calling after a driver tragically killed his wife because he had fallen asleep just as he passed her. Fourteen mysterious lights appear in the sky as earth's impending defeat looms large, broadcast nationwide by television.

Hess' brother is overcome with fear. He asked Hess to offer him words of comfort, as he had in the past. Shaped by his loss, Hess replied that he sees people falling into two categories during uncertain times. One category sees mysteries and uncertainties as coincidence, pure chance. "For them, the situation is a 50/50; could be bad, could be good. But deep down they feel that whatever happens, they're on their own and that fills them with fear." But Hess believed there is another group, a group who sees miracles. "And deep down they feel that whatever is going to happen, there will be someone there to help them, and that fills them with hope." He reasoned that all must decide what kind of person they will be: someone who sees signs and miracles, or someone who thinks we are on our own and just get lucky.[55] A simple choice like this can determine whether we live in fear or hope.

I think we all have that choice. What kind of people will we be in this life? When tragedy befalls us, we can feel as though we are indeed on our own, and that fills us with fear. Or we can feel that whatever is going to happen, someone will be there to help us, and that fills us with hope. For my money, no one on the earth has more right or reason to feel alone in the universe than bereaved parents. They, like few others, had their highest aspirations crushed by a deadly blow, and it's not fixable. For them to again choose hope speaks to a resolute spirit, a gallant courage, and a conviction in the mystique of God. But even choosing to believe we are not alone; to believe in a greater good or higher hope does not disqualify fear's power to make us feel alone in the universe. I must allow for the possibility that many a noble soul has a foot in each world. And they should not feel guilty for doing so.

Life After Life

Mary and Martha were every bit sisters, alike, yet significantly different. Mary was the thoughtful, introspective, nurturing one.

194

Being was a more endearing ethic than *doing*. Martha was the busy bee: disciplined, pro-active, impulsive, and results-orientated. The sisters loved their brother Lazarus. They all were friends of Jesus. Perhaps a reason this story has struck me so is because they could have been my kids. In some ways, they were. Lazarus was sick, and word was sent to Jesus to come and help, but Jesus delayed. I don't know why. John said it was for the benefit of the disciples. It seemed a rather harsh Sunday School lesson if the point of the sermon could only be driven home by a man's death. Regardless, Lazarus died, and Jesus ultimately arrived at Bethany. Predictably, Martha charged out to meet him while Mary silently grieved her brother at home. Martha demanded an answer to Jesus' tardiness. But her demands were tempered by a wistful yearning. I'm not sure if it was hope or mere wishful thinking. "If you would have been here, my brother would not have died. But I know that even now God will give you whatever you ask" (John 11:21–22), she blurted. I must confess I've had similar thoughts. It is a very human response. With Jesus' response, hope invaded pain. "Your brother will rise again."

I have never fully understood Jewish thought on the afterlife. Author Phillip Eichman says the Hebrew religion tends to place an emphasis primarily on the present life. Still, there are many passages in the Old Testament that teach life exists beyond the grave, though blessings and punishment were seen as occurring in the present time or through descendants.[56]

While there is not clear consensus on the resurrection in the Old Testament, some of its writers and readers looked for a bodily resurrection after the Messiah comes, and some didn't. Nonetheless, Martha must have. She spoke to it in a resigning manner, "I know he will rise again in the resurrection at the last day."

I think I know what Martha was saying. Yes, Lord, I believe my son will rise again. A day will come where he will live again. But I want him here now. As stated, I have always hated the cliché, "Well, he's in a better place now." No, he isn't. The best place for him is here—now! I understand Martha's angst. What follows next is mystery to me. I have never tried to add to or delete from the text that has been given. I just allow myself to receive it at face value.

The words are etched in my head and heart: Jesus said, "I am the resurrection and the life. He who believes in me will live, even though he dies; and whoever lives and believes in me will never die. Do you believe this?" (John 11:25–26). The story concluded with the DeMille-like ending. "Lazarus, come out!" Jesus shouted. Wrapped in burial clothes, Lazarus came stumbling out of the tomb. Amazing! Is it true? Do those who believe in Jesus live, even though they die? If so, did Jesus do Lazarus any favors? Doesn't he now have to die all over again? Isn't one time through that merciless passage enough? The point is: Lazarus lived. He always lived, though hid for a time by the shadow of death.

The apostle Paul said, "Therefore we are always confident and know that as long as we are at home in the body we are away from the Lord. We live by faith, not by sight. We are confident, I say, and would prefer to be away from the body and at home with the Lord. So we make it our goal to please him, whether we are at home in the body or away from it" (2 Corinthians 5:8–9). And so I have hope. I have hope that Gabe is at this very minute *at home with the Lord*—alive!

In the wash of visitors the week after Gabe died, my dear friend Neil was there a couple days. One afternoon we walked up the lane to East Cemetery, where we were soon to bury our son. I wanted him to see the spot. Neil and I are alike in more ways than our church and community of origin. Neil is also a pastor. But he is a very insightful one, with a sense of mystic about him. As we walked along the way, he said immediately after hearing that Gabe had died, he had an assurance or vision that Gabe was with Jesus, safe in his arms. Like Martha, my silent response to that was partly wishful thinking. I only want Gabe to be with Jesus if he can't be with us. I can't stand the thought of him being no place. Gabe is not alone. I am not alone. We are not alone. The prospect gives me hope. But my human response is also part, "Jesus! Where were you? Where are you, or—do you even exist?" Whatever happens, are we on our own? And my human view fills me with fear. I've discovered *wishy washiness* does not play well in matters of life and death.

Author N.T. Wright says in the intermediate life that bridges death and resurrection, "there will be a new physicality, which stands in relation to our present body, as our present body does to a ghost." He goes on to speak of this physicality as being more touchable, more sustainable, more present and real than our present bodies. It is not a disembodied spirit that we will occupy in the sweet by-and-by.[57]

I need this kind of thought process. It comforts me like a familiar hymn. It is our *God hope*, even though it seems impossible or unlikely. It places us in a parental love with God that endures until the final act of creation.

- It was paradise to a thief on the cross.

- It was a mansion to fearful disciples in the upper room.

- It is the *was*, the *is*, and the *will be* of our story.

- It is the chrysalis and the butterfly, and both are beautiful.

- It is the best of what is, yet better is coming.

- It is the ecstasy of the wedding night, not understanding that the marriage will be richer still.

- It creates anticipation that all is well—in life and in death.

- It stills my fears when I think of people I have loved and have lost.

- It stills my fears concerning my own mortality.

Likewise, I am resolved to this manner of expectation. A part of me will continue to dwell in the land of theological doubt and distrust. While I retain my human point of view, I will retain its attributes. A foot will always be in each world, and I will feel caught between grief and hope. But something of deity must be at work in the heart of every bereaved person, yes, every mortal person. Something caused Martha to confess, "But I know that even now God will give you whatever you ask." I think that something was hope. Every grieving person longs for it. And so I continue to grieve, but not as those who have no hope. In fact, that is *what* I have.

CHAPTER 9

RIPPLES IN THE POND

No Man Is an Island

No man is an island,
Entire of itself.
Each is a piece of the continent,
A part of the main.
If a clod be washed away by the sea,
Europe is the less.
As well as if a promontory were.
As well as if a manor of thine own
Or of thine friends were.
Each man's death diminishes me,
For I am involved in mankind.
Therefore, send not to know
For whom the bell tolls,
It tolls for thee.

John Donne
Meditation 17: Devotions upon Emergent Occasions

"Strange, isn't it? Each man's life touches
so many other lives. When he isn't around
he leaves an awful hole, doesn't he?"

D o you remember that quote? As one of the great lines from the endearing and enduring movie, *It's a Wonderful Life*, its sentiment now haunted me. Near the end of the movie is a scene where George has been allowed to see how his family and community would have fared if he had never been born. He didn't like what he saw. George felt his life had become a failure, and *not being* was better than *being*. But now he knew he was wrong. Life does matter. The angel Clarence wisely proclaimed: "Each man's life touches so many other lives."

I have always believed that. No one is exempt. It is hard not to entwine your life with another's unless you isolate yourself. I suspect we are designed that way. God told Adam in the garden that it is not good for a man to be alone (see Genesis 2:18). And it isn't. We are meant to be a part of each other. Affiliation is in our emotional DNA. I know some of us are extroverted and some introverted, some are replenished and nourished by crowds and others by solitude. But none of us are intended to be alone. We can't be. We have too many people to touch and be touched by, and we are the richer because of it. I think there is as much celestial pattern in this networking of the masses as in the stars in the heavens. And when a life prematurely ends, a void appears in the pattern. A thread is missing. A picture is incomplete. As Donne suggested: "Each man's death diminishes me, for I am involved in mankind."

Moments before Gabe died he was doing something he loved, something he and I spent a great deal of time doing throughout his youth. He was skipping rocks on the water. This is not an inherited trait, and like pitching a baseball, it takes balance, repetition, and an arm. Gabe often skipped stones. Many of our fishing trips ended with Gabe and me skimming rocks across ponds, rivers, and lakes. And Gabe had an arm. He threw a very hard ball, often hurting my hand when we played catch. That boy could *wing it*. If his Pee Wee and Little League coaches knew what I knew, Gabe might have made a good pitcher. I could throw a rock or a ball a long way when I was younger also. I think it is some kind of measuring stick for manhood to those who grow up in rural Iowa. Boys love to line up on the shores of a pond or lake and see who could throw the rock the farthest. But somewhere between puberty and adolescence, Gabe's throw exceeded mine; it is a humbling thing for a father to confess.

We had a number of chosen fishing holes we often frequented; among others, our favorite ponds were owned by Stanley Vogel, Jerry Dumont, Dave Witte, and Eugene Snakenburg. We were regulars at all these ponds, driving our old green-and-white pickup across fields, ditches, pastures, and barnyards to get to our quarry. That old pickup had a hole in the floor on the passenger side. Gabe thought it was the coolest thing to be able to see the ground through the floor. But this old truck took us to ponds hundreds of times. Gabe and I, and usually a friend or two of his, knew every inch of these ponds, and we even knew some of the fish (as we did catch and release, and often caught the same fish). Eugene's wonderful pond held some of our best memories. Before a winter kill it contained huge catfish. We would toss out our line in the early evening, when catfish are said to bite best. For this, our strategy was a bobber with a ball of "Ol' Whiskers" stink bait on a treble hook. For all of our predictability though, the catfish never once figured it out. We caught a bunch of them. The thing about catching a large catfish on a rod and reel though is it can blur the line between boys and men. On more than one occasion, I have been guilty of commandeering a rod away from its rightful owner when a big one was on the line. I'm not sure if it was because I didn't think they could get it in or because I just wanted to reel in the beast myself.

Eugene's Pond

Gabe was tussling with a big catfish one night at Eugene's pond. I thought he or the pole was going into the pond. So Dad grabbed the pole and successfully landed the fish. It weighed seven pounds. I am amazed at the clarity of that memory. I also recall Gabe being a little out of sorts for not getting to reel in that fish. He should have been out of sorts, and he should have reeled in the fish. He was not shorted on the fishing, however. Gabe reeled in hundreds and hundreds of fish in those years. I remember this part of boyhood myself, and its level of importance in the adventures of growing up.

My dad was an electrician/plumber/furnace man (and other jack-of-all trades). I'd wait for his big panel truck to pull into the driveway so we could go fishing. I didn't realize then how tired a dad can be when he gets home from work. I was simply crestfallen on the nights he said no. But on the nights he said yes, oh, they were great fun. On some trips we didn't catch a single fish, and it didn't seem to matter. The joy was truly in the journey. Every pond was an adventure. I thought I'd never forget the importance of these little father-and-son trips. But early on in my parenting, I did.

I had some wonderful friends in those years and enjoyed trips to the river with them. Adult guy times were certainly important. One time I was getting my gear together, and the guys were coming to pick me up. Gabe saw me getting ready. He immediately got his pole and tackle box ready. He was wearing oversized boots, perhaps mine. "Are we going fishing, Daddy?" "Well, I am," I quietly said. When the pickup pulled up in front of our house, I hopped in with my friends. I turned to look back as we pulled away from the house. Gabe was standing in the yard, holding his fishing pole, watching Dad leave with his "buddies." "Never again," I said to myself. That was the shift in choosing who my fishing buddies would be going forward. And, for the overwhelming part, every fishing trip after that included my son. So we went, over and over, night after night, trip after trip, and I cherished every one. No dad and son ever enjoyed finer moments. These are my best memories of my time with him, and they are absolutely holy to me.

Just south of Eugene's pond was the gravel road that took us to and from this perfect place. We had to cross a barbed wire fence and a deep ditch, some thirty to forty feet from the water's edge to return to the pickup. A ritual took place there after every fishing trip. Crawling under, though, or over the lines of barbed wire, then up the steep side of the ditch, we would toss our gear into the wood-bottomed pickup bed. Without a word being said, we would grab a handful of gravel off the road and let it fly. In the early years, I could hit mid pond with a good-sized rock. By the end of our days on that pond, I could barely hit water's edge, and I was wincing while holding my sore shoulder, but not my son. With something of a three-quarter side-armed throw, he could nearly put a rock on the opposite shore. When he and I got older, he was throwing the rock twice as far as me.

Sometimes I drive down that road and stop at that spot, and I can see that young dad and his boy throwing rocks into a pond. Sigh. I recall something else about rocks skipping across water. With each stone comes a pattern of perfectly concentric circles, drifting farther and farther away from where the rock first hit water. The circles form ripples in the water, first smaller, then larger, before they are gone. And when we each hit the water at the same time, our ripples touched each other's—just like lives touch each other. You are right, Clarence: "Each man's life touches so many other lives. When he isn't around he leaves an awful hole, doesn't he?"

Our lives reach out concentrically starting from us and touch those within our reach, like ripples in a pond. "Remarkable" things can happen when one life touches another. From one perspective, Gabe lived a most "unremarkable" life. He held no higher degrees, won no awards, shared no championships, and appeared on no *Who's Who* lists. I attend some high school graduation family receptions these days and look at the poster boards and tables of ribbons, medals, awards, and certificates. All the while, a videotape is playing in the background of the graduate hitting a home run or scoring a touchdown. I wonder if something is being lost. Those things are wonderful, and a parent is certainly within proper parental protocol displaying them, yet, it seems that what a child does is becoming more important than who a child is. We could be subtly communicating that validation lies in accomplishments. But it is a forgivable and understandable offence. At my children's graduation parties, I displayed every award, certificate, letter, ribbon, medal, and scholarship I could dig up. I carry a fierce fatherly pride for my little brood as well. Still, I wonder if we set them up for an endless cycle of trying to repeat their adolescent successes the rest of their lives.

I attend lots and lots of wedding receptions as part of my pastoral job. At the reception of one wedding I had officiated, the proud dad gave a speech on behalf of his wedded son. He listed his son's accomplishments, reliving his high school and college careers. I certainly don't fault the dad for choosing such, but on Valerie and Tiffany's wedding days, their accomplishments were the furthest thing from my mind.

I always tried my best not to show any favor *or* disservice due to my children's athletic or academic prowess or incompetence. One scene from an old episode of *The Andy Griffith Show* impacted my parenting (actually, many scenes from that wonderful old show influenced me). Opie, not a particularly good student, brought home a report card displaying all A's. Andy was ecstatic and overwhelmed by a fatherly pride. He immediately went out and did something very uncharacteristic; he bought Opie a top-notch new bike. On top of that, he bragged of Opie's accomplishments to Barney, Goober, Floyd, and anyone within reach. He was simply giddy. But the day the bike was presented something happened. Opie's teacher informed him that a mistake has been made—but Andy didn't know this yet. Opie didn't get those A's. In fact, C's and D's littered the report card, as usual. Opie reluctantly accepted the bike, but it didn't *feel* right. Nonetheless, Andy was undaunted, and with a fierce fatherly pride he showcased Opie's accomplishment all over Mayberry. Many fathers see in their sons an extension of their own competencies and prowess, perhaps too much. They feasibly do their sons no favors in the process. Opie saw only one option as Andy continued to create a scenario he couldn't possibly live up to. Knowing his dad would eventually find out the truth, and not knowing how to tell him, he ran away. His validation had evaporated as quickly as his A's. By the time Andy discovered Opie was missing, the teacher had given him the scoop on the report card. Not knowing whether to be mad or concerned (a feeling most dads ultimately know), Andy took off looking for him. When he finally found him walking by a road, Andy sternly confronted him about the report card. What follows next is simply a terrific father/son moment:

Andy: "Opie, where did you think you were going?"

Opie: "I got thinking about it and I figured the best thing was to run away and not to come back until I was able to do something to make you proud of me again."

Andy: (after a long, thoughtful pause) "Ah, Opie, I've got … I've got something I want to say to you. When I thought you got all A's, that was the most important thing in the world to me. And I made it so important that I made it impossible for you to live up to. You're my son, and I'm proud of you just for that. You do the best you can, and if you do that, that's all I'll ever ask of you. Okay?"

Opie: "Okay Pa."[58]

Though we were sternly taught at St. Paul's School of Theology to cite our sources at all times, experience quickly taught me the same rule doesn't apply to dads. So one day, when Gabe felt discouraged over something, I borrowed these words from Andy. Gabe had many discouraging moments growing up. His report cards favored Opie's. I don't recall the particular problem that day, but I do remember putting my arm around his shoulder and saying, "Gabe, you are my son, and I'm proud of you just for that. You do the best you can, and if you do that, that's all I'll ever ask of you. Okay?" Some weeks later, he walked through the family room as I was watching that particular episode, and the dialogue was ironically in that particular place. Gabe heard Andy speak the same lines I had so eloquently and emphatically spoken to him. He looked at me, puzzled, and asked, "Dad, is that where you got those lines?" And I smiled at him and said something on the order of, "If it's good enough for Andy and Opie, it's good enough for us." I was had, but we both chuckled. Regardless of the source, I meant every word. Gabe, Val, and Tiff were my children, and I was proud of them just for that. Their lives had a validation that was not mine to give—or to take away.

People who live "unremarkable" lives often do "remarkable" things—they touch others, just like ripples in a pond. If given time and place on the earth, many humble beginnings can transform into purposeful ends. Church consultant and author Herb Miller wrote a helpful piece entitled, *Give the Chance*:

> Louis Pasteur once had a teacher who wrote this about him: "Pasteur is the smallest, meekest, and least promising pupil in my class." During his childhood, Sir Walter Scott was rated a dunce. The great philosopher Hume was described as "uncommonly weak-minded." Charles Darwin's own father predicted that Charles would be a disgrace to the Darwin family. Napoleon was sent to military school and graduated number forty-two in a class of forty-three. Isaac Newton showed such promise that his parents took him out of school and put him to work on a farm. Yes, many people who at first appeared doomed to a life of incompetency and failure now inhabit the pages of our history books. We never know the potential of a person until they are given a chance. Pasteur wrote his father saying, "Just be patient and trust me. I shall do better as I go on."[59]

From my earthly vantage point, Gabe wasn't allowed sufficient time or place to achieve his potential. He wasn't given that chance. That didn't mean he didn't do some remarkable things. Over the years I have wondered many times what he'd be doing now, how many kids he might have raised, where he would be living, what he would have thought about things, what fish we might yet have caught, and a thousand other *what ifs*. But I am forced to be content with the reality of *what was*. And what was, was still wonderful. It was partly incognito, and I did not know much of the good he had been about until after his death, but Gabe clearly touched many other lives, like ripples do. He was a faithful friend and a tireless buddy. He believed the best about many people when others might have given up on them. He did not judge or condemn (something that cannot always be said of his pastoral father). He could make anybody laugh. He gave freely and could be counted on to help others in need. He was a simple person with simple needs. He was quiet, unassuming, and gentle (mostly). He hated veggies, but loved ravioli. Music, movies, and fishing were his happy places. And his deepest needs were the same as that of every person—to love and to be loved.

Planning Gabe's Funeral

When doing the grizzly task of planning Gabe's funeral, I knew I wanted my dear friend Neil to do the eulogy. By definition, a eulogy is a piece of speech writing designed to praise someone. And in keeping with my practice of celebrating life at every funeral, some well-placed subjective praise certainly seems appropriate. But an early advisor in my clerical training argued that any mortal praise should be balanced by proper doctrinal hope. One of my supervising pastors was a master at this. His funeral sermons were a seamless blend of gospel and mortal celebration. I have made this the aim of every funeral at which I have officiated. I have always rightly strived to stay in that center place by offering a message that was part sermon and part eulogy. But oddly, I really didn't want a sermon at Gabe's funeral. I, a sermon junkie, wanted no part of hearing a sermon that day. I wasn't ready to think about God. Spiritual matters were dangerous ground for me in those early weeks. While Vicki's faith sustained her through these tortuous days, mine strangely seemed to only add to my angst. Maybe if my child had been killed or drowned; or a physical cause had been revealed for his death. But when this boy just drops over dead, with no cause, two weeks before his sister's wedding, well, I just didn't want to hear how much God cared for me that day. From my vantage point, God seemed cruel and especially vindictive. But Pastor John, good and godly man that he is, preached away. And it was okay. However, I heard little of the sermon, except for a few allusions to a text we had picked out for the service:

I remember my affliction and my wandering, the bitterness

and the gall. I well remember them, and my soul is downcast within me. Yet this I call to mind and therefore I have hope: Because of the Lord's great love we are not consumed, for his compassions never fail. They are new every morning; great is your faithfulness. (Lamentations 3:19–23)

John is a wonderful and caring pastor. I hold him in the highest esteem. In the truest sense he is a shepherd of his people. He became my pastor when Gabe died. He probably saw me at my worst but didn't think any less of me. I appreciated that. Regardless, all I recall of his sermon was the emphatic echo of Lamentations, *Great is your faithfulness*. And I wasn't sure about that.

I remember more of Neil's terrific eulogy, particularly two things. Vicki has since listened to the tape of the funeral and could probably restate these things much more accurately than I. Neil said when Gabe was a baby, he reminded him of the Gerber baby, that cherub-like face on the jar labels of Gerber baby food. What a cute little guy. And Gabe was a cute little guy, the cutest in my book. It made me happy to hear Neil remember that face. Later he talked about how Gabe had been skipping stones just before his death. Each stone, as it brimmed across the water's surface, left a symmetrical ripple. And the ripples continued to grow and expand, farther and farther away from the initial point of contact. Each time the stone touches down, it creates a new series of ripples, and as they expand they touch each other. Then they disappear. Neil contemplated a life lesson from that, saying he would have to spend some time considering it. I don't know if he has or not, but I have. I think we all are like ripples in a pond. We grow and expand, farther and farther away from where we started. We touch other ripples we come into contact with, and then we disappear from the earth. So when it comes to matters of purpose, ripples matter.

The Church as One Body

The correlation between connecting ripples and connecting lives also speaks to my pastoral calling. In the church, connected lives are presented as a body, an image that has held some intrigue for me.

The church is, perhaps, the first and best place for one like me to look at the effect of connecting ripples. The Bible says all Christians are one unified body. Holy, apostolic, and universal; people of all ages, nations, and races, and they are one body, at least that is how God apparently intended it. The possibility amazes me. I understand some denominations are connectional; our own United Methodist tradition is. That is a comforting and supportive thought. But one Christian is connected to every other, regardless of tradition or affiliation. In theory, I would then belong to every other Christian who lives, and who has ever lived. In a letter to a church, the apostle Paul addressed this mystery; how one belongs to all and all belong to one:

> You can easily enough see how this kind of thing works by looking no further than your own body. Your body has many parts—limbs, organs, cells—but no matter how many parts you can name, **you're still one body**. It's exactly the same with Christ. By means of his one Spirit, we all said goodbye to our partial and piecemeal lives. We each used to independently call our own shots, but then we entered into a large and integrated life in which he has the final say in everything … . Each of us is now a part of his resurrection body, refreshed and sustained at one fountain—his Spirit— where we all come to drink. The old labels we once used to identify ourselves—labels like Jew or Greek, slave or free—are no longer useful. We need something larger, more comprehensive (1 Corinthians 12:12–13, *The Message*).

Maybe this act of oneness isn't fully realized in the church until the final re-creation. It's a rare thing to see it in a single congregation, much less a universal church. Yet, simply because I have not witnessed the final act of Christian unity does not devalue its place or power. Surely we are sisters and brothers, with what separates us ultimately surrendering to what unites us. It is surely the same with eternity. Just because I have not yet seen paradise doesn't mean it isn't there in all of its glory. If Clarence the angel was right, if every man's life touches so many other lives, then it must surely happen in the Christian congregation. However, I have also seen it fulfilled among neighborhoods, communities, organizations, and even blood families (where it can oft times be the most fragile). And for a while, the world is a less scary place, when you consider that your ripples have crossed the familial lines of another, and there is a sense of belonging because of it.

My Neighbor Ken

Donne is right; each man's death does diminish us. It is one less ripple in the pond. It is one less ripple to touch mine. Clarence, you were also right: "When he isn't around he leaves an awful hole, doesn't he?" Many years ago our neighbor was killed. I never really knew the man though we had visited often over the

The Church is only the church when she exists for others.

–Dietrich Bonhoeffer

years. He had a son slightly older than Gabe. A particular memory I have of him is of an early Saturday morning, when he came pounding on my patio door. I went to see who was causing all the commotion, and there he was, holding a stringer high up in the air. On the stringer was a six-pound northern pike, flopping about as if he had just been caught, and he had. Being a fisherman myself, and knowing there aren't a lot of northerns in southeast Iowa, I said, "Ken, where in the heck did you get that fish?" Of all places, he had caught it in the North Skunk River, a small river just south of town better known for catfish and carp, but on this particular Saturday morning, for northern pike also. This lonely and adventuresome pike had likely swum the long journey up from the larger rivers downstream, perhaps even from the Mississippi itself. Ken was absolutely *boy-like* over the catch, as I would have been. He had caught it on a ditty pole, a single line rigged on a willow branch or another flexible pole that was driven into a steep bank. Ditty poles were deadly for catfish, but apparently also for northern pike.

Ken was a wonderful neighbor. Then, one day, with no warning, while driving to work, a tractor turned out in front of Ken's carpool car. He was dead instantly, and a wife and son suddenly were without a husband and father. I was told a youth was driving the tractor, not of age to drive a car, and perhaps better suited for a bike. But he was put in charge of this immense piece of machinery on a major highway, and a man's life tragically ended. Though I never knew who was driving the tractor, I know the nature of accidents, and I know there surely was loss in his home as well.

> Whenever someone is personally introduced to death for the first time, there is a loss.

Over the next few days, Ken's home was flooded by sympathizers, ham sandwiches, and peach pies. After the funeral, I was at their house and heard the widow say something I have not forgotten, "I never knew so many people cared about us." That sentence stuck in my throat like a fish bone because I realized I was one of those people. Except to do some work, I had not been in that house until there was a death. He was my neighbor, but I never visited in his home—not once—until he died. Why is that? Why does it take death to make us care for each other? Ken's life touched mine, but I showed no care until it was the proper thing to do. Maybe it will always be that way. Though our lives touch like the ripples do, perhaps humanity is now more wired to alienation than affiliation. There was a time in this country when neighbors were "neighborly;" when loss was not necessary to invoke a home visit.

My Brother's Keeper

Cain and Abel is a Bible story I've used for several sermons. I was spiritually shaped by a sermon I heard on the brothers' story. Years earlier, a former preacher of mine used this little drama to powerfully preach on humanity's inclination to neglect care to those closest to us. When Valerie was expecting her second child, she gave me a call one night, asking, "Dad, tell me that Bible story about Cain and Abel again." "Well, daughter, they were brothers. Cain raised crops and Abel raised livestock. They both took an offering from their chosen livelihood to God who, in turn, favored Abel's offering over Cain's. Cain unjustifiably resented his brother, rose up and attacked him, taking his life. God punished Cain by placing him under a curse for the rest of his life. That's the story dear." *"Darn!"* replied my sainted and pristine schoolteacher daughter. "I take it if it's a boy we are going to have a Cain?" I asked, and we did—Kain John. Loving Papa's garden tractor as much as he does, I can see our little Kain becoming a "row crop" man like the original Cain.

A particular line from this story preaches especially well. God confronted Cain after he had taken his brother's life. "Where is your brother Abel?" God asked of Cain. "I don't know," he replied, "am I my brother's keeper?" (Genesis 4:9). "Am I my brother's keeper?" It's a rhetorical question really, with the inference that, yes we are. We must be.

The world works no other way. Only one person mattered to Cain—Cain. We must be our brother and sister's keeper, whether in the church or out. Our commitment to others' needs before our own will say more to the world about our faith than any pious act of righteousness we might achieve. Jesus said to the Pharisees, "But go and learn what this means, 'I desire mercy, not sacrifice'" (Matthew 9:13). James wrote, "Religion that God our Father accepts as pure and faultless is this: to look after orphans and widows in their distress and to keep oneself from being polluted by the world" (James 1:22). A sign of Pentecost was showing concern to the poor by not harvesting the edges of the fields and leaving the grain they dropped during the harvest for those in need to gather (see Leviticus 19:9–10, 23:22). John wrote, "If anyone has material possessions and sees his brother in need but has no pity on him, how can the love of God be in him?" (1 John 3:17). We are designed and equipped by God to connect and care for each other. If there is a single reason you and I are on the earth, it may be just that. No man or woman is an island. "I am involved in mankind," Donne said. Jacob Marley screamed to Scrooge, "Mankind is my business!" It is more our destiny than any other endeavor we might pursue in this short life. From our point of origin, we are created for one thing—to touch another life. It's just like ripples in a pond.

I have said that death is the great leveler. Perhaps it is also the great communicator. Death speaks. Its unwelcome intrusion forces you to contend with pieces of life previously avoided, suppressed, or still unknown. It forces you to step back and see a bigger picture and a greater story than your own.

A Living Memorial

The memorial money that came in from friends and family following Gabe's death touched us.

- What does one do with such money?

- What ways do you spend it?

- How do you invest this money that morphs it from *death* money to *life* money?

- How do we use it in such a way that it continues to tell Gabe's story and touch lives in the doing?

Near our hometown of Sigourney are two small lakes: *Belva Deer* and *Yenruogis* (Sigourney spelled backwards). Gabe loved them both, but since *Yenruogis* had been there far longer, it held more memories. He and I fished and swam there many times. It was on the shoreline of that little lake where Gabe left this world. *Belva Deer* is a new lake, formed several years ago in the wooded valley that ran through a beautiful county park. Gabe and I were forming fishing memories there also. On more than one occasion, I would take my boat out to the lake in the evening, and when rounding a little fishing jetty, I would find Gabe, standing on a rocky shoreline, casting for bass. I would pick him up and off we'd go, as I was chiding him for not telling me he was going there in the first place. One night we drifted around in front of the shoreline and caught dozens of bass. We laughed out loud over our good fortune, much better than how people in a nearby boat were faring. Fishing was the one place we were more friends than father and son. The spot Gabe usually fished is on the north side of the lake, on a contour of land facing the dam, a beautiful spot. It was on the slope, just above that rocky shore, where we decided to invest Gabe's memorial money. The park needed one more shelter, and we thought it a good place. But this was not to be any ordinary shelter. Gabe was a unique person, and we would build a unique shelter.

After having done considerable research, I ordered a rather large kit to build a gazebo, fashioned by the Amish. It would be big enough to accommodate four large picnic tables and a host of folding chairs. When the tandem trailer arrived from Pennsylvania, my brother helped us unload it. From the beginning, the girls determined this would not be known as a gazebo. This was no backyard barbeque spot. Rather, they dubbed it by a more prestigious moniker: a pavilion. Constructing Gabe's pavilion was a family thing, an intense labor of sweat and tears. Like a jigsaw puzzle or model airplane, it came in lots and lots of pieces. The weekend we erected it, it had rained inches, and the thermometer lingered above 90°. The dew point was smothering. Despite the tropical climate, Vicki and I, our girls and their spouses, all gave it our best collaborative effort. The template was down, the uprights were up, the upper rails in place, but the complicated roof system was a bit beyond our formidable skills and desire. I called Van, a carpenter friend of mine, who came out Saturday with his son Cody.

Those good souls provided the expertise, and, along with my wonderful sons-in-law, the necessary muscles to keep the uprights plumb, the corners square, and the eight-sided roof (finally) in place. Despite the obvious emotional motivation for the project, this was hard work. Our boots were caked with mud and our clothes were soaked in sweat. But the good crew remained undaunted. In the week or ten days that followed, Vicki and I went out early in the morning or late in the evening, when it was cooler, and finished the project. I put on the trim pieces, shingled the roof, and installed the cupola. Finally, I installed a plaque on one of the inner posts. It said

Gabe V. Homan Pavilion
Dedicated September 2007
A Place to Laugh Again

And it felt right. It pleased me to have a place where his friends, our friends, or anybody's friends, could gather to fish, grill, and have a good time in a beautiful spot. And we have done it several times with them all in the years that have followed. I've thought Gabe can still touch lives here. On a perfect Sunday afternoon that September, our family, friends, church members, our support group, and many caregivers gathered to dedicate the pavilion, honor Gabe, and to laugh. Pastor John offered a blessing:

> Most gracious Heavenly Father, we have gathered here in this beautiful world which you have created, by a lake you have helped men to build. We praise you for the opportunity to remember anew the life of Gabe Homan. We have been missing his presence among us terribly, and our hearts have been heavy with grief. Through all of this you have given us strength for each new day and situation. We remember how much he enjoyed your creation and how important family was to him. Now we have come to this pavilion that has been constructed in Gabe's memory. This is a place where families can enjoy one another in the midst of your beautiful world. This is a place where we or anyone else who has been struggling with life issues can come and start to laugh again. Father God, in Jesus' name, I bless this pavilion by the power of the Holy Spirit. I proclaim that the Spirit of the Living God will abide here to touch the hearts and lives of all who come to enjoy the shelter of the pavilion, and the beauty of the scenery. May the healing grace of the Holy Spirit always flow to those who come here and sit in time of need. May all who enjoy this pavilion experience your love, mercy, and grace. I thank you for hearing my prayer and hallowing this place with your eternal presence, in Jesus' name and for his sake. Amen.

We have continued our pilgrimage to this now sacred spot. It has often been the gathering place for our family and friends, and sometimes just me, where I sit and take refuge. I prefer coming here more so than his grave. This is a place of life. Three years ago, while visiting that consecrated spot, granddaughter Lily and I walked down to the water's edge. And there, in the shadow of

Gabe's pavilion, we threw rocks in the water and touched each other's ripples.

A Story of Compassion

Several stories in my pastoral portfolio helped me understand the various stages grief took us through. One helpful story came from American journalist, editor, and writer Fulton Oursler, who told how and why humanity must connect with each other in a piece titled, *A Brother in Distress*.

In this skeptical world miracles still occur, when men act their faith as well as preach it, and love gets a chance to show its power; as in the curious adventure of the famous East Indian missionary, Sadhu Subhar Singh. One afternoon the Far Eastern Christian was climbing a mountain road in Tibet. With him traveled a bronze, a Buddhist monk. The two wayfarers were well aware that a storm was rising and that they must reach a certain monastery before dark or perish in piercing mountain cold. As they hastened forward in the icy wind they passed a precipice from which rose a groaning voice; at the bottom lay a fallen man, badly hurt and unable to move. The Tibetan said: "In my belief, here we see Karma; this is the work of Fate, the effect of a cause. This man's doom is to die here, while I must press on upon my own errand." But the Christian answered: "In my belief, I must go to my brother's aid." So the Tibetan hurried on his way, while Sadhu clambered down the slope, packed the man on his back, and struggled upward again to the darkening road. His body was dripping with perspiration when at last he came in sight of the lights of the monastery. Then he stumbled and nearly fell over an object on the ground, and stood, overwhelmed with pity and amazement. Huddled at his feet lay his Tibetan companion; frozen to death. But Sadhu had escaped the same doom because his hard exercise in carrying an injured brother on his back kept his body warm and saved his life.[60]

The Christian in the story embodied us all. He unwittingly saved his own life by saving his "brother's" life. Each life does touch so many other lives. I have little confidence in karma. Triumphs or misfortunes seem more random and less based on rewards or punishment. As Clint Eastwood rightly said in the movie *Unforgiven*, "Deserve has got nothing to do with it." But God's will partnered with human benevolence can accomplish great things.

Nevertheless, I can only focus forward here, seeing where my ripples go from this place, and whose ripples they touch. I choose to believe my future has more to do with personal choice and God's will than fate. I choose to participate in humanity. I am my brother and sister's keeper. Therefore, my life will continue, one ripple at a time. I may not carry a wounded brother to safety, my ripples may be small, but I will keep them coming. My son's life and death demand it. Gabe's ripples have stopped forming. Where he once threw rocks, the water is still. But the world is better because he did. God doesn't waste ripples, not when they intersect as part of a larger pattern. Gabe touched many other lives. Even if being a son were not enough reason, I would be proud of him for that gift he freely gave.

- However we view life, we are not islands.

- We are here for a purpose beyond our own.

- We are here to connect with each other, serve each other, touch each other—just like ripples in a pond.

Angels are always right: "Each man's life does touch so many other lives. And when he isn't around, he leaves an awful hole, doesn't he?"

CHAPTER 10

RELINQUISHMENT

OPEN

How shall I be open to thee,
O Lord who is forever open to me?
Incessantly I seek to clench with tight fist,
Such joy as thou gavest mine open hand.
Why do I consider thy providence,
A light thing, and of light repute,
Next to the grandeur I imagine?
Why spurn I such grandeur as prayed,
Not my will but thine be done,
Such as taught us to pray,
Hallowed be thy name,
Thy kingdom come:
Thy will be done?
Why be I so tight and constricted,
Why must clay shy back,
From the potter's hand,
Who glorifieth clay better,
Than clay knoweth glory to seek?

Christos Jonathan Seth Hayward[61]

M Y DAUGHTERS ARE ALWAYS ribbing me about having a *favorite* of something. This usually means I have a strong liking for one out of several of a kind. When a movie I like comes on television, I'm apt to say, "This is one of my favorites." "Of course it is, Dad," they chuckle. For the most part, I'm probably guilty as charged. I do, however, have some absolute favorites: *The Beatles, Chevrolets*, the *Cubs*, fishing, *Romans 8, Holy, Holy, Holy*, chicken legs and thighs, *The Quiet Man*, and *John Wayne*. In my pastoral library, I have several books of sermon helps, illustrations, and quotations. I find some more likable and practical than others. They have achieved "favorite" status, and I use them repeatedly to make a point, like an electrician reuses the same trusty pliers.

As some sermons do, certain quotations became intertwined in my grief story, influencing my attitude and frame of mind. One, in particular, seemed to prepare me for the most difficult step yet in the grieving process. Attributed to the great holocaust survivor Corrie Ten Boom, the quotation simply said, "I have learned to hold all things loosely, so God will not have to pry them out of my hands." Another version of the quotation (or perhaps an entirely different piece) likewise said, "Hold loosely to the things of this life, so that if God requires them of you, it will be easy to let them go." Corrie Ten Boom's story had a substantial impact on the shaping of my early adult version of Christianity. At the recommendation of my pastor, I read her classic work, *The Hiding Place*. I was amazed at her courage, love, and sacrifice, as God used her to shield and save his people during the blighted days of Nazi imperialism, gas chambers, and death camps. I thought, *shield and save*; this is what God does best, and God does it through people. How wonderful it would be to be used by God for such a purpose. Nothing could make life more significant. But Corrie spoke of what she knew. Altogether, the Gestapo had arrested about thirty members of her family, imprisoning them in a penitentiary, eventually releasing all but her, her beloved sister Betsie, and her father Casper, who died in the prison. Afterward, officials transferred Corrie and Betsie to a concentration camp where Betsie died.[62]

> Clearly, she had known what it was like to have God pry things from her hands. And now, so had I. Like this marvelous woman, I, too, am learning to hold all things loosely in my hands.

Some years ago, in an attempt to improve on my prospects for the hereafter, I took the pledge against humanity's three great mortal sins: gluttony, greed, and garage sales. But as I often remind myself, "… all have sinned …" (Romans 3:23). And they/we continue to do so. One autumn, I fell completely off the wagon—I had a garage sale. I'm pretty sure this will be it, but I'm learning not to make promises I might not be able to keep. Although, having garage sales is not without merit. It is an intriguing opportunity to observe a certain aspect of this consumer-driven society, and it affords you an opportunity to discover a thing or two

I have held many things in my hands, and have lost them all; but whatever I have placed in God's hands, that I still possess.

–Martin Luther

about yourself. If you measure success by the things that leave your property in the back seats of old Pontiacs and on pickup beds, then by all means, we had a successful garage sale. Only three or four bags of *brick-a-brac* were left for Goodwill.

However, if you measure garage sales in terms of financial net growth, then not so much. With a 25 and 50-cent table, and a free section, one can only make so much. It's pretty hard to attach a dollar figure to a memory, and yet, these things were once treasures. When I carried them out of my house to the garage, I knew I was carrying out a good share of my life. As I spread my inventory on the tables and shelves, I felt a certain sigh. Here were wonderful memories on those tables: wall hangings and decorations, favorite VHSs and cassettes, fishing and camping equipment, cookbooks, music books, old books, shelves and chairs, kid's stuff, old tools and garden stuff, dishes and glasses, leftover wedding decorations and flowers—a lifetime's worth. And it all went for pocket change. A man haggled over a $2 sticker on one of my old fishing poles. I caught a number of good fish on that pole—and I didn't sell it to him. Had he been a little more cordial, I probably would have given him that pole.

Most troubling for me was that we decided to part with a number of Gabe's things. It was time. That didn't mean it wasn't painful. The most difficult sale was his stereo receiver. The piece probably cost $300 or $400, and it played all his favorites—loudly. I sold it to some kid for $30. Gabe took great pride in his stereo, just like his dad once did. A day later I wept over that sale. I desperately wanted that receiver back. But, like Gabe, it was irretrievable. Nevertheless, selling it was the right thing to do. I watched as people pawed over my once-prized possessions, and it occurred to me how little value they all had. I was quickly reminded that nothing material we buy on this earth has any real value. I tell my children not to pay more for any item than the value they will receive by owning it. Don't anticipate a profitable resale. This world is such an illusion.

We enslave ourselves to a system that ultimately finds itself on a 25-cent table after we have borrowed it a short time. Even land isn't ours. We may work it and pay taxes on it for a few seasons, but eventually relinquish it to the next bidder. The only land we end up with is about a 4' x 8' plot. I probably will not have another garage sale. A lifetime of memories leaving the building in exchange for the cost of a couple pizzas is just not that good a deal. But perhaps it is just as well. As Corrie Ten Boom advised, I'm learning to hold all things loosely in my hands. Ultimately we will surrender them all. It is called relinquishment.

Saying Goodbye to Gabe's Green Pickup

Another of Gabe's possessions would hold a far deeper pitfall for me than even his stereo—his pickup. I had helped Gabe find and purchase a dark-green Dodge Dakota Sport, but he paid for it entirely out of his personal resources. Soon after the purchase, he annoyed me by tearing out the factory-installed stereo in favor of some contraption capable of making a belligerent thump with all the accompanying annoyances (and my dad thought *The Beatles* were loud). It made this dad suddenly feel very old and grumpy. Regardless, it enabled us to hear Gabe before we could see him. Gabe's pickup became him, and I quickly began to associate every dark-green pickup with his presence. So when he died, it sat there empty in our west yard, like a shrine, and I didn't have any idea what to do with it. I knew I couldn't drive it, and neither of his sisters wanted to either. I couldn't think of selling it. One grief-filled night we all *kind-of* came up with the idea: we'd give it to his good friend Russell. Russell could certainly benefit from a good pickup. It was easy to come up with the courage to tell Russell we wanted him to have the pickup. It was brutal letting it go, and for a long time, I simply couldn't. Vicki would remind me over and over that we promised it to Russell, and we needed to give it to him, and though it was what I also wanted, I simply could not find the strength.

Then one night in an impassioned and emotionally charged moment, I called Russell and said we were bringing it over. He said we could do it tomorrow, but no, I had to do it immediately. Now that I had made the decision, this was not something I could postpone. I walked down to that green Dakota Sport with tears running down my cheek, unlocked the door, and started the motor. I drove directly to Russell's house, parked the pickup, handed him the keys at the door, and walked away. And I felt I was walking away from one of my few remaining connections to Gabe. Despite the pain of this material separation, I knew this pickup would fare better in another driveway.

After giving up the pickup, I felt somewhat relieved. It was the kind of thing where the anticipation of the event was much worse than the event itself. The only time I struggled was when I saw Russell driving it around town. I couldn't help but think that's Gabe's pickup, *dammit*, and he should be the one driving it. Sometimes I would imagine it was Gabe behind the wheel. Inside I would pretend that none of this hell had happened, and he was just out cruising around.

One day I was heading home from a long day in the church. A skiff of snow had fallen that afternoon, and I was on the cell phone with my brother Larry as I drove into Sigourney from the west. As I looked ahead, I could see the flashing lights of police and emergency equipment. And then I saw it, crumpled up, on the shoulder of the highway, a dark-green Dakota Sport pickup.

"It's Gabe," I screamed to Larry. "He's been in a wreck!"

"What?" Larry responded.

"Gabe, Gabe's been in a wreck," I shouted. "His pickup is just ahead, all smashed up."

"It's not Gabe," Larry answered.

And then I realized, no, it wasn't Gabe. I was amazed at how quickly my worried dad side had reappeared. But Gabe's pickup was now gone. Russell had fishtailed on the slick road and ran directly into an oncoming, larger pickup. Fortunately no one was hurt, but the pickup was totaled. I didn't know how to feel about what had just happened. At first I was angry with Russell for not taking care of Gabe's pickup. But then, I thought there might be some providence and/or mercy here. No longer would I have to see that pickup, and be reminded of Gabe. Now, it was really gone, just like its one-time owner. It was one more thing pried out of our hands.

Christianity's Stained-Glass Words

Jesus knew relinquishment. When I first encountered him in Sunday School, I learned all the stories, but I didn't know what they meant. Words like justification, redemption, repentance, and salvation meant little to me. I called them *stained-glass* words. Regardless, they were finding entrance into my way of looking at the world. We endure many awkward, formative years as we ascend toward emotional and physical maturity. It's clear to me there are formative years in our pilgrimage toward Christianity as well. Perhaps the earlier we are introduced to the Bible's mysteries, the more likely we are to embrace them. Wise Solomon advised, "Remember your Creator in the days of your youth, before the days of trouble come and the years approach when you will say, 'I find no pleasure in them'" (Ecclesiastes 12:1–2). I suspect we give our children a greater gift than we realize when we nudge them toward those first wobbly spiritual steps. Like learning to walk, everybody's got to start somewhere, and I took my first spiritual steps early on.

I've always been prone to a concrete learning pattern. If a teacher told me something was true, it must be true. But even as a boy, I questioned how Jesus the man could also be Jesus the God. The first language I ever heard to explain the incarnation was: *very God* and *very man*. Perhaps it was simply more church stained-glass window talk, but I eventually kind of got it. For God to be flesh meant that Jesus must be all God and all human. As aforementioned, I am by no stretch a theologian or biblical scholar, but I was growing to comply with the image of Jesus as God.

The little Methodist church where I grew up had the famous painting of Jesus by Warner Sallman that was in every Methodist church. Jesus is portrayed with his sandy-brown flowing hair, perfect tan, beautiful features, and penetrating eyes. Entitled the *Head of Christ*, one admirer wrote the following about its meaning to her:

> There is something about Warner Sallman's pictures that makes me feel ... that this artist had felt Christ's presence when he made the images ... and you can feel Christ's presence ... conveyed ... to you through his images. From the image of the head of Christ I can see righteousness, strength, power, reverence, respect, fairness, faithfulness, love, and compassion. From the way the hair in the image is highlighted in the back and highlights around the front of the head and face there seems to be a holy radiance emitted from the image, depicting the qualities mentioned above. (Correspondence file, Sallman Archives, Anderson University)

This is what God looks like, I reasoned. And when I prayed as a child, this was the God to whom I prayed. Perhaps it was a reason I embraced God growing up. This was a trustworthy, handsome God who could do anything. I had absolute confidence in the God who was in that picture of Jesus. Yes, I made the executive decision early on not to have an issue with Jesus being God. In fact, for me, that was the whole point of the story. But it wasn't as easy to accept the idea of God being human. I have always had trouble with that. To think that God would be vulnerable to the same human maladies I am vulnerable to is a much larger step of faith. I have heartburn, high cholesterol, backaches, and sinus drainage. Did God put up with all that? They didn't have statins or acid blockers in Jesus' day. Does God get depressed, mourn, weep, and fear like I do? Isn't this what it is to be fully human? I know one of the reasons the Jews rejected Jesus as the Messiah was because he died on the cross. They apparently couldn't conceive of a God who would volunteer for martyrdom, which has always amazed me, since they had Isaiah's prophetic description of the suffering servant before them. "A man of sorrows and familiar with suffering," Isaiah said of the promised one (Isaiah 53:3).

I know many Pentecostal and full-gospel brethren would consider me a heretic for this, but I don't think God or man can be fully who they are intended without suffering. If that is so, then Jesus, that beautiful Jesus in the picture, must suffer, or he is not God at all. Nowhere is suffering more keenly known and felt than in the Garden of Gethsemane. This lonely place by the Mount of Olives seems the perfect place for the humanity of Jesus to be fully seen, just like a picture on a sanctuary wall. It was in that orchard of olive trees where Jesus taught relinquishment by example. Teacher and historian Ray Vander Laan reveals keen insights into Jesus' visit to the Garden of Gethsemane:

> The word Gethsemane is derived from two Hebrew words: gat, which means "a place for pressing oil (or wine)" and she-manim, which means "oils." During Jesus' time, heavy stone slabs were lowered onto olives that had already been crushed in an olive crusher. Gradually the slab's weight squeezed the olive oil out of the pulp, and the oil ran into a pit. There the oil was collected in clay jars. The image of the gethsemane on the slope of the Mount of Olives where Jesus went the night before his crucifixion provides a vivid picture of Jesus' suffering. The weight of the sins of the world

pressed down upon him like a heavy slab of rock pressed down on olives in their baskets. His sweat, "like drops of blood falling to the ground" (Luke 22:44), flowed from him like olive oil as it was squeezed out and flowed into the pit of an olive press.[63]

Nonetheless, I think what got pressed out of Jesus in the garden wasn't *blood*, but *will*. And that is what ultimately gets pressed out of us. Like Jesus, every person will be pressed by life to the point where they must say, *not my will but thine be done*. When those words come out of Jesus' mouth in Matthew, Mark, and Luke's gospels, it still stuns me, like death. If Jesus was God, how can he say this? Yet, if Jesus was man, how can he say this? Men want their own will to be done. From childhood, we learn to seek our own way. Men are more prone to competition and assertiveness than congeniality and amiability. The Jesus in the picture I learned to trust as a child should get his own way. He shouldn't give up so easily.

Jesus Christ Superstar

Being a child of 60's and 70's pop music, I loved the rock opera, *Jesus Christ Superstar*. This is probably a sad commentary on my formative years and may speak disparagingly regarding my formal education, but there was a time I had every word of that rock opera dedicated to memory. For this middle-of-the-road fellow, any hybrid of Bible and rock n' roll seemed a great idea. It appeared to give new life and great passion to this *passion play*. My favorite piece of the opera came near the end and was simply entitled, *Gethsemane*. It felt inspired, and at that point in my life, I thought Tim Rice might have captured the moment better than the gospel writers. I still am moved when I hear those last lines:

God, Thy will is hard,
But you hold every card;
I will drink your cup of poison,
Nail me to your cross and break me,
Bleed me, beat me, kill me, take me now …

Before I change my mind.[64]

Much to my delight, I recently stumbled across that wonderful old CD in a music store and have listened to it many times since. I suspect I have re-dedicated it to memory, as much as my nearly six decade-old memories will allow. And every time I hear those lines, I am troubled. The incarnation mystery revisits me.

- Could God really be a human?

- What kind of bargain was struck in heaven that required this?

- Did Jesus have an option?

- Could he have changed his mind at the last moment?

- Did he have to drink that awful cup?

The human side of him wanted out. The God side held life loosely in his hand. "Father, if you are willing, take this cup from me; yet not my will but yours be done," he prayed (Luke 22:42). But God wasn't willing.

Something about this fallen world needed Jesus' death on a cross. Now standing in the shadow of my son's death, I feel a kinship with the man who whispered these words in a place where heavy slabs of stone were lowered onto olives already crushed, and crushed them further. I did not have an option in my Gethsemane, and perhaps Jesus didn't either. I could have prayed "not my will" for anything, but not about my children. True, I'm the overprotective dad. Concerning them, Mom and Dad are the ones who love them most, and know what's best for them. They are indeed more precious than life to me. I used to say I would take a bullet for them or their mother in a heartbeat, and I meant it. What manner of prayer could relinquish the fate of my children to another caretaker? Yet, if there is no choice to be made, if it is already laid out like an itinerary, then it is our only prayer. I wish I knew. As I grow older, and more and more people I know and love pass over to the other side, I am becoming persuaded that this is the epicenter of Christian faith, "not my will but thine." Relinquishment. But it's so hard.

My "God Moments"

I have had a few epiphanies in my life, which I call *God moments*. If God could talk to Moses through a burning bush, then I reasoned God could surely talk to a self-respecting Methodist. Nearly thirty years ago I had two God moments in close succession. I now think they were partly in preparation for my loss. The first one happened over my lunch hour one ordinary day. I was probably more disciplined in daily devotions back then, and often used my noon times for them. One particular day I had been praying when I had a strange sense of being lost. Not spiritually lost, rather lost in the sea of humanity as a drop of water would be lost if dropped into a great ocean. It was a weird feeling, not really supernatural, as if I had a great vision, but more like a sense of foreboding. I felt so small, and wondered if God ever noticed me, if my prayers went higher than the ceiling. I breathed out these words, "God, I need to know that you see me and know me, and that no matter whatever happens, you won't forget me. I can handle anything as long as I know you won't forget me."

I went to get my guitar to work out some feelings. I lifted up the piano bench to retrieve a songbook I had been using. Lying there on the songbook was a bookmark—just a bookmark. As I picked it up to move it, I was stunned. At the top of the bookmark was the image of a child's face engraved in the palm of a huge hand that was reaching down. Below was a scripture: "Can a mother forget the baby at her breast and have no compassion on the child she has borne? Though she may forget, I will not forget you! See, I have engraved you on the palms of my hands ..." (Isaiah 49:15–16a). Instantly, I believed God had spoken to me. Vicki worked at the Sigourney hospital back then. Having never seen that bookmark before, I ran to the phone and called her at work. "Where did you get that bookmark?" I demanded. It turned out she had never seen it before either. Yet it was there, right on a book I often used, and it said exactly what my heart hungered to hear. Moses at the burning bush had no greater encounter with God than I did at that moment. There are times in our lives where we need to be reminded that God has not forgotten us. My son's death was that time for me.

It was later, the same summer, when my second God moment occurred. That summer I first came into contact with Catherine Marshall's *Prayer of Relinquishment*. I don't recall the exact details of how I came to acquire the prayer like I do with the bookmark. I found it nonetheless. It was on a 3 x 5 index card hidden by the Spirit somewhere in my house, waiting for the day God would reveal it to me. I knew the first time I read this prayer that it was given to me for a reason. I read it carefully, line by line, again and again. I anticipated a day when this prayer would be mine, not by authorship or right, but by experience. I dreaded the possibility, knowing that a prayer of relinquishment would matter only if something had been taken away from me—something precious. And I had precious things: Vicki, Gabe, Valerie, and Tiffany. I couldn't bear the thought of losing any of them. I would happily take God's (or fate's) intervention to prevent a time when I would need such a prayer. But the time came nevertheless, and nothing seemed powerful enough to prevent it. The day I fearfully anticipated finally arrived on June 18, 2005. On that day my fingers were pried open, and I reluctantly relinquished something precious out of my hand. The prayer was prophetic:

THE PRAYER OF RELINQUISHMENT

Father, I have pleaded before You,
This deep desire of my heart—
Yet, the more I've clamored for Your help,
The more remote You have seemed.
I want to trust You, Father,
My spirit knows that even when I feel nothing,
That You are here,
That You love me,
That You alone know what is best for me.
Perhaps You have been waiting,
For me to give up self-effort.
So now, by an act of my will,

> I relinquish this to You.
> I will accept Your will—whatever that may be.
> To You, Lord God,
> Who alone are worthy of worship,
> I bend to the knee with Thanksgiving,
> That this, too, will
> Work together for my good.
> Amen.

I had prayed for Gabe for years. He struggled more growing up than the girls did, but that wasn't the real reason for my prayers. Perhaps it was that I worried about him more; perhaps it was because he was a bit of a rebel; perhaps it was something much deeper. But I wore out the knees in several pairs of pants praying for him. I suspect it is part of the reason prayer became such a chore for me in later years. Regardless, I prayed fervently for my children, and somehow, especially for Gabe. Still, the more I clamored for God's help, the more remote God seemed—just like with Catherine Marshall.

I had to know more about the woman who wrote this prayer that seemed crafted just for me. I began reading several articles about her life and voluminous professional work. I learned that while in college she met and married Peter Marshall, the same Peter Marshall who would become U. S. Senate Chaplain. When Peter took the pastorate at the New York Presbyterian Church, Catherine was only 23. Four years later their only son, Peter Jon was born. At the height of their ministry, Catherine was diagnosed with tuberculosis. For three years, she fought depression and isolation. Despite prayer and faith, monthly chest x-rays showed no improvement. Her journal became her spiritual solace where she recorded her daily talks with God and the hope God provided. This is what she wrote:

> Only one way was left. Perhaps I had held back one heart's desire. So after many days of struggling, I handed over to God every last vestige of self-will, even my intense desire for complete health. Finally I was able to pray, "Lord, I understand no part of this, but if You want me to be an invalid for the rest of my life—well, it's up to You. I place myself in Your hands, for better or worse. I ask only to serve You."[65]

Catherine would ultimately recover from her illness, but tuberculosis would not be the only thing she would have to relinquish into God's hands. In 1949, with their son Peter Jon only nine years old, her husband died suddenly. "'Surely goodness and mercy shall follow you all the days of your life,' was His (God's) personal pledge to me and to a son who would now sorely miss his father," Marshall wrote.[66] As with Corrie Ten Boom (and with me), Catherine Marshall learned to hold all things loosely in her hands. She learned relinquishment. But it was more than that; she learned to pray relinquishment. Perhaps it is the only authentic prayer for one to whom relinquishment had already forced its life lessons. I have likewise learned to pray relinquishment because of her.

In the years that have passed since Gabe died, I have read that prayer multiple times, more in a literary sense than a devotional one. I have poured over the lines, wondering how they might have prepared me for the day our son died. As with Jesus in the Garden, there was a crushing of self-will here, and a relinquishment to another's will. There was a resignation that this, somehow, will work out for good. I still do not understand that line. Romans said the same thing, "And we know that in all things God works for the good of those who love him, who have been called according to his purpose" (Romans 8:28). All things, I ask? I have no idea what the writer to Romans meant. Peter wrote, "So then, those who suffer according to God's will should commit themselves to their faithful creator and continue to do good" (1 Peter 4:19).

Lessons in Letting Go

I have spent the duration of my years of grief pondering the possibility: can good come out of great sorrow or tragedy? Regardless, I am coming to grips with an ultimate truth that does arrive. There is relinquishment. Of course, it is an easy thing to relinquish something already taken from you. But to pray in such a manner for things you still hold in your hands, even precious things—is that possible? Or is it still a matter of more continuing education. Both my pastoral and electrical careers require yearly continuing education. I sit through those twenty hours of Power

Point and lecture and leave wondering if I am now more educated than when I walked in the door. I have always felt this was probably more a statement of my ability to focus than on the instructor's ability to instruct. Nevertheless, there are more important moments in life where we must focus on the instructor. I do not want to repeat this lesson.

Rev. Henry Lyte was a Scottish pastor of a parish church among lowly fishing people at Lower Brixham, Devonshire, England for 23 years. Despite physical frailties, he had a strong faith, and was a tireless worker with a reputation as a writer, poet, musician, and an excellent preacher. He coined the phrase, "It is better to wear out than rust out." Rev. Lyte was beloved by his parishioners, but his failing health was forcing him to give up his parish and the work he loved.[67] A few months before his death, he rallied to preach one final sermon and to celebrate one last Holy Communion. The date was September 4, 1847. On the evening of that day, he walked out to the cliffs overlooking the sea at the end of his garden. There the setting sun reminded him of the words of Cleopas and his companion to Jesus on the road to Emmaus, "Abide with us, for it is toward evening, the day is far spent ..." they said (see Luke 24:13–35). And in less than an hour, he had written the beloved hymn, *Abide With Me*.[68]

That comforting hymn had an unexpected impact on me recently. A random selection, we were singing it at the nursing home during my monthly communion service there. This first Friday ritual started innocently while suggesting to the resident United Methodists that we take communion together. It seemed a proper thing to do. But each month the congregants grew, finally moving us out into the dining room. Now it has become a full-blown church service, and it gives me great joy. Nonetheless, we were singing this great hymn, and as the verses began to unfold there seemed to come to me a voice of the Spirit—certainly another *God-moment*. Yes, I've had moments before when it seemed that God's very presence filled a room. For me, that day was one of those mystical moments. Surely, Lyte felt such when he wrote those words:

Abide with me; fast falls the eventide;
The darkness deepens; Lord, with me abide.
When other helpers fail and comforts flee,
Help of the helpless, O abide with me.

I decided to look longer, deeper, into these words penned from a good man in relinquishment's conservatory. I suspect many of us have known those dark times, when helpers fail and comforts flee. It is a terrible feeling of aloneness and helplessness. Every single person who lives will know a time when he or she loses power and control. It is in those hours when we, too, long for Jesus to abide with us. The word has a connotation of dwelling or staying with. When the darkness closes in, and we may feel abandoned by all, Jesus will stay. And yet, it's a stronger word than that. He will dwell with you. In passing the staff of leadership to Joshua, Moses assured him, "The Lord himself goes before you and will be with you; he will never leave you nor forsake you" (Deuteronomy 31:8a). I once offered that text to a woman who asked her abusive husband to move out. Pause a minute from your busy life and ponder those words, "He will never leave you nor forsake you." Matthew ended his gospel with these words of Jesus to his disciples, "I am with you always, to the very end of the age" (Matthew 28:20b). Are words like these even possible to believe or embrace without a relinquished heart?

I need thy presence every passing hour.
What but thy grace can foil the tempter's power?
Who, like thyself, my guide and stay can be?
Through cloud and sunshine, Lord, abide with me.

Perhaps, the deepest level of human poverty is the loss of awareness of our need for God. It is something that has found a separate place in our collective consciousness, becoming increasingly impotent and irrelevant to our lives. I sometimes think that difficulties and sorrows are a gift because they resurrect a moment-by-moment awareness of God. Suddenly we awake to the fact that ultimately we are dependent upon and accountable to our creator. As my seasons of grief unfolded, it became clear that I would not survive alone. I needed someone. And the question has been: could I trust God to be that someone? "I need thy presence every passing hour," wrote Lyte. Illness and loss remind us of that, and so does loneliness or addiction or a hundred other maladies. Israel often sought the Lord during times of famine, captivity, or defeat. Sister Wendy Beckett wrote, "If your life is difficult, it could well be that you are more open to God than someone like me whose life has been so sheltered."[69] If I could warn the church to be alert for one deceptive sin, it would be this: beware of losing your daily awareness of and dependence upon the Savior of your souls. When you do, you become defenseless against this world. Acquisitiveness will not teach you that. Relinquishment will!

> I fear no foe, with thee at hand to bless;
> Ills have no weight, and tears no bitterness.
> Where is death's sting? Where, grave, thy victory?
> I triumph still, if thou abide with me.

Here is where the hymn becomes too marvelous and yet troubling to me, for I have known death's terrible sting. The grave seems still to be gloating with its loathsome victory. Death seems incredibly final and cruel. Yet, Lyte sings of triumph, if thou abide with me. My human experience continues to challenge such a radical concept, but a still small voice persists in speaking of victory. It is that voice that can build into a triumphant crescendo if we dare utter it. It is a voice of relinquishment.

Dr. Arthur John Gossip preached a sermon several years ago entitled, "When Life Tumbles In, What Then?" He preached it the day after his beloved wife had suddenly died. He closed his message with these remarkable words:

> I don't think you need to be afraid of life. Our hearts are very frail, and there are places where the road is very steep and lonely, but we have a wonderful God. And as Paul puts it, "What can separate us from His love? Not death," he writes immediately. No, not death, for standing in the roaring Jordan, cold with its dreadful chill and, conscious

of its terror, of its rushing, I too, like Hopeful in *Pilgrim's Progress*, can call back to you who one day in your turn will have to cross it, "Be of good cheer, my brother, for I feel the bottom and it is sound."[70]

"I triumph still, if thou abide with me," wrote Lyte. Absolute relinquishment. It's amazing.

> Hold thou thy cross before my closing eyes;
> Shine through the gloom and point me to the skies.
> Heaven's morning breaks,
> And earth's vain shadows flee;
> In life, in death, O Lord, abide with me.

Relinquishment and Dying Well

Every time Holy Week rolls around, I find myself attracted again to the story of the penitent thief, crucified alongside Jesus (see Luke 23:32, 39–43). Though scripture and church tradition regard this man as a *ne'er-do-well*, his life remains something of a mystery. Some legends suggest he was something of a Judaean Robin Hood who robbed from the rich and gave to the poor. What I do know is he was fully human, like me. He lived an imperfect life with some regret, and now he found himself nailed to a cross. But this man also lived his life with an eye upward. He somehow believed there was something more. And in his honest petition, *Jesus, remember me,* he found it. Earth's vain shadows gave way to Jesus' promise of paradise.

The founder of Methodism, John Wesley, once wrote that he wanted Methodists to die well. I think I grew up believing religious people did that routinely, like Enoch who went out for a walk with God and was no more, for God took him (see Genesis 5:24). But in truth, we are all human, and like holding on to what we know. I certainly do. So we ask: Will our faith really hold us up? Is there an abiding peace? The apostle Paul thought so. "Whether we live or die, we belong to the Lord," he wrote (Romans 14:8). And Rev. Lyte thought so. The final words of his last sermon were, "My desire is to induce you to prepare for the solemn hour which must come to all by a timely appreciation and dependence on the death of Christ."[71] He could have simply said, "Let me introduce you to relinquishment." What an abstract concept: dwelling on the solemnity of Christ's death brings tranquility to our lives. It is a peace found by thieves on crosses, by apostles and poets, and by folks like you and me— relinquishment to the sovereignty of a God we rarely understand.

> Relinquishment to the authority of God comes only when
> we loosen our grip on the things we have grasped so firmly.
> It is the great letting go that comes to us all, yet some more
> reluctantly than others.

I have wanted this book to be as real and honest as I was capable of expressing myself. Parental grief is a brutal foe. We often become a different person; even to the point of thinking we are losing our minds. I have tried to be completely open with my own experience so that perhaps one bereaved person will read this and not feel so alone, nor think he or she is going crazy. Perhaps someone who provides care and counsel to a bereaved parent will have a bit more empathy and understanding.

But as I have said, I am also a person of faith, deep, and personal. For much of my Christian formation I was under the illusion that authentic, victorious Christian living and profound grief and suffering were mutually exclusive ideals. I certainly no longer think so. In fact, for me, growing in one experience leads to growing in the other. Nothing about my journey would have been by my own choosing. But it is my journey, nonetheless. This past Advent I preached a series of sermons on the four candles of the Advent wreath: hope, peace, joy, and love. The sermon on peace consisted of four inspired points: we must have peace with our past, peace with our future, peace with our neighbor, and peace with our creator. Peace with my past is the hardest for me. I was preaching in theory only because for all my contemplative journaling, group therapy, and soul angst, I am still bewildered and beguiled by what has befallen our family. So the image of simultaneously living in grief and hope has comforted me.

This Father Is Two Things

As Jesus was two things: *very God and very man*, so I am two things: *very grieved and very hopeful*. I have a foot in two worlds. And I have relinquished myself to that very present reality. Both worlds are unfinished works. In the years to come, as grief and hope continue to cement their relationship with me, my formation will continue. The clay is still in the hands of the potter, and I am at peace with that.

One final place where trouble lingered for me though, was in the perceived breaking of a promise by God. This I still could not relinquish. I had a *bone to pick* with God, and I would not relax my grip on it. Before Gabe died, I had spent about one year in the book of Isaiah. Verse by verse, I would listen to what the prophet (or prophets) might be saying. Often, I felt akin to the Ethiopian eunuch when asked by Philip, "Do you understand what you are reading?" And like the eunuch, I too would reply, "Well, how could I, unless someone guides me?" (Acts 8:30–31). Sometimes I have felt particular scriptures might mystically be isolated and applicable to my life scenario. That was the case on the final day I spent with the book of Isaiah.

As I have said, my prayer life was fifty percent Gabe and fifty percent everybody and everything else. I don't know why. But I always had an inherent fear for him. When having a driver's license brought him some independence, he would go fishing all over the county, by himself. I gave him a fatherly order: you can go to ponds by yourself, but when you are walking the riverbank, take a buddy. Of course, this went in one ear and out the other. Many times he would go fishing, and darkness would fall before he got home. Worried Dad would run out to the river looking for him. If that boy only knew how much I fretted over him in those years. But with the final words of Isaiah before me, I had prayed that morning that God would protect and watch over Gabe, as I had a thousand other times. And then my eyes fell on the 22nd verse of the 66th chapter, the third from the last verse in this mammoth book. It was as if God wrote it in response to my many prayers: "'For just as the new heavens and the new earth which I make will endure before Me,' declares the Lord, 'So your offspring and your name will endure.'" The date was June 6, 1995. I wrote this down in the margin of Isaiah's final chapter. I absolutely knew this was a promise from the Holy One to me that Gabe would live. He carried my name. He had to live or God would be a liar. That is how I saw it. And the promise gave me peace.

Two days later, June 8, I was prayerfully re-reading this verse. Perhaps it was my own longings or perhaps it was the voice of the Spirit, but in a God-moment, I heard words in my inner-soul that I immediately wrote down in my Bible: "My hand of blessing shall be upon Gabe, and I shall not forsake him, neither by day or by night." While it may have been my own subconscious longing, I felt this was God's own word to me concerning my greatest fear. I was ever more convinced God would watch over Gabe, and he would live, prosper, and have children. I was utterly convinced of this promised outcome. When Gabe died, part of my disbelief was that God seemed like a liar. I wondered if I might have misread much of my spiritual savvy and perceptiveness. I began to question everything, and doubt even more. Could such a sacred bond as this be so summarily dismissed? If so, then what hope is there for further promise; further assurance. This breach of contractual authority and trust with heaven was beyond my ability to understand. It was un-relinquished. I was the man after God's own heart. God and I were friends. And I built a wall, separating myself from God.

I include these intimate and private stories to reveal how serious I took my faith, and my profound trust in God and prayer. Gabe's death diminished all those things and placed my relationship with God in peril. But I recognize the walls around this shattered reality will eventually tumble because time will require it. Repeated visits to the 22nd verse revealed to me that the *new heavens and the new earth* will likewise endure; they just aren't here—yet. And I am coming again to believe that my name and offspring yet will endure, for the promise just hasn't been fulfilled—yet.

Peace with our past must and will again be found. It will persistently knock until we open the door to it. We cannot change what has been, so we embrace it for what it was and look to what will

be. Part of what will bring those walls down is the growing embrace
of hope that Gabe endures, just not here. And a day of completion,
of fruition, is coming. Like Jericho, there will be a crumbling of the
walls of separation. And part of what will help bring the walls down
is the growing number of miracles that have come into my life since
Gabe died, among them, my grandchildren:

Lillian Gabriel-Homan Polniak

Kain John-Homan Polniak

Graham Homan King

Sutton Vincent-Homan Polniak

God told me my name and my offspring would endure. Perhaps they
are, just not in the way I would have dreamt or chosen. But my mom
was right, "My grandchildren are my children." I treasure them
more than I will ever find words to tell them. God has used them to
place some sense of purpose and order back in my life.

I saved a story to close this book that seems to comprise my
understanding of life now. And yes, it's one of my favorites:

> From ancient Greece comes the story of a woman who died
> and arrived at the River Styx to be ferried to the realm of
> departed spirits. Charon, the ferryman, told the woman
> that she was permitted to drink of the waters of Lethe if
> she wanted to forget the life she had just left. "Of course,"
> added Charon, "you would then forget past joys as well as
> past sorrows."
>
> "Then I would forget all I have suffered," said the woman.
>
> "And your many occasions of rejoicing," reminded Charon.
>
> "But my failures—I'd forget them too," continued the
> woman.
>
> "And also your triumphs," said Charon.
>
> "And the times I have borne people's hatred," added the

woman.

"True," said Charon, "but you also forget how you have been loved."

The woman stopped to weigh the whole question, and finally decided not to sip of the waters of Lethe; it was not worth being rid of the memory of life's sorrows and failures, if one must at the same time lose the memory of life's happiness and love.[72]

I suspect every human life has known both the good and bad, or we have not known what it is to be fully human. In my great letting go, I am not prepared to relinquish the memories of my happiness and love, even if it meant I could forget how much I have suffered and sorrowed. But I would not relinquish them either, only some of their bitter intrusions. I am convinced that our lives need both, with the melancholic sweetness they bring.

> I am surrendered to the life I now live. It is a life lived in two worlds, contrasting worlds: doubt and faith; grief and redemption; pain and purpose; bitterness and transformation; self and significance; regret and contrition—
> hope and sorrow.

And I am relinquished to the outcome of the process. I am still learning to yield my pain, my bitterness, my many regrets, and my sorrow. I never dreamed I would lose a child to death. That kind of thing happens to other families. But no, it doesn't. It happened to my family. Our son is dead. So I must leave him now in the hands of the One who loves him unconditionally and completely, like a Father, like I loved him.

The day Gabe died, the day before Father's Day, he left me an unopened Father's Day card in the kitchen, addressed *To Daddy— from Son*. He hadn't called me Daddy since his childhood. I have since thought it strange that he left a Father's Day card the day before Father's Day, as if maybe he knew he wouldn't be there that day. I have never been able to open that card. I will someday, but for now it is safely tucked away in my dresser drawer where important things are kept. I have been asked why I haven't read it yet. Perhaps the reason lies somewhere between the fact that this is the last I will hear from him (until that final day), and the fact that I am still in deep grief, and I am not ready.

Regardless, life beckons me now to move forward. So I lift one foot up to higher ground—to hope. But I leave one foot in human mire—in grief. I have a foot in two worlds, and I am resolved to that. The part of me in grief I will leave much like Gabe's unopened Father's Day card, tucked away in a safe place to be opened another day, when I am ready. The part of me that rises to hope turns my face to the future: my wife, my children, my grandchildren, my purpose in this world, and my place in the next. It is a new creation, and I am a different man. And regardless of my past or my future, I will keep my face turned to my God, who loaned me a son for a season while teaching me to pray, "Thy Kingdom come, thy will be done, in my life, just as it is in heaven." It's the only thing a relinquished soul can do.

CONCLUSION

THE TRIP IS BRIEF—
ENJOY IT

Destiny

I remember the morning,
Early fall, I recall.
They say miracles are precious and rare.
Is it so? I don't know.
Dare I ev'n hope?
But a miracle came to me;
Rather was giv'n to see.
I wasn't in the room
When the wonder occurred,
Yet it came—just the same.
She was beautiful in bloom and birth.
Then I wept and I slept.
But this was no dream.
A life was given unto us—unto us.
What part of me could be so entrusted,
With such a gift—such a gift?
If treasure can be placed in earthen vessels,
Then I see it could be me.
This could be my appointed destiny.
Can the gift be diminished by the steward?
Then what cost? Is it lost?
A cherished miracle ceasing to be?
But he walked, and he talked.
Yet, like vapor or dew, he was quickly gone.
Life; how tender and fragile the gift.
The clay returns to the potter much too soon.

Vincent D. Homan

Wisdom guru, Criswell Freeman wrote, "A good fishing trip, like a well-cooked meal or a well-lived life, always ends a little too soon." Like the Roman poet Horace knew, a good fisherman likewise knows the value of the day. Horace wrote, *Carpe diem, quam minimum credulity poster!* Meaning: *Seize the day, put no trust in tomorrow!*[73] My son and I were fishermen, and fishermen know one golden rule about the craft: the best day to go fishing is the day you can. It is the day that matters most, and days are fragile and fleeting. Every time you go, something changes: the water level, the barometric pressure, water clarity, movement of a stream, the fish's aggressiveness, or nature itself. As with the angler, everything about fishing is always in a state of flux. Much can be observed about the rites of life by watching what happens when you park an old pickup by a small farm pond over the course of a summer, as we often did. Ponds go through their change, and so do boys. Freeman quotes the philosopher Albert Camus who wrote, "Real generosity toward the future lies in giving all to the present."[74] So it is that the day you can go is the day that matters most. And we went—again and again. But summer is short, and so can life be, so let us savor every moment.

I found myself sitting in my boat one night, as the day turned into dusk. Enough fish were in the live well for a meal, and plenty were returned to the water to fight another day. Still, I lingered, not wanting the trip to end. The water sparkled in the twilight, frogs were beginning their evening serenade, ducks were coming and going, the birds were filling the air with their resonant sounds, fish were starting to feed on top—ah, all seemed right with the world. But the trip did end, the boat went back into the shed, tackle box back into the cabinet, and I went back to *civilization*, a savored moment indeed.

While the world toils and struggles in its quest for a better tomorrow, it sometimes misses a perfect today. The Hebrew sage

255

wrote, "Do not boast about tomorrow, for you do not know what a day may bring forth" (Proverbs 27:1). Life's untidy, and uncertain realities are no cause for ambition or idleness. Rather, they are a reason for savoring and seizing moments, recognition of our complete dependence on an unseen faith, and awareness that we are vulnerable in this world. Since the loss of son Gabe, my life has been a pilgrimage toward that trinity of truth.

"What is your life?" wrote the apostle James. "You are a mist that appears for a little while and then vanishes" (James 4:14b). Yet I am convinced this world is a wonderful place, and offers us more promises and possibilities than we expect, but tomorrow is not one of them. So we make the most out of this day. Savor it and use it for good; it is irreplaceable. And trust tomorrow to God. Angling author, Sparse Grey Hackle (Alfred W. Miller, 1892–1983) wrote, "The trout do not rise in the cemetery, so you better do your fishing while you are still able."[75] Indeed, the trip is brief, so let us treasure the moments that make up our lives. Like people, each moment matters.

Endnotes

1. Into the Storm

1. Brook Noel and Pamela D. Blair, *I Wasn't Ready to Say Goodbye* (Milwaukee: Champion Press, LTD., 2000), 120.
2. Ibid. 120.
3. Douglas R. Hare, ed., *Interpretation, A Bible Commentary for Teaching and Preaching, Matthew* (Louisville: John Knox Press, 1993), 169.

2. Grief and Redemption

4. Robert Browning, *O Never Star,* Yahoo! Voices.com, http:// voices. yahoo. com/o-never-star-poem-hope-8297777. html?cat=42.
5. Bereaved Parents of the U.S.A., http://www. bereavedparentsusa. org/BP_NewlyBer. Htm.
6. Perry H. Biddle Jr., ed., *Abingdon Funeral Manual* (Nashville: Abingdon Press, 1990), 98.
7. Ralph W. Sockman, *The Meaning of Suffering* (New York, N.Y.: Woman's Division of Christian Service, Board of Missions, The Methodist Church, 1961), 104.
8. Maxie Dunnam, as quoted in *The Workbook on Coping as Christians* (Nashville: Upper Room Books, 1988), 99.
9. Carol Luebering, as quoted in *Coping With Loss* (Cincinnati, Ohio: St. Anthony Messenger Press, 1989), 30.
10. Gordon S. Jackson, ed., *Quotes For The Journey, Wisdom For The Way* (Colorado Springs, Co.: NavPress, 2000), 171.

3. Pain and Purpose

11. Khalil Gibran, *On Pain*, PoemHunter.com, http://www. poemhunter.com/poem/on-pain/.
12. David Van Beima, "Mother Teresa's Crisis of Faith," *Time* (Aug. 23, 2007): 3, http://www. time. com/time/magazine/ article/0,9171,1655720,00. html#ixzz20FLJJQlU.
13. Ibid. 1.
14. Jerry Sittser, *A Grace Disguised* (Grand Rapids, Michigan: Zondervan, 1995), 43.
15. Ibid. 36.
16. Jeanne Guyon, *Experiencing the Depths of Jesus Christ* (Goleta, California: Christian Books, 1981), 38, 39.
17. Nicholas Wolterstorff, *Lament For A Son* (Grand Rapids, Michigan: Wm. B. Eerdmans Publishing Co., 1996), 96.
18. Chaim Potok, *The Chosen*, http://potok.lasierra.edu/Potok. chosen.quo.html.

4. Bitterness—The Paralyzing Sting of Loss

19. John Bowring, *The Heart Knoweth Its Own Bitterness*, PoemHunter.com, http://www. poemhunter. com/poem/ the-heart-knoweth-its-own-bitterness/.
20. Abraham Lincoln, goodreads.com, http://www. goodreads.com/quotes/141073-in-this-sad-world-of-ours-sorrow-comes-to-all.
21. Dr. Catherine M. Sanders, as quoted by Drs. Brook Noel and Pamela D. Blair, Brook Noel and Pamela D. Blair, *I Wasn't Ready to Say Goodbye* (Milwaukee: Champion Press, LTD. 2000), 120.
22. Ann Hood, Comfort, *A Journey Through Grief* (New York, N. Y.: W. W. Norton, 2008).
23. "There Is a Balm in Gilead,"*The United Methodist Hymnal* (United States of America: The United Methodist Publishing House, 1993), 375.
24. Howard Clinebell, *Basic Types of Pastoral Care & Counseling* (Nashville: Abingdon Press, 1984), 221, 222.

25. Albert Camus, Thinkexist.com, http://thinkexist.com/quotation/in_the_midst_of_winter-i_finally_learned_that/12613.html.

26. Bob Deits, *Life After Loss* (United States of America: Fisher Books, 2000), 138.

5: His Eye Is on the Sparrow

27. Erma Bombeck, as quoted in *Illustrations Unlimited*, James S. Hewett, ed., (Wheaton, Illinois: Tyndale House Publishers, 1988) 380.

28. Deitrich Bonhoeffer, Letter from Tegel prison 16 July, 1944, http://www.inwardoutward.org/author/dietrich-bonhoeffer.

29. Lyrics, Millard, "I Can Only Imagine." *All that is Within Me*, CD (Nashville: Simpleville Music, 2001).

30. Lyrics, Martin, "His Eye Is on the Sparrow," 1905, Http://nethymnal. org/js/ads1. Htm.

31. Ralph Sockman, as quoted in *The Meaning of Suffering* (New York, Woman's Division of Christian Service Board of Missions, The Methodist Church, 1961), 133.

32. Ibid. 132-133.

33. Lyrics, Green, "When the Church of Jesus," *The United Methodist Hymnal*, (United States of America: The United Methodist Publishing House, 1993), 592.

6: In Search of Significance

34. Henry Van Dyke, *Life*, PoemHunter.com., http://www.poemhunter.com/poem/life-10/.

35. Rick Warren, *The Purpose Driven Life* (Zondervan: Grand Rapids, 2002), 17.

36. Stephen D. Bryant, ed., *The Upper Room Daily Devotional Guide*, September-October 2003 (The Upper Room Inc.: Nashville, 2003), 11.

37. Edward Everett Hale, *I am only one*, Wikiquote.org, http://en. wikiquote.org/wiki /Edward_ Everett_Hale.

38. Helen Keller, *I am only one,* Thinkexist.com, http://thinkexist.com/quotation/i_am_only_one-but_still_i_am_one-i_cannot_do/10674. html.

39. Mitch Albom, goodreads.com, http://www.goodreads.com/quotes/133061-the-way-you-get-meaning-into-your-life-is-to.

40. Henri Nouwen, *The Way of the Heart* (Ballentine Books: New York, 1981), 25.

41. Donald Miller, *Searching For God Knows What* (Nelson Books: Nashville, Tennessee, 2004), 92.

42. Kirk McNeill and Robert Paul, *Reaching for the Baby Boomers* (Nashville: The General Board of Discipleship, 1989), 21.

43. Ernest Hemingway, BrainyQuote.com, http://www.brainyquote.com/quotes/quotes/e/ernesthemi131095. Html.

44. Kirk McNeill and Robert Paul, *Reaching for the Baby Boomers* (Nashville: The General Board of Discipleship, 1989), 22.

45. James S. Hewett, ed., *Illustrations Unlimited* (Wheaton: Tyndale House Publishers, Inc, 1988), 470.

46. Attributed to Bessie A. Stanley, *What is Success?,* The Ralph Waldo Emerson Society, http://emerson.tamu.edu/Ephemera/Success.html.

7: Regret and Contrition

47. Frederick Buechner, *Wishful Thinking* (San Francisco: HarperSanFrancisco, 1973), 34, 35.

48. Sister Wendy Beckett, *Sister Wendy on Prayer* (New York: Harmony Books, 2006), 22-24.

49. Ibid. 105.

50. Ibid. 105.

8: Hope—A Mourner's Manifesto

51. N.T. Wright, *Surprised by Hope* (New York: HarperOne, 2008), 16.

52. Ibid. 7.

53. Susan Salisbury, "Tragedy inspires search for 'Faces of Hope,' book Obama mentioned at Arizona memorial," *Palm Beach Post*, January, 13, 2011, 2, Http://www. palmbeachpost. com/money/tragedy-inspires-search-for-faces-of-hope-book-118426.

54. N.T. Wright, *Surprised by Hope* (New York: HarperOne, 2008), 190.

55. *Signs*. Dir. M. Night Shyamalan. Perfs. Mel Gibson and Joaquin Phoenix. 2002. DVD. Touchtone, 2003.

56. Phillip Eichman, *What Does The Bible Teach About The Resurrection*, http://www.doesgodexist.org/JanFeb11/Bible.Teach.Resurretion.html.

57. N.T. Wright, *Surprised by Hope* (New York: HarperOne, 2008),

9: Ripples in the Pond

58. *The Andy Griffith Show*. Opie's Ill-gotten Gain (Episode 103). Nov. 18, 1963. Pro. Aaron Ruben. Dir. Jeffrey Hayden. Perfs. Andy Griffith, Don Knotts, Frances Bavier, Ron Howard, and Aneta Corsaut. Wri. John Whedon. DVD. Paramount Pictures, 2005.

59. Herb Miller and Douglas V. Moore, ed., *300 Seed Thoughts: Illustrative Stories for Speakers* (Lubbock, TX: Net Press, 1986), 133-134.

60. Ralph L. Woods, ed., *Wellsprings of Wisdom* (Norwalk, Connecticut: The C.R. Gibson Company), 45-46.

10: Relinquishment

61. Christos Jonathan Seth Hayward, *Open*, JonathansCorner. com, http://JonathansCorner. com/open/.

62. *The Hiding Place Summary*, TheBestNotes.com, http://thebestnotes.com/booknotes/Hiding_Place_Summary/Hiding_Place_Study_Guide03.html.

63. Ray Vander Laan with Stephen and Amanda Sorerson, *Faith Lessons on the Death and Resurrection of the Messiah* (Grand Rapids, Michigan: Zondervan Publishing House, 1999), 124.

64. Lyrics, Rice, "Gethsemane (I OnlyWantTo Say)," *Jesus Christ Superstar*, CD (New York: Leeds Music Corp., 1969).

65. Barbara Lardinais, *Prayer of Relinquishment*, HannasCuupboard.com., http://www.hannahscupboard.com/prayer-relinquish.html.

66. *Meet Cathrine Marshall*, Christianbook.com, http://www.christianbook.com/html/authors/107.html.

67. *History of Abide With Me Hymn*, Suite101.com, http://suite101.com/article/history-of-abide-with-me-hymn-a36157.

68. Carlton R. Young, ed., *Companion to the United Methodist Hymnal* (Nashville: Abingdon Press, 1993), 185.

69. Sister Wendy Becket, *Sister Wendy on Prayer* (New York: Harmony Press, 2006), 43.

70. James S. Hewett, ed., *Illustrations Unlimited* (Wheaton, Illinois: Tyndale House Publishers, Inc.), 140-141.

71. *History of Abide With Me Hymn*, Suite101.com, http://suite101.com/article/history-of-abide-with-me-hymn-a36157.

72. Ralph L. Woods, ed., *Wellsprings of Wisdom* (Norwalk, Connecticut: The C.R. Gibson Company), 79.

Conclusion

73. Freeman Criswell, ed., *The Fisherman's Guide to Life* (Nashville: Walnut Grove Press, 1996), 15.

74. Ibid. 15.

75. Ibid. 15.

BIBLIOGRAPHY

Albom, Mitch. goodreads.com. http://www.goodreads.com/quotes/133061-the-way-you-get-meaning- into-your-life-is-to.

Beckett, Sister Wendy. *Sister Wendy on Prayer*. New York: Harmony Books, 2006.

Beima, David Van. "Mother Teresa's Crisis of Faith." *Time*. Aug. 23, 2007. http://www. time. com/time/magazine/article/0,9171,1655720,00. html#ixzz20FLJJQlU.

Bereaved Parents of the U.S.A. http://www. bereavedparentsusa. org/BP_NewlyBer. Htm.

Biddle, Perry H. Jr. *Abingdon Funeral Manual*. Edited by Perry H. Biddle. Nashville: Abingdon Press, 1990.

Bonhoeffer, Deitrich. Letter from Tegel prison 16 July, 1944. http://www. inwardoutward.org/author/dietrich-bonhoeffer.

Bowring, John. *The Heart Knoweth Its Own Bitterness*. PoemHunter.com. http://www. poemhunter. com/poem/the-heart-knoweth-its-own-bitterness/.

Browning, Robert. *O Never Star*. Yahoo! Voices.com, http://voices. yahoo. com/o-never-star-poem-hope-8297777. html?cat=42.

Buechner, Fredrick. *Wishful Thinking*. San Francisco: HarperSanFrancisco, 1973.

Camus, Albert. Thinkexist.com. http://thinkexist.com/quotation/in_the_midst_of_winter-i_finally_learned_that/12613.html.

Clinebell, Howard. *Basic Types of Pastoral Care & Counseling*. Nashville: Abingdon Press, 1984.

Companion to the United Methodist Hymnal. Edited by Carlton. R. Young. Nashville: Abingdon Press, 1993.

Deits, Bob. *Life After Loss*. United States of America: Fisher Books, 2000.

Dunman, Maxie. *The Workbook on Coping as Christians*. Nashville: Upper Room Books, 1988.

Eichman, Phillip. *What Does The Bible Teach About The Resurrection*, http://www.doesgodexist.org/JanFeb11/Bible.Teach.Resurretion.html.

Gibran, Khalil. *On Pain*. PoemHunter.com. http://www. poemhunter.com/ poem/on-pain/.

Guyon, Jeanne. *Experiencing the Depths of Jesus Christ*. Goleta, California: Christian Books, 1981.

Hale, Edward Everett. *I am only one*. Wikiquote.org. http://en. wikiquote. org/wiki /Edward_ Everett_Hale.

Hare, Douglas R. *Interpretation, A Bible Commentary for Teaching and Preaching, Matthew*. Edited by Douglas R. Hare. Louisville: John Knox Press, 1993.

Hayward, Jonathan Seth. *Open*. JonathansCorner.com, http:// JonathansCorner. com/open/.

History of Abide With Me Hymn. Suite101.com. http://suite101.com/article/ history-of-abide-with-me-hymn-a36157.

Hood, Ann. *Comfort, A Journey Through Grief*. New York, N. Y.: W. W. Norton, 2008.

Illustrations Unlimited. Edited by James S. Hewett. Wheaton, Illinois: Tyndale House Publishers, 1988.

Jackson, Gordon S. *Quotes For The Journey, Wisdom For The* Way. Edited by Gordon S. Jackson. Colorado Springs, Co.: NavPress, 2000.

Keller, Helen. *I am only one*. Thinkexist.com. http://thinkexist.com/ quotation/i_am_only_one-but_still_i_am_one-i_cannot_do/10674. html.

Lardinais, Barbara. *Prayer of Relinquishment*. HannasCuupboard.com. http://www.hannahscupboard.com/prayer-relinquish.html.

Lincoln, Abraham. goodreads.com. http://www.goodreads.com/ quotes/141073-in-this-sad-world-of-ours-sorrow-comes-to-all.

Luebering, Carol. *Coping With Loss*. Cincinnati, Ohio: St. Anthony Messenger Press, 1989.

Martin, Civilla. "His Eye Is on the Sparrow." 1905. Http://nethymnal. org/ js/ads1. Htm.

McNeill, Kirk, and Robert Paul. *Reaching for the Baby Boomers*. Nashville: The General Board of Discipleship, 1989.

Meet Cathrine Marshall. Christianbook.com. http://www.christianbook. com/html/authors/107.html.

Millard, Bart. "I Can Only Imagine." *All that is Within Me*. CD. Nashville: Simpleville Music, 2001.

Miller, Donald. *Searching For God Knows What*. Nelson Books: Nashville, Tennessee, 2004.

Noel, Brook, and Pamela D. Blair. *I Wasn't Ready to Say Goodbye*. Milwaukee: Champion Press, LTD., 2000.

Nouwen, Henri. *The Way of the Heart*. Ballentine Books: New York, 1981.

Potok, Chaim. *The Chosen*. http://potok.lasierra.edu/Potok.chosen.quo. html.

Rice, Tim. "Gethsemane (I OnlyWantTo Say)." *Jesus Christ Superstar*. CD. (New York: Leeds Music Corp., 1969.

Salisbury, Susan. "Tragedy inspires search for 'Faces of Hope,' book Obama mentioned at Arizona memorial." *Palm Beach Post*. January 13, 2011. Http://www. palmbeachpost. com/money/tragedy-inspires-search-for-faces-of-hope-book-118426.

Signs. Dir. M. Night Shyamalan. Perfs. Mel Gibson and Joaquin Phoenix. 2002. DVD. Touchtone, 2003.

Sittser, Jerry. *A Grace Disguised*. Grand Rapids, Michigan: Zondervan, 1995.

Sockman, Ralph W. *The Meaning of Suffering*. New York, N.Y.: Woman's Division of Christian Service, Board of Missions, The Methodist Church, 1961.

Stanley, Bessie A. *What is Success?*. The Ralph Waldo Emerson Society. http://emerson.tamu.edu/Ephemera/Success.html.

The Andy Griffith Show. Opie's Ill-gotten Gain (Episode 103). Nov. 18,1963. Pro. Aaron Ruben. Dir. Jeffrey Hayden. Perfs. Andy Griffith, Don Knotts, Frances Bavier, Ron Howard, and Aneta Corsaut. Wri. John Whedon. DVD. Paramount Pictures, 2005.

The Fisherman's Guide to Life. Edited by Freeman Criswell. Nashville: Walnut Grove Press, 1996.

The Hiding Place Summary. TheBestNotes.com. http://thebestnotes.com/booknotes/Hiding_Place_Summary/Hiding_Place_Study_Guide03. html.

The United Methodist Hymnal. United States of America: The United Methodist Publishing House, 1993.

The Upper Room Daily Devotional Guide, September-October 2003. Edited by Stephen D. Bryant. The

Upper Room Inc.: Nashville, 2003.

300 Seed Thoughts: Illustrative Stories for Speakers. Edited by Herb Miller and Douglas V. Moore. Lubbock, TX: Net Press, 1986.

Vander Laan, Ray, with Stephen and Amanda Sorerson. *Faith Lessons on the Death and Resurrection of the Messiah.* Grand Rapids, Michigan: Zondervan Publishing House, 1999.

Van Dyke, Henry. *Life.* PoemHunter.com. http://www. poemhunter.com/ poem/life-10/.

Warren, Rick. *The Purpose Driven Life.* Zondervan: Grand Rapids, 2002.

Wellsprings of Wisdom. Edited by Ralph L. Woods. Norwalk, Connecticut: The C.R. Gibson Company.

Wolterstorff, Nicholas. *Lament For A Son.* Grand Rapids: Wm. B. Eerdmans Publishing Co., 1996.

Wright, N. T. *Surprised by Hope.* New York: HarperOne, 2008.